THE LETTERS

OF

A LEIPZIG CANTOR

BEING

THE LETTERS OF MORITZ HAUPTMANN

TO FRANZ HAUSER, LUDWIG SPOHR, AND OTHER MUSICIANS

EDITED BY

PROF. DR. ALFRED SCHÖNE

AND

FERDINAND HILLER

TRANSLATED & ARRANGED BY A. D. COLERIDGE.

VOL. II.

NEW YORK
VIENNA HOUSE
1972

Originally published by Novello, Ewer and Co., London and New York
and Richard Bentley & Son, London, 1892

First VIENNA HOUSE edition published in 1972

International Standard Book Number:
Volume I . . . 0-8443-0007-1
Volume II . . . 0-8443-0008-x

Library of Congress Catalogue Card Number: 75-163789

Manufactured in the United States of America

HAUPTMANN TO HAUSER.

78.

LEIPZIG, *September* 26*th*, 1842.

DEAR HAUSER,—

Lo and behold, we have arrived, we have entered in and taken possession, we are settling down in the old nest, known as "The Cantor's Residence!" Everyone, high and low, does his utmost to be kind and friendly. I should never have time to tell you, how good everybody has been, but when all is said and done, I don't feel at home—very far from it, as yet. The secret is safe with you, who are eighty miles away. I cannot help telling you, that I feel no vocation for my present post. I have always had to do with individuals, never with corporations. I get on fairly well with M. or N., but I am all at sea with a heap of people; a man in my position ought to know his own mind, and have no scruples; he should, at all events, *believe* that he is doing right. It was impossible to foresee at a distance all the little side issues, and they hamper me dreadfully, though they would be nothing to regular men of business, like most of those I see about me. I started my rehearsals—singing-lessons I should rather call them—eight days since: they are doing my G minor Mass, three numbers of which I mean to have performed, next Sunday, in the *Thomaskirche*. The lads hit the right note at their first shot, but it is screaming rather than singing. I was present on two occasions, when Pohlenz conducted selections from Cherubini's fourth Mass, and was pleased with the performance, which I can honestly say impressed me more favourably than any I ever heard in the Catholic Church at Dresden; it is difficult to get such a fine movement as the *Gloria* of that Mass performed there. What sort of figure will my Mass cut in comparison? I mean to give the *Kyrie*, *Gloria*, and *Credo*. Wednesday, I have an

orchestral rehearsal in the hall, on Friday in the Church.
Oh, that you could be with me here, my old and loyal friend—
my friend of many winters! All the people here are summer
friends, and how I shall get on in rough weather remains
to be seen. I can't make up my mind about your Moritz; I
should like to feel myself firm in the saddle, before asking
him to join me. . . .

The local paper makes a good deal of my installation; there
is a biographical sketch too, but I have not yet seen it. In
strictness, I ought to have made a Latin speech; Weinlig did,
so I am the first to distinguish myself by shirking the law.
The Rector, however, harangued in German for nearly five
quarters of an hour--very fine I daresay, but I don't grudge
him the gift . . . I shouldn't care about anything, if I could
only play the piano. Pianists are as plentiful as mushrooms.
I don't know how they manage it, unless they are born to it.
We had better resign ourselves once for all, as a certain
person says, however hard it may be; it is better than a fit of
despair every other day. But no! We all think we ought to
be able to do it, because so many can do it—and that's a great
mistake! It is not the want of time, it is the want of concentration; one has too many things in one's head, to be able to attend
to the mechanical exercise; for a short time it's right enough,
then away go the thoughts, and the fingers " err and stray
like lost sheep." It causes a twofold evil in my case,—directly,
as I can't get on; indirectly, as my pupils see that I can't get
on. I am like a bad rider, who can't keep his own seat, and yet
has to drive a four-in-hand. What is it to them, that the
fellow may be able to do something else besides riding? All
they want is a good equestrian. One thing I am very sure of,
and that is, that if all does not go smoothly, I shall anticipate
my *congé*. *Cernere mundum, cernere se ipsum, cernere se cerni.*
I believe I am quoting Spinoza; the last two phrases, in some
measure, apply to me. Perhaps excess of energy as a theorist
does hinder my practical effectiveness. Well, some have
one gift, some another! . . .

Yours,

M. H.

79.

LEIPZIG, *November* 13*th*, 1842.

DEAREST HAUSER,—

Why this unusually long silence, when I am longing to hear whether you are coming, and when,—with Moritz or without him ?   When David wrote to you about the fiddle, I have no doubt he added, that he would gladly promise to give Moritz lessons.   Mendelssohn returned here a few days since, and stays the whole winter through, to conduct the Concerts.   He said yesterday, that people were very well pleased with the Thomas Choir, or, as he put it, that the Choir was quite another thing now ; but I feel a qualm, when I hear him make these remarks, for I am not sure whether he is in jest or in earnest, and I am very touchy on the point.   I like the post well enough, but the post does not like me. I am wanting in penetration, in activity of mind, I am doubtful whether I can adapt myself to the conditions required by the office.   I feel as if they would never become a part of me, as if I should always be in opposition.   Take an instance !   I am so stupid about remembering faces and names, and here they expect me to know every one of my sixty pupils, when I find it quite impossible to criticise more than a few.   I am too old to enter a sphere so completely new to me ; at my time of life, it is hard to alter one's method,—though I have always wavered as to what is really my vocation.   I am Jack of all trades and master of none.

H. is still at me about the editorship of the *Musikalische Zeitung*, and wants me to take it up at the New Year.   C. F. Becker, the organist, has been editor up to this time, the firm undertaking the responsibility, but it was only a temporary arrangement, and when it seemed probable that I should be appointed at Leipzig, they made up their minds to offer me the post. . . .   We have any number of Concerts here just now ; for the future, I expect we shall pick and choose amongst them.   On an average, the *Gewandhaus* Concerts are pretty much like the rest, with the exception of the Overtures

B 2

and Symphonies, which go splendidly. For the sake of these, one can put up with the rest of the programme. I don't mean to say that the other things are badly done, far from it! but they are not always equally interesting. It's the old, old story, *tout comme chez nous,* Airs by Donizetti and Mercadante, Concertos for flute, keyed trumpets, &c., and a quantity of pianoforte music, which last never attracts me to a public hall. As a rule, one new piece sounds to me just like another. Henselt (who played at H.'s, when he was on his way through) is still my favourite pianist. His compositions, too, have more character in them, although Thalberg's very pretty combinations sound marvellous, when you consider that only one person is playing. But I would rather hear the piano in a room, where it fills all the available space, than in a hall, with sixty men standing by, their instruments in their hands, doing nothing but stare. Even if they play an accompaniment, it does not improve the effect; that metallic tone will not blend with any other. Many people think the want of sustained power an absolute defect in the piano, but I cannot agree with them—nay, I believe it to be rather an advantage, except when an attempt is made to combine it with other instruments that have this power. I have read nothing at all lately—in fact, I have scarcely looked at a book in my library, except for reference. My mind is too much agitated for study. . . .

Yours,
M. HAUPTMANN.

80.

LEIPZIG, *February* 13*th,* 1843.

DEAREST HAUSER,—

It will do you good, once in a way, to learn how to wait for an answer that never comes; but believe me, I meant no harm! When I was at Pultava, the tutor of the Prince's children had a brother in Geneva, about four hundred miles away, who never would answer his letters. After his patience was quite exhausted, the tutor sent him an unstamped letter, written on the thickest paper he could get, and when the brother opened it, he found nothing but the words, "Write, you rascal!" You are a good fellow, after all, not to serve me in the same fashion. Your letter was delightful.

We are to open our Leipzig *Conservatoire* in April next. I daresay you read the *Musikalische Zeitung?* You will find there a prospectus, explaining some few details. Between you and me, I feel no great confidence in the scheme, from what I have heard of the staff of teachers. Not one of them knows how to set about his work, for though we have all instructed single pupils in our time, we have no experience of classes. I head the list of the uncertain. The *Musikalische Zeitung* does not overtax me in any way, but I cannot do anything to improve it. For a man of my capacity, I have far too many irons in the fire; each is a mere nothing in itself, but they take up all my time. We have plenty of Concerts, and nearly all of them are good. Mendelssohn's music to Goethe's *Walpurgisnacht* was given the other day, and a rare fine thing it is, this Cantata, or *Ballade*, as he will have it! Anything so healthy, fresh, and jubilant, I have not heard for ages. We have had his new Symphony too. I thought it very beautiful, but I had heard too much music that evening, and besides, I was a little out of sorts. Berlioz also gave a Concert, treating us to some of his mad stuff; it *is* quite mad, but that being so, I like it. I don't think it is either *affectation* or *inspiration*, it shows a certain *limitation* in him, to aim at such a thing. *Du reste*, he succeeds very well, and you cannot but admire his success. There is nothing beautiful about it, and the Leipzig people, so far from being impressed, were put out. He is coming here again, to conduct his *Romeo and Juliet*. . . .

The *Musikalische Zeitung* gives me more than enough to do, though this may seem a paradox, for a registrar would serve the purpose just as well, my duty being merely to read through long-winded articles and vapid reviews, and to distribute them among the various numbers, as best I may. It's a waste of time; I am a bad hand at such work.

I don't quite know how to advise you about Moritz. Music in every branch is to be taught at the *Conservatoire*. Fancy

Pohlenz as a teacher of singing! Schumann takes the piano, David the violin, Mendelssohn and I, composition. How I'm to set about it, I don't know, but we must make a start somehow in April next—not on the 1st, Mendelssohn exclaimed against that! Supposing you were to send Moritz, and I were to help him as much as I could, out of lesson hours? . . . I have lately been rehearsing, with orchestra, some of Bach's sacred Cantatas. *Hear, O Thou Shepherd of Israel*, is wonderfully fine. Yesterday we did the *Kyrie* and the *Gloria* of the Mass in G. The instrumental effects, here and there, sound curiously enough; it is always part against part, one consisting merely of ten basses or six violins—the other of a flute or oboe; there is seldom anything except two oboes, as you know. One is forced to pick and choose the numbers that are really practicable; to do them all would be hopeless. I should like to know how they managed those Cantatas in the old days; and what sort of an effect was produced. I think it cannot always have sounded well. I wonder whether the basses really sang all such passages as these, quite clearly :—

or whether they merely existed on paper. Melodious those passages may be in themselves, that is, in the common acceptation of the word *Melody;* vocal melody, melodious accentuation of words, they often enough are not; they are *rococo.* Just now we are rehearsing a bit of Giovanni Gabrieli. That's the sort of stuff, to teach a choir how to sing! . . .

We take great delight in the local *Kunstverein,* not so much in the pictures which are there permanently, though some of these are very good, as in the Saturday Exhibitions, when they light up the gallery of an evening, and the place is filled with engravings, drawings, lithographs, &c. Weigel, Börner, Puttrich, anyone who has anything interesting to show, lends it for the occasion. Yesterday, for instance, the walls were covered with Overbecks and Steinles. Another time, they had different examples of Architecture, Painting, and Sculpture from Munich. These Saturday Exhibitions are only intended for *connoisseurs*, but on Sunday morning the general public is admitted. However, I went with Susette in the evening. I have not got a Pianoforte Edition of the G minor Mass. We are to have the *Kyrie* and *Gloria* at a *Gewandhaus* Concert, unless Berlioz's *Romeo and Juliet* stands in the way. . . .

Spohr says that things in Cassel are going from bad to worse; the Prince, and the head of the police, who wishes to curry favour with him, keep all outsiders away. Ernst only passed through. The Milanollos gave a Concert in Marburg, and then went back again. Two different operas are ordered for every week; the Prince never allows the same work to be repeated, till after a long time has elapsed, so that a really good performance becomes impossible. Now that I am outside Cassel, I can hardly conceive such mismanagement; when I was there, I was quite accustomed to it. . . .

Yours,
M. HAUPTMANN.

81.

LEIPZIG, *June* 13*th*, 1843.

. . . So far, I find a good tone prevailing in the School here; the lads stick to their work, and are interested in it, and as they have to prepare for so many teachers, their hands are pretty full. Your Moritz goes right by instinct, we have no difficulty with him at all; he can't go wrong if he would. . . .

Mendelssohn sets his pupils exercises in composition, which they write off-hand, to show what they can do. Sometimes these are difficult enough; he will even give them a quartet. I think he is wise in combining practical work with the abstract study of Harmony and Melody. Whilst giving private lessons, and trying to adapt my teaching to the powers of a single pupil, I have now and then found it difficult to keep the proper balance. The seven years' apprenticeship, required by the Italian *Conservatoires*, would

not do here; one, or two years at the most, is supposed to
be enough for a smattering in every branch of learning, and
we think ourselves lucky, if here and there a pupil strikes the
right path under our guidance. But remembering in what
a crude state I had to let them go, I have been pleased
to find, when I happened to come across specimens of
their work in later years, that there was nothing bad
in it — nay, that a good deal had developed, which
still lay underground at the time they left school. You can't
manufacture a poet, he must be born; and poetry lies at the
root of the whole matter. You can form an artist in the
abstract, and train him to write correctly, and if he learns
that much, it is a satisfaction to the teacher. Many are poetical
by nature, who never learn how to write. . . . I feel myself
out of place here. I have not written a note, since the day I
first thought of coming; all my old work, however poor it may
be, seems to me like the fruit of a better time, and this thought
makes me moody or melancholy, just as the fit takes me.
Comparing small things with great, I feel like Goethe, when he
was asked to read aloud his *Iphigenie*, on his return to
Pempelfort, after the French Campaign. It reminded him too
vividly of the time he spent in Rome; he could not do it.
My wife, and my darling little child, are now my only joy. I
daresay bodily indisposition has something to do with my
indisposition for work, and constant wish for change. I have
to put a good face on it, when people congratulate me on my
honours, and all the time I am sick at heart. One would
rather write music as Rousseau did, just to escape the burden of
office, just to be able to write something else. Give me a house
of my own, that I can pay for myself, rather than a coveted
official residence like this, where I am not my own master!
We are enjoying a week's holiday, and I am just expecting
Moritz, that we may hold a *Conservatoire* at home. I fear we
shall lose Mendelssohn, an event we could not foresee. Of
course he will have to go to Berlin some day or other, and I
doubt whether he will give up his summer excursions, which
no one could grudge him; but it will be a bad look-out
for the School. . . .   Yours,

                                                  M. H.

82.

LEIPZIG, *October 3rd*, 1843.

. . . Yesterday my G minor Mass was performed, in the *Thomaskirche*, by special request; it was given without any omissions, in accordance with the wishes of the members of the orchestra. The work was well done, and well received. People remarked on the real progress made by the Choir, but I am not sure whether this was not the effect of imagination, and I think the good will of the Choir may have had something to do with it. Mendelssohn, who passed through here on Friday last, was present; next day he went to Berlin, and returned in time to conduct the first Concert on Sunday, the 2nd. Yesterday was a very busy day with me; at 8 a.m. a rehearsal in the Church, followed by another in the *Gewandhaus*, and then Mendelssohn and I went off together, to see the Bach Monument. Knauer, the sculptor, has completed it, from a design of Bendemann's. I have seen the same sort of thing in Catholic Churches. Bach's bust stands in a niche of the upper lantern, where there is just room enough, and no more, for the colossal head and stately wig; the other three sides are adorned with bas-reliefs, representing ecclesiastical allegories. The conception and execution of the bust are equally good; the monument faces our windows, which look out on the Promenade. Mendelssohn has raised money for it by giving concerts. It is not a big affair, being only about twelve *Ellen* high; but like all such things, it will cost quite enough money. Mendelssohn, David, Susette, and I dined at the Hotel de Bavière afterwards—as it is fair-time, the *table d'hôte* was crowded—and after that we paid the sculptor a second visit, for I wanted Susette to see the bust. We wound up our evening at the Subscription Concert. The new decorations, and the furniture of the hall, cost 6,000 *thalers*. They give the Symphonies there quite splendidly; we had Beethoven's in A major. Schloss has a lovely voice, and she sings admirably. Clara Schumann played. . . .

Yours,

M. H.

83.

LEIPZIG, *December 18th*, 1843.

. . . Yes, I spared no pains, the one year that I studied under Spohr in Gotha. I had two motives for hard work—one, my own delight in a thing that required my undivided attention; and secondly, the thought "In a year's time, you must be a made man!" My very anxiety left me no time for idleness. I often see young people now, spending their time as many a student spends his at the University, and trying to redeem it all in the last term. Well, they may just manage to get a livelihood on that system, but Art is not a matter of memory, it is a power. I dare not advise any pupil to leave the *Conservatoire*, so long as I am on the staff. Already I have been told—nay, I was well aware—that I have given offence, by declining to advise some students to join, though I felt certain it would not suit them. I can't say what I should have felt in my young days, but I do not see the good of shifting a pupil about from one quarter of an hour's lesson to another. Spite of it all, our numbers steadily increase. We have over sixty students already, so the authorities have consented to build us a house. Since Mendelssohn left, we seem to want a head, though perhaps we shall extend our branches all the farther. Of course there are *Conservatoires*, that get on without a Mendelssohn. The King has ordered the *Hofcapelle*, of Berlin, to sing the *Missa Papæ Marcelli*, with words taken from the German Bible. I fancy Mendelssohn will make a face at this, although he holds Catholic Church music rather cheap. Perhaps, if he once sets to work at it in good earnest, he will come round. That was my case. I became so enamoured of the music, that it monopolised all my thoughts, and for a long time, I did nothing else but pick to pieces and reconstruct the various parts of the work. I dote upon it still. I was just as much in love with Bach's Church Music at one time, but now, when I hear the eight-part Motets *growled* by the Thomaners, and after them the eight-part *Tu es Petrus* of Gabrieli, it is patent to me, that one is vocal and sacred music as well, and the other is neither. Once a wig always a wig, though it hides the head of a genius. *

---

* Fitzgerald's criticism of Handel is on the same lines : " I think Handel never gets out of his wig : that is, out of his age."

I am, on the whole, delighted with Mendelssohn's new batch of Songs; Nos. 2 and 4 are particularly good. Without being over-punctilious about the musical accent on certain words, I must say I think a little more care might have been bestowed here and there, especially in passages where high-pitched notes are given to unimportant syllables. Much, however, depends on the singer, who can do a good deal to mend this. *The Midsummer Night's Dream* is to be performed on Christmas Eve ; I don't suppose I shall be able to go, but it's sure to be repeated. It is, and ever was, an evening sacred to family joys, and this year our little Helen is to have her first Christmas tree. Don't tell that to the enthusiasts ! What would they say to my giving up " an æsthetic feast " for that reason ? You know how I love that expression ! One reason why I am glad to get rid of the *Musikalische Zeitung* is, that I shan't have to see it so often. . . . As for the Lectures on Æsthetics and History, I don't much mind. There has been no talk about the former, and the latter only occupy one hour a week, from 6.30 to 7.30 p.m. It's a good lesson for the students, to watch the historical development of Art in all its phases. Of course they criticise and find fault right and left, but you know what superior beings these young fellows are—so much wiser than their teachers ! *Nolens volens*, they get hold of a thread, and it serves them in after years to string together beads, which would otherwise have been scattered and lost. . . .

Schumann has written an imposing work, called *Paradise and the Peri;* the words are taken from Th. Moore's *Lalla Rookh.* At first sight, you would think it was an oratorio. There have been two performances. Take it for all in all, it's a very beautiful work. The author has found his way out of the fog, and learnt how to enjoy loveliness and simplicity. He and his wife are now starting for St. Petersburg and Moscow. They will be absent from four to six months. Not a cheerful look-out in winter ! . .

Yours,

M. H.

84.

LEIPZIG, *April 8th*, 1844.

. . . From the beginning, I never thought it a wise
plan, to set our pupils down to write a quartet or a symphonic
movement, when they were still incapable of making two parts
move together correctly. If they are hardy and foolhardy
enough to insist on trying, it's a good sign, though it's sure
to be a regular jumble, and we have a right to expect in
exercises such correctness, and proper conformity to musical
grammar, as shall ensure a tolerably agreeable effect. But
this is very difficult in a quartet. They have heard quartets
of course; they have been pleased with the involution, they
like to hear everyone playing something different; they try to
do the same, and instead of purifying themselves, they only
sink deeper and deeper into the mire! It's a mere waste of time,
in my opinion, and it is utterly impossible to clear up the
faults in such a piece of work. By the time you get to an
historical composition, it is too late to begin arranging the
various members, and counting to see whether the number of
fingers is right, &c. To be sure, the attempt shows whether
or no there is talent; but then you must begin from the very
beginning. In many instances they may, by degrees, work
their own way out of the desert, but as a method, I think it
highly unsuitable. . . .

Joachim of Vienna, who is now on his way to London,
seems to have learnt his art easily enough. He was a rare
clever boy in early days, when he entered the good sound
school of Böhme—and now he practises perhaps an hour daily.
A short time since, he was called upon, quite unexpectedly, to
play Spohr's *Gesangscene* at the *Gewandhaus;* he had tried it
for the first time with David, a few days before. The solo
part was missing, but the lad played the piece by heart, in a
style that would have charmed Spohr himself. The *Gesang*
was given with exquisite purity and feeling, the intonation
was as pure as a bell, and the tone unfaltering in the most
difficult passages. . . .

Our Oratorio, on Palm Sunday and Good Friday, was the
St. John's Passion, a work much to be respected, particularly
the first chorus, the Jews' choruses—*e.g., Were He not a
malefactor,—Crucify*—and several Airs, some of which I was
obliged to omit. There is a fine bass Air with a lute part,
which I arranged for the violas and clarinet (lower register);
the two *Viole d'amore* parts I gave to the violins. Susette
sang the alto Airs very beautifully; I gave the second, which
is accompanied only by the *Viola da Gamba* and bass, to the
Corno inglese, and the figured bass to violoncellos and violas.
The effect was very fine, and everyone was pleased. The bass
song, answered by the chorus with *Whither?* made a great
impression. All went off smoothly. . . .

Yours,

M. H.

85.

DRESDEN, *June* 20*th*, 1844.

. . . The one object of the Epicureans was, pleasure
for pleasure's sake, so it is commonly supposed that they
passed their lives in sensuality and frivolity, regardless of all
but themselves. In reality, it was the reverse of this, else
they could have had no pleasure in life. They ate the simplest food, and but little of it; they drank pure water, and
they were more concerned about other people than about
themselves. It was virtue founded upon egotism, but after
all, every feeling that I entertain for another is *my own*
feeling, so I had rather no one did anything to please me,
unless at the same time he pleased himself, and virtue for
virtue's sake seems to me positive egotism—a compact made
with the conscience, and the heart no part of the bargain!
. . .

Yours,

M. H.

86.

LEIPZIG, *July* 30*th*, 1844.

. . . Make Moritz take a draught of some musical
Lethe, in order that he may wash away something of
Mendelssohn's influence, and learn to invent a little on his
own hook. It is all too Mendelssohnian, so much so, that
were we to eliminate the master's thoughts from the pupil's
score, we should be left with a blank sheet of paper. I forgive a certain amount of imitation in a young man's earliest
works, but here it is too rampant. In Mendelssohn, too,
through all the drapery, we see the accurate drawing and
fine articulation of the separate parts—*we* see it, I say, but
all beginners do not, and when they imitate the folds, they
let them fall anyhow, and the body is not thought of. You
remember Michael Angelo's remark upon Bandinelli's statue
of Hercules, in front of the *Palazzo Vecchio* at Florence?
" The back looks just like a bag of melons." . . .

Dear Hauser, how am I to get a copy of Bach's B minor
Mass? The *Kyrie* and *Gloria* are so vilely printed, that I
don't care to have them. If you could get me a copy in
Vienna, I should be very much obliged. Mendelssohn has
one, but Heaven knows when we shall see him, or when he
returns to Berlin! I wonder if you have the scores of the
forty-three Cantatas, the parts of which are in our School
library? I have had two of them scored, but it is weary
work, and if I knew of anyone who had them already, I would
rather get them copied. I should be especially glad of any
sacred compositions suitable for an orchestra. The vocal
difficulties are no great hindrance; the real hindrances are
the *Viola da Gamba*, the flutes, and *Oboi da Caccia;* if there
are no other instruments, and it is impossible to substitute
the organ, it is impossible to give this music in a church.
And then there are so many solos! I wonder if they ever
were well sung! I look around amongst our best singers,
and it is hard to find anyone who could manage them. We
have given, out of Marx's selection, *Du Hirte Israel, Herr*

deine Augen, Herr gehe nicht ins Gericht, besides *Bleib' bei uns,* and the Mass in G. I should so like to have done *Gottes Zeit,* but I don't see my way to the orchestral part. There are the two flutes, and the two *Gambas* again ; nothing else. And what terrible pieces those are, with nothing but a *basso continuo!* Even if the organ be employed as an accompaniment, it. is too hard in tone, and will not blend with the voice ; it is only effective in the loud passages of a chorus. A good piano would perhaps be better; it sounds very well, even in church. . . .

Yours,

M. H.

87.

LEIPZIG, *August* 13*th,* 1844.

. . . I mean to enjoy the B minor Mass. Of course the students make rough work of it, and no one supposes they will sing it as it ought to be sung ; but we shall have a performance of some sort, and as they never get beyond a certain point, we shall not want six months for rehearsals. What a misfortune it is, that the tenor part should be so much higher than our present pitch, and that for the most part transposition is impossible, because of the instruments ! But we must not make too much fuss about it, else we shall never get anything done. It is no use lowering the violin pitch ; to do that, we should have to enlist the sympathies of the whole world, and in common fairness we cannot ask too much. . . .

Gade is a very clever fellow ; he has plenty to do still, but the stuff is there. Too much of his work is mere colour and depends too much on colour for its main interest. His Leipzig admirers were greatly annoyed by Kahlert's criticism of his Symphony, in the *Musikalische Zeitung,* because it did not praise him up to the skies. Surely, he was right in saying, that a composition, to be good, must stand the test of an arrangement, without losing the greater part of its interest ; a good picture makes a good engraving. Mozart can be played from A to Z on the piano. No doubt, a good

deal of Beethoven's Ninth Symphony would have to be
sacrificed in the process, and I am far from saying that the
merits of a work depend *entirely* on this test. I only say
that instrumentation should not be the principal thing.
Mendelssohn has given a regular death-blow to all such
composers as Reissiger, Marschner, and Lindpaintner.
Perhaps, after all, our good Dresdener is the shallowest of the
whole lot. I make you a present of every one of them, vain
as they are of their skeleton compositions, touched up now
with a green brush, now with a blue. Why do Lindpaintner
and Reissiger persist in writing operas ? That beats me.
Each of them has written a dozen, not one of which is ever
heard of. Bellini has written five, all of which are performed
all the world over; let them be what they will, they are performed,
for all that. The innocent creatures fancy that they have
composed sterling German masterpieces, too good for the
public; this is the reason why *they* are not performed.
Perhaps they are much finer things than *Don Juan* and
Figaro ! Somehow or other, the public likes Mozart.

I, as you know, am not enthusiastic about the so-called
Romantic School, the main characteristic of which is,
Absence of form, and therefore a mere negation.
I grant you, Art requires new material, after a period
during which she has only busied herself with forms;
but though at first these new subjects may appear
to be somewhat accidental, and not in accordance with
the rules of Art—*i.e.*, not perfectly rational—they are always
natural. Josquin is an instance; he was voted *bizarre* and
extravagant by his contemporaries ; it was the same with the
Venetian School and with Beethoven. At first, people think it
intolerable, but if there is anything good in it, it has the effect
of making everything that preceded it, except the very best,
tasteless and *fade*. The best will not lose by it—nay, it will
gain, for the hosts of parasitical plants that have climbed round
it and drawn their sap from it, die off, and leave the tree to
grow young again. After all, I would rather have a fragment
of Berlioz than all the works of Reissiger. It is like the
water of our Pleiss—cataracts and waterfalls, and now and
then a brilliant rainbow in the midst of the spray. Berlioz

has just written a big volume on Instrumentation, and dedicated it to the King of Prussia. Schlesinger is the publisher,
and it costs ten *thalers;* I daresay there are five *thalers'* worth
of remarks on different kinds of drumsticks, but, on the other
hand, you may get the fair equivalent of your remaining five
in the rest of the work. It is no great praise, to say it is
very likely the cleverest book that has appeared on the subject.
The Germans are much stupider than the French. It is only
our very best that is good, though when it's good, it's very,
very good. . . .

Yours,

M. HAUPTMANN.

88.

LEIPZIG, *September 23rd,* 1844.

. . . We mean to give Spohr's *Fall of Babylon,* at our
next Concert in the *Thomasschule.* Don't quote me, but I
have often been irritated at rehearsals, to find that a man of
Spohr's age and an experienced writer of vocal music, should
persist in writing so unintelligibly for the Chorus. He is even
worse than he was in his younger days. Many of our boys,
who are first-rate readers, are puzzled to sing certain notes
which lie side by side; here is one instance out of many :—

Spohr may see no difficulty, because the notes lie close to one
another on the keyboard, but here are B flat minor and B
minor in close proximity, and to bridge over the whole of the
intervening space between them and D sharp, E, F sharp, we
should require Peter Schlehmil's seven-league boots. It is
impossible to hit the right note, without some conscious process of modulation ; in this instance, the singers come to grief,
and the instrumental basses must drag them along over the
offending passage. I defy Spohr himself to sing it. A singer

can't get hold of the notes ready-made; he has to make them first of all for himself, and he should be able, at the same time, to imagine some sort of connecting link between them. . . .

Yours,
M. H.

89.

LEIPZIG, December 22nd, 1844.

. . . We can't do anything out of the way this season. Instead of attending Christmas rehearsals, here I am, shivering with cold, behind a stove. I had wanted to give a performance of Beethoven's Mass in D, Op. 123, but we had got no farther than the *Gloria*, when I fell ill; so did the soprano, who suddenly turned into an alto. The tenor also, and several of the chorus, are on the sick list. The *Gloria* gets very wild towards the end. I daresay many people think it all a divine inspiration. Speaking for myself, I abominate, in church music, all those quick transitions from *Allegro* to *più Allegro*, *Stringendo*, and *Presto*, and I abominate them most of all in great composers. They begin beautifully enough, but it only lasts a minute or two, and then off they go on the track of this vulgar idea, which never can be anything but vulgar, however choice the workmanship. If you betray the effort to be choice, you become commonplace immediately. The *Kyrie* is not far-fetched, it begins and continues in the beautiful traditional manner, only with more exultation about it, and the other vocal parts of this number are well within the range of the ordinary voice; later on, the music is utterly unmanageable—instrumental, in fact, throughout. Surely, Beethoven was too much absorbed in himself to make a sacred composer, even in his Masses. In the C minor Mass, I often think of that scene at Carlsbad, described by Bettine, who tells us how Goethe and Beethoven, whilst walking together, fell in with some grandees, and how Goethe bowed respectfully, and Beethoven clapped his hat firmly on his head, folded his arms, and aired himself as Goethe's superior; *ça perce quelque fois*, even in Beethoven's finest things, which I admire as much as anybody. . . .

I suppose you have heard about Spohr's Opera, which is to be given at Cassel on New Year's Day? The libretto of *Die Kreuzfahrer* is an arrangement from Kotzebue, the joint production of Spohr and his wife, he distributing the scenes, she supplying the verses. From what I hear, I fear it is likely to join the *Berggeist, Pietro,* and *Der Alchymist,* which have long ago been shelved, even at Cassel. I marvel at Spohr's attempting another opera, after having so long foresworn the practice, when he has seen so many beautiful scores wasted. It is discouraging for a man in the decline of life, and he has spent a great deal of time over this last opera—in fact, he hardly wrote anything else for a whole year. Did I tell you about *The Fall of Babylon,* which we did in the Thomaskirche? I can't remember. The Church was crammed, and the receipts amounted to more than we usually realise by four concerts. It was a brilliant performance, and the solo parts were given to competent singers, not to members of our own body, as in Weinlig's time. I did the same thing, when we gave *Samson* last year, and the receipts on that occasion doubled those of former years. The audience thought the music very Spohrian—too secular; secular it always will be, if it is overcharged with a man's individuality, be he Spohr or anybody else. Take him for all in all, I respect the man, and I will not hear him run down, for his sound and complete artistic knowledge entitle him to general esteem. Much of the music of our time may show greater intellectual force and *esprit,* but I think no one has a right to despise Spohr's artistic instinct; you should take the best of a man's work as your standard; compared with one of his Violin Concertos, all the rest are rubbish—you *can't* compare them for a moment. I always find the best composers treat him respectfully; in fact, the regard in which he is held is almost a criterion of quality.

Yes, you are right, it is a good thing to be at a *Conservatoire,* because you get opportunities of studying music with others. I was much tickled by your Vienna arrangement of one year for Major, and the next for Minor keys. I find it hard enough, to keep asunder subjects which a teacher should keep asunder. How am I to set about it? How am I to treat

c 2

Rhythm, Melody, Modulation, &c., as different subjects? And yet such departments and plans of study figure well enough in a prospectus! Happily for me, I am confined to teaching Harmony and Counterpoint, though even here I am not thoroughly satisfied with my work, for I get to know but little of my pupils from this one side. They learn their drill like a company of soldiers; it is only the awkward squad that gets noticed.

I have allowed Moritz to write some songs lately, wishing him to keep well within a limited range; he can understand what I say to him about such simple things as these, and overhaul them for himself. They have much of the modern spirit, but they seem to me to be clearer and less pretentious than his previous efforts in this *genre*. I cannot force my pupils to write long contrapuntal exercises, and, after all, there is no good in forced work. I think that Moritz has a certain feeling for Counterpoint, but in general his school-fellows have none whatever. Knowledge can be acquired in different ways, and every method may have its good points, but youngsters are blindly enamoured of their own ideals, and have no enthusiasm for anything besides. In my earlier days, I used to make scores from the parts of Spohr's Symphony in E flat major, his C minor Clarinet Concerto, and many other things. It was purely a labour of love. I had no eye to the main chance. But there are all sorts of worshippers; there is such a thing as worshipping blindly and there is such a thing as an intelligent worship. . . .

Yours,

M. HAUPTMANN.

90.

LEIPZIG, *March 15th*, 1845.

The authorities on Metre seem to me to go wildly wrong here, independently of the system of division into groups of four bars. But it is tiresome to be often in doubt, as to whether a passage is to be taken as the first or second part of a Period, and when the sequence only elucidates this.

In such a case, one would wish to hear part of the Period over again, but the music goes on notwithstanding. Every painting, apart from the special story it represents, should be a picture, the composition of which has its own intrinsic value. So, too, in poetry, the rules of metre must be observed. If these are neglected, it degenerates into prose; it is no mere rhythmical grouping together of words, just as they come. I find, in the more modern music, the composers often think themselves superior to that which is in reality above them, the knowledge of which would enable them to realise all that is artistic in humanity—I mean that instinct for arrangement —that feeling for form, which should be proof against a torrent of emotion. It is this that we find, on the whole, in Beethoven, a man pre-eminent in the discovery of so much that is new, for which there was no place to be found earlier. . . . His music to *The Ruins of Athens* was given at our last concert; it is very uneven in style, and very unequal. There is a pretty and characteristic Chorus of Dervishes, besides the familiar *Crown ye the Altars*, which has often been done before. Towards the end, it reminds me of *Die Schwestern von Prag*, or the *Sonntagskind*. The overture is a patchwork, made up of subjects, half of which are trivial, and half of which are odd. As a rule, I prefer Beethoven writing on his own account to Beethoven writing for others. David played a pretty, delicate Violin Concerto of Mendelssohn's; it must be a grateful work for the performer. The best of the new Symphonies was by Lührs, a young Berlin composer; Markull's was a failure, and Hesse's one of the ordinary type. Gade's very effective overture would have been all the better, had he given us less of the sea gulls, which fluttered about by dozens in *The Hebrides*. I suppose, if we have marine painters, we are entitled to have marine composers; but when it all turns to water, even if there be a dash of salt in it, enough is as good as a feast. A man is far less likely to repeat himself, if he paints portraits. . . .

Yours,

M. H.

91.

LEIPZIG, *May* 31*st*, 1845.

. . . He never will become a great violin player; he is too old for that, and assuming life-long perseverance and industry (which is asking a good deal), he is not far enough advanced, to make such an effort advisable. I am another instance of a man beginning too late; it's as hard to get one's hand in, as it is easy to get it out again.

I think I have already told you, that we gave Beethoven's Mass twice in the Church. Much of it is, I admit, of the colossal order, and I doubt whether any man, who ever wrote a Mass, wrote with such lofty intentions, but I cannot learn to like the music, notwithstanding. To oblige Härtel, I wrote an account of the performance in the *Musikalische Zeitung*, but it went against the grain to do so. The use, or abuse, I should say, of the voice, irritates me beyond bearing. What an absurdity too, to write all the music in such a way, that no singer can sing it as it stands, without the aid of instruments! I like the *Kyrie* very much. The end of the *Gloria* is unbearable. . . .

Have you seen or heard anything of the new edition of Handel's works, published by the Handel Society? The first two volumes are out; one contains four Anthems in honour of George II.'s coronation, the other, *L'Allegro* and *Il Penseroso*, a sort of Cantata. I should be better pleased, if we were allowed to make selections, for a good deal of useless music is sure to appear—like this *Penseroso*, for instance. The Anthems are rather commonplace Handelian ware, but they will be available for our Church music. Whilst underlining them with the German text, I found, to my joy, how naturally the music grew out of the words and phrases, and this greatly lightened the task. If you only fit the words well to the beginning of each musical section, or to the introduction of any new phrase, the whole thing is safe. I have not myself underlined the words in the score, I have left that to the copyist, because he can't go wrong. It would be impossible to do this with the best of our modern music, for here the composer often adapts and writes in the words himself, whilst he is working at the piece. . . .

I set down the slow progress of French musicians in Rome to the fact that they come unprepared, and do nothing whilst they are there. But if you are talking about the way painters imitate the antique, I think the blame rests with David, Gerard, &c., rather than with the more modern professors. I find, in the later works that adorn the Galleries of Versailles and the Luxembourg, the strongest national characteristics; they are so clever and so expressive, that the contempt of our big, blundering Germans, who affect to despise these efforts, only shows their own pitiable conceit. I think just the same of composers, with their affectation of deep feeling in operatic music. Why, the tenth opera of a writer, whose first work was said to be full of promise, betraying only a certain want of knowledge of stage-business, is just as ill-suited to the theatre as the first. Three performances, and back it goes, just as the first went. Think of Lachner, Lindpaintner, and many others; think of Spohr, with his *Pietro*, his *Alchymist*, and his *Berggeist!* Surely, it is part of a composer's duty to be a good judge of librettos. Here is Hiller to the front again, with yet another opera good music, vile libretto—and yet he knew the importance of it, and took plenty of time over his work.

Felicien David has been here. Mendelssohn was much pleased with his Symphony; his other compositions are rarely heard. If a composer now-a-days succeeds in writing anything that pleases the public, instead of writing a second, he wanders about the world, trading on his first and only production. Spohr goes to Dresden in July, to conduct his *Kreuzfahrer*. We also hope to be there for a few weeks. . . .

Yours,

M. H.

92.

PRAGUE, *July* 26*th*, 1845.

. . . The day before yesterday, we heard Gluck's *Armida*
in Dresden. Schröder Devrient is excellent. Such crowds of
people flock to hear this opera, time after time, and it is such
a favourite, that for this reason alone we are bound to respect
it. I think Gluck's operas have something of the impromptu
about them ; it is as if a highly imaginative man were to lay
the text open on the piano, and to sing off the whole story
from beginning to end, in a fit of inspiration. Many people
would think this the highest praise, but then he may be
defective in other points. . . .

Yours,

M. H.

93.

LEIPZIG, *October* 12*th*—19*th*, 1845.

. . . I found a book on my return from Vienna, and
a letter from Härtel, requesting me to review it. I haven't
had time for it yet. It is a posthumous work of Weinlig's
on the Fugue, a fat volume, though the examples take up the
greater part of it. The author explains in his Preface, that
Marpurg's work, the only satisfactory one on the subject,
being out of print, he has undertaken to write another ; but
after Weinlig's death, Sechter brought out another edition of
Marpurg, so all Weinlig's labour has been thrown away.
Marpurg has one decided advantage, for he has taken his
examples from first-class works, in most instances from
Sebastian Bach himself, whereas Weinlig has written his
own—the out-of-the-way examples, as well as a great many
completed models. I highly commend his industry, but as an
incitement and an encouragement to the study of Fugue, the
work is comparatively a failure, for the exercises are dry,
mechanical, soulless, the product of that dead-alive period of
the Fugue after Sebastian Bach's time, when all vitality was

gone, and it had degenerated into mere formalism. I shouldn't think much of a young musician, who could sit down to work through the book, from beginning to end, without skipping a good deal; it would be a sign that he had no talent whatever. He had much better stick to Marpurg, and his bits of Bach, Frescobaldi, Buxtehude, &c., for Marpurg lived in an age when the Fugue was at its best, and he himself was animated with the true spirit of it. But the prescription Weinlig gives for making Fugues, is a worn out, bony old skeleton; he teaches you not form, but deformity; not Bach, but everything that Bach avoided.

Mendelssohn has published six Organ Sonatas; he played me three of them, and I thought them very fine. They are really suitable for the organ, and I like that artistic simplicity which is the special charm of his more recent works. Take, for instance, his last new Pianoforte Trio, in which I am glad to see, that he does not fuss himself about the particular effect of every phrase. Only I hope he will not go so far as Spohr, who in his later and latest compositions, persists in working on in the old mechanical groove. Comparing such things as these with Mendelssohn's earlier works, I see the stream has become a waterfall. There is a great difference between a pond and a puddle, though each reflects the same objects on the bank. The papers are full of scandal about the musical arrangements at the Beethoven Festival, and to-day, I see, Professor Breidenstein has received from the King of Prussia the Order of the Red Eagle; I suppose he will console himself with that. People thought, from Spohr's visit to Berlin, that he too would be decorated, but I have not yet heard of anything of the kind. Such a fellow as Spohr must live to be a very old man, if he is ever to get more than that one solitary Cross, bestowed on him by the Prince in a fit of ill-humour with Feige, for the sole purpose of annoying the latter. He would often enough have taken it away again afterwards, if that had been possible. . . .

I suppose you have heard of the death of old Mieksch, at the age of eighty-one. He taught singing industriously up to the very last, having lived through a long period of musical history in Dresden. You and I have seen many things come and go, but we found *Don Juan* and his contemporaries already to the fore; an octogenarian like Mieksch knew what music was before their day, and had witnessed the transition. One would think that *Don Juan* must have appeared on the scene like the *Commendatore*—but perhaps not; may be, it did not seem so great at the time, for such works as the *Opferfest* were named in the same catalogue with Mozart! And the *Zauberzither* was acted as well as the *Zauberflöte*. Such music as that in the *Wasserträger* must have created a great sensation, there had been nothing like it before. Spohr probably got his tendency towards what he calls " interesting harmonic progressions " from Cherubini; but Cherubini, happily for himself, remained Italian, and his " interesting harmonic progressions " are invariably saturated with pure melody, which makes them more transparent and less compact; they are never introduced, except when they can be appropriately used, and they occur more frequently in the instrumental than in the vocal part, to which latter chromatic passages do not easily accommodate themselves, as his vocal music is more diatonic in style. The chromatic style is based on change of key, and if it be made a primary instead of a secondary motive, the effect is harsher, more indefinite. Every vocal interval must be rationally defined or definable, if it is to be sung at all; were it otherwise, the composer himself would not hit the right notes. Talking of that, reminds me of the passage in my *Salve Regina*—

G sharp, c sharp,   C sharp, D natural,   B and E.

which although quite natural in its direct course, is generally a stumbling-block to competent singers, and impossible to the incompetent, who invariably get flat at the end of the piece. From the + onwards, it goes on purely at the pitch already reached; the difficulty really is to pass, within two bars, from C sharp minor to C major, although the steps themselves are clear enough. The g in the soprano always gets too flat, compared with the foregoing e. My Motet was once given by

a few amateurs at Schelble's, and I never heard it sung better
in tune ; for all that, I never feel quite comfortable—if the
music is agreeable to hear, it should also be grateful to the
singers, for as much effort is required to understand as to sing
it.   Although the difference expressed by the ratio 80 : 81
(the so-called syntonic Comma*) seems a small one, it is in
reality very important ; it is the difference between e as, for
instance, the third of C, and E, the fifth of A ; not of the C
minor triad with this C, for in that case, it would be the third

   64 : 80
    4 : 5
  a C e

but of the A major triad, reached by a series of fifths from

  1 3 9 27 81

C = C. G. D. A. E.   On the piano, it becomes the same note
by temperament, but the singer does not temper ; he takes
either the one or the other, and if he takes one of them in a
melodic sense, while the harmony demands the other, he
palpably sings out of tune.   When the Chorale *Ach Gott und
Herr*—

is accompanied in C, the A is the third of F major—

* If I sing

      *
  c d e f
    d e f♯ g
      *

then, in the first instance, d stands to e as 9 : 10, and in the second instance as
8 : 9—*i.e.*, the same proportion as existed in the first instance between c and d.

but in the transition to G major—

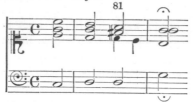

it is the fifth of D ; in the first instance it is eighty, in the second, eighty-one.   Should the singer have thought of the a as a third of f, it would be too flat for the D major, and he will have to glide into the fifth of D, for to remain between the two, as the pianoforte tuner is obliged to (so that all thirds are too large, and all fifths too small on the tempered key-board), is a thing a singer cannot possibly do, without singing false.   So it is not at all true, to say that the above melody may be treated in either way, for a different melody is produced by each treatment, and yet only one of these can be the one required.   Such a thing could not occur with the hexachord system *ut, re, mi, fa, sol, la*.   If the terminology has to be abandoned, it is still a matter of regret, that in our modern music (I mean that of our musicians), the feeling for what was expressed by that terminology should have become so rare, that they get their knowledge of Nature from a mere machine, determining vocal music by the pianoforte, restrain-ing a living curve within a dead circle, which is an unnatural thing that never occurs, nor could occur, in Nature, during a state of progress.   The *mi contra fa*, the *Diabolus in Musica* (I speak merely of pure vocal music) is but little heeded now ; people fancy that they have got beyond it, so to vocal music there must always be a pianoforte accompaniment, if it is to go off well.   The later Venetian School gets quite crazy over the great discovery that a flat and g sharp are the same note. Compare the last page in Winterfeld's book, which gives a bit of Marenzio, and see how the music wanders about through the different keys in enharmonic changes ! No one in our day would be able to write such a thing, subjected as we are to a rational order of modulation—yet there it proceeded from unity, which, once abandoned, can never be regained. . . .
—Yours,   M. HAUPTMANN.

94.

LEIPZIG, *January 7th*, 1846.

. . . I have not felt much inclined to go to concerts lately, partly on account of my health. I heard a few pieces, when Jenny Lind sang, but I happened to be particularly bad that evening. She delighted every one, and all the world is looking forward to her coming back again. " I don't think much of that," you will say; but there is no *arrière pensée*, except that I was not in a humour to listen. . . .

I got through a good deal of reading during my illness; *Les Mystères de Paris* in thirteen volumes, and *Consuelo* in eleven. When I am well, this would be impossible. I have to stick to the old books, and if, on rare occasions, I do take up a new volume, I make very little way with it. Once is quite enough for such a big book as *Les Mystères*, and there is no need to read it again; for the language is so vivid, so truthful, that one feels as if one were an actor in the scene. After that, I looked into one or two German novels, such trivial, sentimental, wearisome stuff, that the attention is sure to wander, whether you will or no; you are always thinking of the toiling author, whose existence you scarcely suspect, in the French. The worthy Bettina tried to do something of the same kind in *Dies Buch gehört dem König*, but people won't read it. It is a book, I suppose, as it stands bound up on a shelf with others, but there is nothing inside it. Everyone reads *Les Mystères*, and you can't put it down till you've finished it. Bettina's volume sticks in the throat like a stale bit of bread; it has as many divisions as a tapeworm. Now the French work, with all its simplicity, awakens a keen interest, because in spite of many episodes, it is a whole; there are perhaps fifty characters in it, but one can take in the plot at a glance. It is like a good picture— Leonardo's *Cenacolo*, for instance—with its thirteen figures, full and tranquil at the same time. . . . It is not mere unity nor mere plurality, but a representation of varied characters, which anyone can take in at a glance—

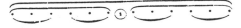

Of course, pictures admit of a still larger number of figures, and the same remark applies to compositions. . . . George Sand begins very finely, but then come long, unprofitable wastes of sandy desert, all she has thought, all she has read, all she has learnt, she never spares us anything—she leaves her story hanging in the air for half a volume or more —she makes the delay yet more wearisome, because she chooses to account for it by unnatural dialogues and interminable soliloquies, which are no sort of compensation, and only dull the brilliancy of the vivid situations that precede them. French writers should confine themselves to French life only. In *Consuelo* the action takes place in Germany, Bohemia, Austria, Prussia, but we never feel firm ground beneath our feet, only the hazy uncertainty of the authoress. As I said before, a composer should be as careful as a painter or a novelist, to arrange his work in such a manner, that it is possible to take a bird's-eye view of the whole. A good composer will always do so, and very often, the only merit of one who is not otherwise a good composer, consists in this. No other quality, not even originality, can make up for the want of a definite plan. That is why I hail the least trace of it in the writing of a beginner, and it is all the dearer to me, because it is difficult for the teacher to awaken any feeling in that direction, unless the pupil comes half-way to meet him. The wildest consequences result from the mere prescription of certain hard and fast rules; the pupil is quite satisfied, he thinks no fault can be found with him, because he has done just what he was told to. . . . Of course, young musicians hate the word Form; they think it means conventionality. All the same, they are quite content to be the possessors of a pair of eyes, a mouth, and a nose in the middle, like other folk—like Beethoven himself. He certainly was not a conventional writer, but in his greatest compositions, he never neglected Form. I envy you your *Belvedere*, for I am often bored by music, and sigh for some other recreation, which is not to be found here, except in our *Kunstverein* and in private collections of modern pictures, and these are as nothing, beside the paintings of the old masters, which have been carried down the stream of time, and will never be swamped by it.

Spohr has just written a Quartet for two violins, tenor, and cello, with an orchestral accompaniment; we shall hear it soon. His sixty-two years seem to have no effect on him, he is always on the go; that incessant activity and love of work command deep respect. Once he has planned a new scheme he is sure to execute it unfailingly. Few men like him have realised the accomplishment of their own ideals, for when once he has taken a thing in hand, all humming and hawing, all dilatoriness and *laisser aller* are odious to him, dear old fellow! He will leave no fragments, no unfinished sketches behind him. We are to hear the Third Act of the *Kreuzfahrer* at the Subscription Concert. I see no reason why he should not go on writing for years to come. . . .

Yours,
M. HAUPTMANN.

95.

LEIPZIG, *Maunday Thursday*, 1846.

. . . When we had read your last letter, Susette and I cried out simultaneously, "I should like to have it printed!" It would be nice, if one could have the letters one is fond of printed and bound up in a volume—so much easier to find what one wanted! Goethe's later letters look much better in print than his earlier correspondence with Lavater, &c., which wants the flying penmanship of the *Sturm und Drang* period. It is quite a different thing, in neat, orderly type. . . .

A *Liedertafel*, consisting of some eighty ladies and gentlemen, has just been started here; we owe it chiefly to Mendelssohn. The meetings are held once a month, song and supper (N.B. No Seneschal present!). Part-songs have to be written specially for the occasion. Only one was asked for, but when you begin, you may as well go on. Lots of people would write a dozen, but I remained content with half that number, for as everything has a beginning, so must everything have an end. I send you the *Zigeunerlied*, the *Abendlied*, *Waldeinsamkeit*, &c. . . . I was not made to be the overseer of a troop of boys, and I shall never get accustomed to it,

however long it may last. "This is no home for spirits," as
Iphigenie says. It is hard to transplant one's self, late in life,
and feel at home again—though that must depend on each
man's disposition—for I remember outsiders who came to
Cassel, and felt more at home there, after two years, than I
did after twenty. But anyhow, I bring my home with me,
that's one comfort! Surely, the State should be opposed to
marriage ; it is a state within the State.

Mendelssohn has written an Oratorio called *Elijah*, which
is to be given at Birmingham in May. Perhaps it will stand
in the same relation to *St. Paul*, as his later music to *The
Midsummer Night's Dream* does to the Overture ; not so full,
but more even! I like everything of his, early and late, and
if, after *Faust* and *Götz*, he gives us *Tasso* and *Iphigenie*, let
us rejoice in them all! He is always busy, always producing.
Œdipus and *Athalie* have not yet been heard out of Berlin.
Some of the last new Songs without Words seem to
me less interesting than the others—the sort of thing
he could improvise at any time. The other day, we had
a performance of Gade's dramatic Cantata, *Comola*, a subject
taken from Ossian. The work, which is fresh and pretty, was
well received ; but it is not clearly designed nor well put
together. Our doctor, who, I fancy, is no musician in the
ordinary acceptation of the term, says that it sounded to him
just like a Recitative from beginning to end. Now, though
the conventional Recitative never once occurs in it, the doctor
is not far wrong. As Recitative is only defined by the text,
the light and shade of the spoken phrases, and is rather a
tract of ground, which we must get over, than a place to halt
and sojourn in, so in *Comola* there is too much mere
transition ; we travel through beautiful scenes, but there are
no resting-places. I don't mean that the old-fashioned Aria
is an absolute necessity, but you feel the want of movements
which are rounded and complete in themselves. When we
have gone a long way, we want to arrive somewhere, else we
get tired. Had we a musical Goethe, he would inveigh against
such things, just as the poetical Goethe fell foul of the
Romantic School, although he surely knew how to recognise
talent, in whatever direction it lay.

We are going to repeat Bach's *Passion nach Johannes* on Palm Sunday and Good Friday. I have no doubt that the *St. Matthew Passion* was a later composition; it is far the finest of the two, but the choruses are harsh and barbaric in their grandeur, and the choral writing is closer and more condensed than any I ever met with. All the parts in the four-part choruses are continuously employed, with scarcely a break, and yet there is no padding, it is all organic. We only do five of the Arias, the most beautiful of which are the Arioso for the bass and the last contralto song. These are accompanied by a *Corno inglese* instead of a *Gamba*, and as nothing but the bass is given in the score, I have, as discreetly as I could, added middle parts for violas and cellos. It was a real success, and the audience was delighted with the effect. Susette sings the first and last songs, and they are well within her range. . . . Mendelssohn will soon be off again. He goes first to Liège, to conduct his *Lauda Zion*, and after that, to Birmingham, for *Elijah*. Though in the service of two Royalties, he is bound to neither, and besides, he is well enough off to be independent. He deserves all he gets, and he is the architect of his own fortune—an honest, persevering worker, to be commended accordingly. Not so the man who works by fits and starts, or from a momentary passion. . . . I doubt if Mendelssohn could accept, *en permanence*, a dependent position; it would go against the grain. Happy the man with a competence, enough to keep him from compulsory working at a task for which he has no aptitude nor natural inclination, and the pursuit of which hinders him from more profitable occupation; more profitable because, whether the result be great or small, it is what he was sent into the world to do. I believe that everyone has his own place in the scheme of things; how pleasant it would be, if he could only find it ! . . .

Yours,

M. H.

96.

. . . Mendelssohn is hard at work upon his *Elijah*, which he has to finish for Birmingham by August. I am greatly pleased with the *Lauda Zion*, which he has written for the Festival of Corpus Christi at Liège. It reminds one a little, at the beginning, of the *Lobgesang* and similar works; but later on, it becomes quite Latin in character. It is not easy to define the change, but it seems to me that the German Psalms, which anyone can sing for himself, which are more subjective, and should be treated more subjectively (not that I would alter them on that account), blend with all that is most characteristic of Mendelssohn in his music, more readily, than does the rock-like Latin hymn, to which he is here confined. Do you know his C minor Trio, dedicated to Spohr? It is a great favourite with me—plain, grandiose pianoforte music, deeply pathetic in parts, and highly effective. It sounded glorious on our Streicher the other day, when Mendelssohn played it with Spohr. He talked at first of having one of Härtel's pianos brought over, but he did not know, or had forgotten the Streicher upstairs. The tone was brilliant—it literally sang— and as for the playing, you know Mendelssohn can play upon anything! Surely, none but a pianist can write good pianoforte music, extracting, not the poverty, but the wealth of the instrument. Quartet-like part writing for the piano soon palls upon me; on the piano, multiplicity is unity, that is its compensation, and that quality it possesses above every other instrument. You may call this inability to sustain an equal strength of tone a defect, but there is also something musically beautiful in the natural dying away of the sound, and the avoidance of single, long-held notes is a special pianoforte effect. If a man has to force himself to remember this, if the feeling be not innate in him, he will never do any good; he is no better off than a writer of songs, who is out of sympathy with the human voice. . . . Mendelssohn, talking of Cologne Cathedral, the other day, and the music he heard there, observed that every instrument, trombones included, sounded poor, whereas two human voices filled the whole space directly. They mean to celebrate Mass in the nave, in 1848, though it will still be without a roof; I suppose it will take a little longer to finish that, and the towers! In St. Peter's, even the human voices do not sound, unless they can muster, as they do at Cologne, 2,500. . . .

Yours,

M. H.

97.

LEIPZIG, *June 5th*, 1846.

. . . Pianoforte playing, however elaborate, is an easier matter than violin playing; for one violinist, there are a dozen pianists. But a violinist can get on better without composition; he is like a singer, for nobody expects him to write his own songs, so long as he reflects his own spirit in their interpretation. Jenny Lind can sing *Norma* a hundred times, when another *prima donna*, however competent, could sing it but once. Think of the number of utterly worthless concertos for the violin, written by Frenchmen, which have been played repeatedly, because the performers saw in them an opportunity of making a name for themselves! It is just the same with singers; trash suits them almost better than the few compositions, which make too great a claim on the audience as music. . . . I wish we did not go so often to *Don Juan*, simply because a particular *prima donna* happens to sing; it is so great an opera, that the *ensemble* ought to be perfect. No one expects this in an Italian opera; the composer did not intend that we should. I am very glad to hear what you tell me, about Moritz's progress in composition. Never mind his dislike to counterpoint! That's the fault of our age. Young people look on it as a restraint, a chain forged by their masters, and now-a-days everyone must be free. But surely, there is more freedom in an eight-part Motet of Bach's, than in a sentimental Song without Words of the modern school. Mere sentiment, even in a good sense, is as little satisfactory in music as in any other art; there must be solid work, and that too in the good sense of the word. Goethe, when he was in Italy, recast his *Iphigenie*, exchanging prose, which he did not think strong enough, for verse, which—as he expressed

D 2

it—gave more predominance to Form. It was by paying attention to Form, that he secured its immortality. The earlier version has been reprinted among the posthumous works, enabling us to measure accurately the difference between a play in metre and a play written in so-called poetic prose, which, however closely it may approach the sphere of art, can never penetrate the circle. Anyone capable of distinguishing the difference between poetry and art will easily understand this. I don't mean to imply that a man need overtax his strength, in order to produce a work of art. Handel, who used to write an Oratorio in a fortnight, could never have had leisure enough for slaving at Counterpoint. But he had prepared himself by long study, beforehand, to claim this exemption, and he was a master of his craft. The tension of the open E string of a violin is thirty pound, if it is to sound large E; when the peg is fixed, the pull, although no longer actively exerted, as it has been in tuning, is yet essential to the existence of the sound; in the same way, the facility of a master proves that he worked hard to begin with.

The music in Félicien David's *Wüste** is very pretty, and I shall gladly defend it against those who try to run it down, but he has not put enough work into it; it shows more natural talent than real merit. Of course, from its very slightness, it is pleasanter to listen to than a more pretentious work, but it would not bear playing over and over again, like a Quartet of Haydn's, or a Fugue of Bach's. It is a happy inspiration, but when you have heard it once, you have learnt all that there is to learn from it. Besides, it seems to have exhausted the powers of the composer, for in a new work of his, which has been performed in Paris, he has assisted at the burial of his own reputation. I daresay, after all, it is just as good as we should have expected, just as good as his *Wüste*, but he was bound to write something better, after the extravagant praises bestowed upon him,—and of course that was impossible, with the very limited gifts at his disposal. . . .

Yours,
M. H.

The Desert.

98.

LEIPZIG, *August* 14*th*, 1846.

. . . It is rare to come across a good singer, but harder still to find a good singing-master. If a man will sing badly, let him do so; but it is a dreadful thing, to make your livelihood by teaching people to sing badly, who might learn to sing well, if they had the chance. Herr Risse, Herr Biene, and Mad. Drewitz profess to teach singing in Dresden; their pupils combine every imaginable fault, and their singing is so bad, that they might have been taught by the Nightwatchman. I think that Julia's schoolchildren, taught by her, sing delightfully, though they don't pretend to be finished artists. Her plan is, to sing a passage to them, and they imitate it as best they can. They have no mysteries about registers, head and chest voice, combinations of tetrachords, &c. But if they are naturally musical, it's a pleasure to hear them; if they are not, there's an end of it. We were talking the other day about Tichatscheck (not a great favourite of mine), and one of our Professors said, that in a *forte* passage, he allowed *half the phase* of the body of sound to strike against his teeth! A brilliant and instructive remark, wasn't it? And you should hear the tone produced by the speaker in question! The Lord knows where he allows *his phase of sound* to strike, but the effect is like the bleating of a calf. . . .

If I had a boy, I wouldn't send him to an *Alumneum* like this, even if he couldn't get his classics anywhere else. Better no Latin and Greek at all, than Latin and Greek only! All other subjects are secondary, in these old-fashioned institutions. I should send my boy to school, to learn how to behave himself, and how to hold his own, but I shouldn't let him live there. I don't think the young people are happy, for they are always fighting against the restraints of their school life. I suppose it can't be helped, but I should have thought a boy might learn what he learns at school in a far shorter time, if the powers of his mind were concentrated, and directed only to what is strictly necessary. I have heard that Rode, the

French violinist, found Franz practising ten hours daily, when
he went to see him in Dresden, and getting on worse and
worse. Rode told him that he very rarely exceeded one, or at
the most, two hours a day, but he devoted this time entirely to
conquering new or difficult passages. Here, we go through every
note of our Concertos, from A to Z, all day long, which is not only
unnecessary, but positively harmful. The result of too much
mechanical practice is to make easy things difficult, without
making difficult things easy. Concentration is the one thing
needful ; a chiroplast does nothing anywhere. This accounts
for the difficulty of acquiring mechanical skill, when we are
past our youth. It is not because our joints are stiff, it is
because we have too much to think about, and our thoughts are
but too apt to stray from an occupation, which cannot long
absorb a man with any pretension to brains. One might
manage eight hours one day, but not an hour for eight days.
I heard yesterday that Franz Liszt is setting some of
Petrarch's Sonnets to music, a curious combination of ancient
and modern ! I doubt Liszt's powers of writing for the voice;
his four-part songs, they say, are very unvocal. . . .

Yours,

M. H.

99.

LEIPZIG, April 8th—10th, 1847.

. . . On Palm Sunday and Good Friday, in place of
the Oratorio of the Passion (I did not know where to find
another), we had Astorga's Stabat Mater and Bach's Cantata,
Gottes Zeit. The Stabat Mater is really beautiful, the solos
highly effective ; I think, as a piece of workmanship, it is far
greater than the Stabat of Pergolesi. There is a Trio, a
Duet, and an Aria, which are perfect specimens of their kind ;
they are neither old-fashioned nor modern, they are for all
time ; rare enough in music ! Bach's Gottes Zeit, too, is one
of his finest works, though of course the result is not quite
what one could wish, when one cannot pick and choose in the

Chorus. I remember a performance of this Cantata at Schelble's, with a small choir, made up of a few good sopranos and altos, Schelble the only tenor, and you the bass. How delightful was the effect of that passage for soprano solo and chorus : *Ja komm' Herr Jesu!* And yet, I shall not be convinced that Bach intended it to be given as it is now,— unless you can show me that it is so in the MS. The alto Chorale, with the bass solo, is a different thing altogether. It is a lovely work, from first to last. . . .

I should like to get into the country this summer, if only for the sake of the children ; they are so happy out of doors, it is a real grief to them to have to come in again. They love the flowers and butterflies, and it is natural and right they should. Of course they can go into a hired garden here, but it takes such a long time, to get a procession of babies under weigh ! One wants a garden of one's own. I have never been able to manage even a few weeks in the country. We must have got into a very unnatural way of life, when Nature, harmless, beautiful Nature, seems so impracticable ; and yet it really is so—we are bound by a thousand chains. Art has devoured Nature, though there is very little trace of it in her works. . . .

Becker, our organist, is publishing a chronological Catalogue of Music up to the year 1700,—a very meritorious undertaking. He would not go beyond that date, for, at that time, the printing of music ceased for years, until Breitkopf took it up again. Bach's compositions were wretchedly engraved on tin or copper, and after 1700, the date of the year, which was all important to Becker, is wanting. It is highly desirable, that reference should be made to the earlier music which is only to be found in libraries, but it was impossible to get a complete list, so the idea had to be abandoned. However, the Appendix is to tell us about such ancient music as is still to be found in modern collections, and the way to get at it—though nothing will be included that cannot be procured through the trade, as at present constituted. It is a good thing for us, that there are bookworms of this description, who have a mania for collecting and classifying, and never lose patience over their work. There are plenty who

can begin such a task, but there is no merit whatever except
in the finishing of it.

I suppose you have heard about Spohr's Jubilee, on which
occasion the Electoral Prince is said to have surpassed himself in graciousness, strewing flowers with his own hands
before Spohr, who, of course, had to appear on the stage at
the gala performance. It seems rather silly, to have conferred on him the title of *Generalmusikdirektor* of Cassel, a
post he virtually filled before as *Kapellmeister*. However, it
gives him the right to appear at Court, to dance at the royal
balls, and eat the royal dinners. I think he is to be con-
gratulated on his Prussian Order, a compensation for neglect
in former days.

You have not come upon any serviceable Motets in
Munich ? If orchestrated, they might do for us on Sundays ;
if not, on Saturdays. The Prefects are ordered to supply the
library every year with twelve new Motets, but where are
they to get them ? We are in the same fix with regard to
orchestral works. Fischer offered me three Masses, in score
and parts, for five-and-a-half *thalers* the other day, but I
wouldn't take them at a gift. I could almost envy the
Dresden *Kapellmeister*, who can furbish up any old stuff they
like, and not be thought the worse of. I, poor wretch, am at
my wits' end every week ! We can't go on for ever repeating
the few good things we have, and even if I had the right to
give bad music, like my colleagues at Dresden, I have not
the heart to do so. It grieves me to see how the Mass suffers
at the hands of composers, who in other matters are much
more punctilious. Hummel never dreamt of disfiguring his
pianoforte pieces with such commonplace trash as is to be
found in his Masses ; anything, it seems, was good enough
for sacred music. Weigl too, when they asked him if he was
still at work, is said to have answered: " Now I have no more
ideas, I must take to the Church." Mendelssohn has given a
good impulse in this direction, not only by writing first-rate
Church music himself, but by writing it whilst he is still a
young man. As a rule, it has been the monopoly of superannuated musicians, who found they could no longer succeed
in secular works. There is less risk in writing a Mass, or

setting a Psalm, than in producing an Opera or a Symphony; people don't pay to go to church, and no one looks a gift-horse in the mouth. . . .

Yours,

M. HAUPTMANN.

100.

LEIPZIG, *June 12th,* 1847.

. . . I am very glad you find that you can use *Ueber allen Gipfeln* as an *Ave Maria.* The words of the *Ave Maria* can be more easily adapted to sentimental music of this kind, than any other sacred text. The Rector here had substituted other words for my *Salve Regina,* so that we might sing it in church, but they brought out a sort of unreality and effeminacy, which were not conspicuous in it before. Of course, Palestrina's *Salve* is another thing—and not a bad thing in its way! on the contrary, it is very fine. If one could but fire the hearts of the people, singers and hearers alike! But they complain that the end never comes, they think it wearisome, they long for the four-to-a-bar periods, &c. The consequence is, that even the singers prefer my Motet with the original words. When I was in Bohemia, I often heard congregations singing hymns, which were more like songs in respect of metre, rhythm, and melody, instead of our chorales.

Thibaut, however, is quite right in his views of modern church music, though they apply more directly to Catholic, than to Protestant churches. In the Protestant school, Sebastian Bach and Handel are still first and foremost in respect of genuine feeling; the clothing may be old-fashioned, but there is plenty of earnestness and depth within. The intro-duction of the orchestra made too much of the clothing, and clothes get out of fashion; in our time, vocal music, which ought to stand on its own merits, is in reality in-strumental music translated. Witness those "interesting harmonic progressions" and tiresome pedal-points, where the bass gets lockjaw, and is degraded into a dead machine, whilst the other parts are still supposed to represent actual persons! I am just fresh from an experience of this, for I have been making my pupils sing a short stanza of my own, in which a dead pedal-point in the bass, such as I have described, is a conspicuous feature. I doubt if any of the singers felt as keenly as I did, how far short it fell of the proper effect; but such a passage is more tolerable in a chorus than in a solo, and it is just as unnatural to express words on a note, lying frozen, as it were, at the root of the harmony, as to dwell for an unconscionable length of time upon a single syllable. Strange that it should be so easy to see what we had better do, and so hard to do it! Even Goethe felt the difficulty; when it comes to practice, " We act as we are wont to act."

What you say about the minor scale is quite correct; the descending g in A minor can be accompanied with a⁷; at the same time, the note G does not cease to be the lower Fifth of D, or the Prime of the G minor chord, and a c e g is, after all, not a mixture of the chord of A minor and C major, but the A minor chord, with the beginning of that series of triads, of which the A minor is the last.

$$\ldots \ldots | \overset{\frown}{\text{G b D f A c E}} | \text{g sharp H} \ldots \ldots$$

As every truth must be corroborated by instinct, one can feel quite well that in the key of A minor A c E | G is something different from what it is in the key of C or F major a C̆ e Ğ.

Thus, in the former, the interval c G is no Fifth, but is to the Fifth as 80 : 81—*i.e.*, the difference (not the apparently trifling difference of number, but distinctly a difference of Nature)— called the same in pianoforte nomenclature, although it appears in the system of Fifths, now as I. and afterwards as III.

As in the series . . . B flat d F a C e G b natural D⁺ . . .

the d is different from big D, and the a is no Fifth to the D, and the chord D | F a in C major is not the D minor chord, but just as b D | F is only a triad on paper, not at all in reality, but only a bringing together of the extreme limits which enclose and define the key; so b D | F is, of course, more than D | F a, neither of them being sufficiently definite, inasmuch as the one might be interchanged with E g sharp | B | D f |, the other with d F a in A minor and F major. Thus G b D | F is fixed for and belongs to C major and minor, whereas g sharp B D f belongs to A minor. With regard to the enumeration and nomenclature of the intervals, my pupils never get much instruction from me, little more than occasional remarks. Perhaps I give them too little, for, as a matter of fact, the students learn to understand the subject more from without than from within; and, after all, a nomenclature may serve a good purpose. But I really cannot find time, to make a regular, tabulated form of Intervals. I should have to change my ways, and begin with them. I could not introduce the augmented Third, although the notes in it are seen in your example of the diminished Sixth—

which might occur in G minor :

a flat C e flat g b flat D f sharp A c sharp E :

for I might let a flat and c sharp be heard one after the other, in the harmony, without losing the sense of Tonality, G b flat D. It is quite evident, that a flat, in your illustration, sounds with the c sharp as a suspension, and it concentrates most compactly all that has to be grasped together. Other anomalies, such as that passage of yours—

where E flat, c sharp and g sharp are sounded together, are not to be accounted for by direct means. That is, the figure is to be regarded by itself, as a parasitical plant, like the mistletoe on the oak, which is rooted in the tree, but yet has an organism of its own; or like a monkey, jumping about on a stalking camel. E sharp can never be anything else but the Third of c sharp; thus the $\begin{cases} a \\ f \end{cases}$ sharp which is represented

(VII 70)

by the tree, or the camel G : V, f sharp is of itself a I, whose V is c sharp.

Here, at all events, each chromatic interval has its meaning, as one of the three possible *momenta* of the harmony, and it can have no other meaning; for instance, g g sharp a : as C V. E III a I or G V, a : V—I; but they are not to be referred to the underlying chord, any more than the monkey's gambols would be explained by the anatomy of the camel. We should quickly dispose of such combinations, if we took them for what they are, conglomerates, having no effectual existence, and of which the component parts hardly cohere, and hardly affect one another. So, too, the intervals of harmonies upon a pedal bass, which, if we wish to compute them from the pedal note, are quite inexplicable, because they have no direct relation with it : for just as connected melodic notes may be heard together with a prolonged chord, so connected chords may be heard together with a prolonged note, but the place of such a note in the Tonal system can only be a pivot upon which the harmony turns—*e.g.*, in C major, not F or D, but :

$$
\begin{array}{cccc}
\text{F} & \text{C} & \text{G} & \text{D} \\
 & & 1-\text{v} & \\
 & 1-\text{v} & 1-\text{v} &
\end{array}
$$

—*i.e.*, G before the close, C after the close; G for the authentic and C for the plagal close. On G turn tonic and dominant, on C subdominant and tonic; it is only those chords that can be referred to the pedal note; they rest upon it, and so serve to combine that which occurs between them, and is alien to the pedal note.

You are right in saying, that to judge by the singing world of our time, it is difficult to explain, how people could have sung the ancient music correctly without accidentals. All accidentals are, as we ought to know, only the signs to show if a tone is the *mi* or *fa* in solmisation : the b *durus* or b *mollis* of the old tetrachord; b *durus* is harsh and angular to look at (♮), and b *mollis* pleasant to look at (♭); the first,

when rapidly dashed off, developed into ♮ or ♯, for both these forms have the same signification in ancient music (where usually there was no other signature at the beginning of a piece but a b), and the so-called Quadrate (Natural), being rather like b, has (by Germans) been called h (Natural). This was the origin of our unspeakably silly musical alphabet, a h c d, etc., instead of a b c d, etc. Now, however, it may happen that in a purely melodic part, a note may be a *mi* or b *durus*, where the harmonic condition of the sequel does not admit of it; how then is the individual singer to know this, until he has heard the whole ? Such things often happen, not only in the music of the oldest composers, such as Ockenheim, Josquin, and the like, but even in the music of the seventeenth century. It is clear to me, that our major and minor—*i.e.*, a single tonality, and at the same time an infinite number of such had to be evolved, and that the earlier so-called Modes, in limited number and function, are only the result of a narrow conception. So in Creation, transition had to be made from all created things to self-conscious Man. Our scale, compared with that of earlier times, is like the Christian Religion among or above other religions. One must nevertheless acknowledge the beauty of ancient compositions, though classing their system of scales not above but below our own. Surely, a sound horse is more beautiful to look upon than a sick man. The higher organism is always more subject to disease than the lower. The old scale never gets out of itself, and consequently cannot return to itself; without the chord of the dominant Seventh, nothing can be rightly grouped together into unity. But together with this modern power, we have to face the possibility of dismemberment and sentimentality—disease, in fact. The former was too general, the latter is too much individualised; the former had too little cadence and articulation, the latter has too much. This holds good in all that concerns metre in musical matters. It is just as little possible, to write with the old key-system, in our manner of rhythmical and metrical construction, as to write in our modern system of keys, preserving the old melodic continuity. Each must have its own counterpart. . . .
—Yours, M. HAUPTMANN.

101.

LEIPZIG, *August* 20*th*, 1847.

. . . A few Sundays ago, I went to Dresden, on purpose to be present at a performance of *Tannhäuser*, an opera by Wagner, which I am glad to have heard, as I knew next to nothing of his music. His aims and tendencies are utterly foreign to the purposes of Art, he aspires to that which no artist should aspire to, and could he realise his aim, it would be the destruction of all Art. For he admits, and properly too, that *Tannhäuser* is not music at all. What is it then? Musical declamation? Surely, the mere setting of words to sounds does not constitute music; real music consists in so combining words that they form a whole as regards feeling, just as the combination of words is the rational sense of speech. When Wagner sets *Welch ein seltsam Leben*,* he flies off at a tangent on the word *seltsam*, and *Welch*, the beginning, has no sort of unity with *Leben*, at the end, even as a musical phrase; of course, there is no question of periods. Everything else that people find fault with in this opera, the noises, the overloaded harmony and instrumentation, is merely relative; there are very brilliant and effective passages, but the main fault, the purpose he has in view, makes the whole thing valueless. With Wagner himself to conduct it, and the unlimited means of a Court Theatre at his disposal, a splendid *mise-en-scène* and a fine orchestra, the Dresden people will go to see it for a time, and even believe that it would be very lovely, if only they understood it—if they could but see the stars for the fog—but it won't live; the music has no substance in it. Wagner had his operatic scores, in his own handwriting, lithographed and published straight off; *Tannhäuser* was issued before the first rehearsal. . . . He is, as you know, his own librettist, and the book, taken by itself, *not* as a libretto, is the best part of the whole thing. Besides this, he superintends all the stage arrangements, even to the smallest detail, and here he shows great skill. He is more of a conjuror than an artist. . . .

---

* What a strange life!

I have just finished a Chorus for men's voices, *Ehre sei Gott in der Höhe*, with accompaniments for two horns and three trombones ; it was a commission for a wedding. It is my first effort in writing for male voices only ; *in abstracto* I hate four-part songs for men, though *in concreto* I must confess there are good examples of it—*e.g.*, Mendelssohn's. The strain of producing a double contrast from the high and low registers of the human voice, is repulsive to me, whereas twice two is a perfectly natural distribution between male and female voices. Of course, the actual notes can be reached, but the very high and the very low in such a range do not blend together. A bass growls the deep f, a tenor screams the high e ; voices so different in character and strength are hopelessly at variance, and even when they go well together, the music soon gets monotonous ; we have bare agreement, nothing more. In the long run, I am always bored by men's voices, and I don't care in the least for the Festivals which are so popular now-a-days ; I must have choral parts, male and female, properly distributed. I suppose you have heard of our recent meeting of musicians here ; Herr Brendel, who represents music, philosophy, and æsthetics (you can't beat that !) at our *Conservatoire*, presided. Well, they met last Friday and Saturday—in the morning for speeches and learned talk, in the afternoon for music, in the evening for a supper, with Fr. Schneider in the chair. He and Moscheles, who lives here, were the only distinguished people present, as far as I know ; the others were nobodies. I shirked. I couldn't see the necessity of it beforehand, and now everything that was to be discussed has been discussed, and everything is in a fair way to remain just as it was, I see it still less ; yet they are actually talking over the plan for next year's meeting, already ! I cordially dislike all the æsthetic and philosophical presumption, which marked Brendel's earlier Lectures, and Schneider assured me, that it was very conspicuous in his Inaugural Address. He said that music was only just beginning to be intelligent again—namely, through the explanations of such gentlemen as had once read their Hegel through, and appropriated to their own use the mere catchwords of professional skill. Of course, Sebastian Bach and Mozart did not know what they were about—the

dawn began with Beethoven, and after him came daylight!
To illustrate all this verbiage, an amateur, Frau Brendel,
played a Sonata by Flügel, and no one, not even Schneider,
could make out in what time it was, and which was the
beginning, which the end. When Brendel lectured on modern
music in the *Gewandhaus*, he never alluded to Mendelssohn,
though he said a good deal about Schumann. He
thinks that Mendelssohn has so imperfectly realized
the proper aim of Art, that he has slender claims to be called
musical,—which is tantamount to saying that, according to his
views, Mendelssohn's music has no form. Then we have
another gentleman, Lobe, who says that every artist must
come to grief, unless he proposes to himself something
definite, "objective," as he calls it. He recently published, in
his own paper (Härtel's), an analysis of the Overture to
Don Juan, and taking as a motto Goethe's words, " The
real artist never does a stroke in vain," he actually dis-
sects every bar, so as to show in what way Mozart meant it
to be characteristic. Oh, that Mozart could have read it!
I can hear him saying in his mongrel Viennese German,
" What a pack of jackasses you all are ! " though I daresay
his language would not have been quite so choice as that!
It is such folly, to attempt to define music in this manner.
Musical expression is general, and it answers to an infinite
number of particulars at the same time, like an algebraic
formula, which may be taken to stand for many different
numbers.   When I say $a + b = c$, and another person maintains that this is equivalent to saying $1 + 2 = 3$, he may be
perfectly right ; but he who affirms that $2 + 3 = 5$ is right too,
and so on *ad infinitum* with others, who attribute other special
values to a and b. It is owing to the higher nature of algebra,
that in all these special cases and values, it only expresses
their relation, that in which they all are one; I may be thinking of apples and pears all the time, and my friend of the
distance of Sirius. . . .

Mendelssohn, I hear, is writing some inaugural music for the
opening of Cologne Cathedral, a delightful task, apart from
any of the disturbing influences of time and circumstances.
He had heard an instrumental piece performed in the

Cathedral, and with a well-appointed orchestra too, but it made no kind of effect; afterwards, when the choir sang without accompaniment, the effect was splendid. It is conceded on all sides, that flutes and violins are out of place in a church, though we have never been able to get rid of them; but nothing sounds so mean as stringed instruments, unless there is such a mass of them, that you cannot hear the thin, scratchy tones of the catgut. At Dresden, they have plenty of first violins, and are overweighted with basses; but apart from the composition itself, the whole thing is bad, for one hears next to nothing of the voices, and the orchestra is mere buzzing. . . . The Bishop has substituted a vocal movement for the Symphony, which used to do duty for the Graduale. This might have been a change for the better; but, on the one hand, the choir is too small, and, on the other, the new compositions, written for the purpose, by members of the band, such as Morgenroth, Dotzauer, and Reissiger (who threw off a dozen of them in no time), are, like the old Symphonies, poor, trivial, and sentimental. Of course they cannot use the ancient music, that would mean ancient singers, nor do people like Reissiger want it, for they imagine they can do much better, more particularly as the chord of the diminished Seventh was not then invented. Take it out of their pretty little compositions, and there wouldn't be much left—so they don't think there can have been much in the old masters. . . .

Yours,

M. H.

102.

Leipzig, *November 3rd*, 1847. *Evening.*

Dear Hauser,—

I write to you in a very anxious and depressed state of mind, for Mendelssohn is so ill, that we are much alarmed. About three weeks ago, he had a sudden attack, the feet and hands became cold as ice, the head feverishly hot, and these symptoms were accompanied by loss of consciousness.

He was with some friends at the time, and they had to take him home. However, it all passed off, and after a few days, he felt pretty well again. Since that time, he has had several more or less bad relapses. I found him, a fortnight ago, looking weak and tired, though he seemed on the way to recovery. Next day the pains in the head became violent, but these were greatly relieved by copious nose-bleeding, and so he rallied again. It was currently reported here, a week ago, that he was dead, but I went in all haste to the house, and found him looking certainly better than before. There was no foundation for the rumour. Since last Sunday, however, there has been a real change for the worse, the doctors are now greatly alarmed by the congestion of blood to the head, and this evening we hear that he is very ill indeed—news which was, alas, confirmed, when we called to enquire! The nature of the disease makes one feel very anxious. Hofrath Clarus told us, even on Sunday, that they feared an effusion of blood upon the brain. I cannot forget, that Raphael and Mozart died in their thirty-seventh year. Sad, sad! I easily lose hope now, when I hear that anyone is ill. . . .

I sent at once for Father Singer's book on Music, *Die Metaphysischen Blicke.* It is a poor thing, not a bit better than many former treatises, written on the same subject. The book is wanting both in technical knowledge and in philosophy. It is hopelessly wrong, too, on the subject of Temperament, which, he says, is a *sine quâ non* of the existence of music in our time. Why, I ask, is our music alone to be affected, by the fact that C sharp and D flat are apparently so close to one another, that a clever pianoforte tuner can only tune them to one note, equally available for both? We musicians should fare well enough, if each note stood independently for itself. The Circle of fifths is as little a matter of practice as it ought to be in theory; it ought not to be taught, for at best it is but a makeshift. But Singer makes out Temperament to be a thing of far higher importance—he considers it as the element of evil, which has found its way into the world, and has banished all purity, &c. For naturally in the succession of fifths, not merely the difference between C and C sharp and D flat has to be considered, but also that between E as a third of C and as a fifth of A, and so in respect of all notes viewed as thirds and fifths; so he says that the neighbouring chord of A minor cannot occur in C major, without Temperament, because the e is so different in both. Why didn't he consult some person conversant with the subject, who would have enlightened him, about these expressions, before he had his book printed?

The e̊ in the A minor chord has actually nothing in common with the É where it occurs in the series of fifths, but is in fact a part of the C major Triad, and is the pure fifth of the a which belongs to the chord of F : F a C̆ e̊ Ğ b D f sharp A c sharp É. But if the A major chord follows that of the C̊ major, it can only be defined by the a – e given by C major, and it is not the e which would be different, but the c sharp would not be the same that it is at ○. There are in music no such predetermined notes as are found lying mechanically, side by side, on a piano ; on the contrary, each one settles the matter for himself, in his own consciousness. Has a singer a fixed c, c sharp, d flat, e or E in his voice, and is vocal music—pure polyphony, I mean, which none but very borné people associate with Temperament—beyond the pale of modern music? I have known people go so far as to say, that a singer ought to learn intonation from a piano tuned in equal Temperament, for otherwise he would be unable to sing in tune. I ask only as to the possibility (necessity is out of the question) of thinking of a g flat, when f sharp is played, or in a work written in G major, of thinking of a chord with g flat in it? This is only one of the many points that arise, from a misapprehension of the subject. And then such chords as—

which we are about as likely to come across as fir cones in the top of orange trees! This arises from a false idea of augmented and diminished Intervals, from the supposition that a note can be screwed up or down, that the difference between a major and a minor chord consists in the *"deepened"* third, &c., for a *third*, like a fifth and an octave, can only be *one thing* (what we call a major Third), hence—

$$\overgroup{C\ e\ G}, \qquad c\ \overgroup{E\flat\ g}.$$
$$\text{I-III} \qquad\qquad \text{I} - \text{III}$$
$$\text{I} - \text{V} \qquad\qquad \text{I} - \text{V}$$

I do not care to insist upon this elementary knowledge. It is an *aperçu*, which a number of learners are not likely to get at straight off; but don't let us add to the many falsities and half-truths, already existing, others which are still less intelligible, and don't let us make extravagant pretensions to new and enlightened ideas.

4th—Early, 7.30.

I have just returned from Mendelssohn's; he has passed a very restless night, and is in the greatest danger. That was the bulletin, in Schleinitz's own handwriting. I saw nobody but a maid-servant, who was in great distress. His brother Paul has arrived from Berlin. What will become of us to-day? So much that is beautiful has been crowded into this short life—he is famous—he is happy in his home—he has deserved it all. What grief to think of his poor wife and children, if he should die! "Nothing but love makes the existence of Man a necessity," says Werther. True enough! The world goes its old way, but who can stand in the gap, when our nearest and dearest are taken? Thank God, that we are forced to live so much in the present; but for that, which of us would have a moment's happiness? It is only very young and very thoughtless people, who can enjoy really high spirits. I think, to a certain extent, we do well to keep in mind the sadness of the world. It is not right to withdraw from it altogether. Let us help our fellow creatures to bear their burden, as best we may, and when we may—else it will be too late. . . . Another series of Mendelssohn's short eight-part Anthems, taken from the Psalms, must be coming out now in Berlin. He brought them to me one day, when they were in manuscript, and asked me about the counterpoint. I thought them very beautiful, and very well suited to the voice, but I am not sure whether they would do for the Catholic Church Service. They were written for the

Cathedral Choir at Berlin. In the eight - part movement, there were passages in which it would have been difficult for the eight voices to move without constraint; I said something about this, and afterwards he wrote a German Mass (I think), in which, he told me, that he had endeavoured to confine himself to harmony that moved freely in eight parts. He brought this work to me for my opinion, but we happened to be in Berlin at the time. I go on and on writing about Mendelssohn, trying to forget how hopeless his condition is now! It is eight o'clock, and we have no better news; though he has been quieter throughout the day, the doctors are just as anxious. Dr. Härtel has gone to Berlin to fetch Schönlein, the King's body physician; they expect him this evening. Schleinitz, who is continually with Mendelssohn, has become much more despondent in the course of the day. The concert is put off. . . .

5th,—Early.

My letter ends with the saddest news. Mendelssohn passed away yesterday evening at nine o'clock, quietly and peacefully; he was unconscious the whole day, but there was no suffering. Alas, for the poor wife and children! Schönlein arrived in time, but it was seen from the first that the illness was mortal, beyond the reach of human skill. He was first attacked on Sunday, October 10th, whilst in the act of rehearsing some numbers of the *Elijah* with Frau Frege, at her own house. Benedict, who happened to be in Leipzig, brought me the news on the Monday. I was rather unwell, and had to postpone my visit until Wednesday, when I found Mendelssohn on the sofa, and he was in good spirits, and glad to talk. Next day he got worse. Later on, he thought he was going to recover; his troubles seemed more mental than physical. The following day he was not so well, and since that time, I suppose no one but Schleinitz has been admitted. I never saw him again.

Anything in this letter that does not relate to the one subject, was written merely to distract my mind, for I spent the whole of yesterday in grief and anxiety. Farewell, dear Hauser! My kind greetings! Yours,

M. H.

103.

DEAR HAUSER,—

Herewith, I enclose the programme of the last honours paid to Mendelssohn. It was a very beautiful, impressive ceremony, and the intense and universal sympathy made it much more than a mere pageant. The procession, followed by crowds, passed from the house to the Paulinerkirche, where the coffin was placed upon a lofty dais, draped in black, and surrounded with candelabra. The orchestral platform was also draped in black. There was a full orchestra, and a chorus of five hundred voices. The programme will tell you the rest. After the address, the chorus, "Happy and blest," from *St. Paul*, was sung with marvellous effect. Whatever may be said against modern Church music, and I myself have said a good deal, such a chorus as that was most appropriate; it is one of the loveliest things Mendelssohn ever wrote. It was the first thing out of *St. Paul* that I heard, when Feige and I were passing through Leipzig in 1836, and Mendelssohn was still a bachelor, living *en garçon*, in Reichel's garden. On that occasion, he played me several things from his Oratorio, the corrected proofs of which he had just received from the printer; I remember how that particular Chorus charmed me. We all thought Pastor Howard's address very fine; by *we*, I mean all of our household, for many of the Leipzig *haute volée* are not satisfied with it. What do they want? Nothing satisfies them. Perhaps they wanted a sermon on the *Lieder ohne Worte*, or a minute analysis of Mendelssohn's pianoforte playing, or what not? Howard was a dear friend of the Mendelssohn family, and loved him well; others were friends too, and loved him in the same way. Everybody can speak—that is not an art which has to be learnt, like pianoforte playing or painting, and no one expects a display of theological learning on such an occasion as this. So everyone can realise Howard's position, when he stood by Mendelssohn's coffin. It would be only good natured, if they were to ask themselves, what they would have said, if they had had to stand there. But they never think of that. What we do hear is, that they are " not satisfied." For my own part, I thought, and I still think that Howard's address was very appropriate; he is a dear good fellow.

I wrote the above about a week ago, but was unable to finish my letter, owing to press of business. The King of Saxony has written a very touching letter to Mendelssohn's widow; he feels his loss keenly. To-day His Majesty is at Leipzig, and he will be present at the Concert to-morrow, when we do the *Walpurgisnacht*. . . . Have you seen Schiller's very interesting Correspondence with Körner ? It is yet another proof of the wonderful energy and unceasing activity of two men whom the world justly remembers. Of course, many others, of whom the world hears nothing, may have been equally laborious; but then, the necessity of their profession or occupation probably makes it imperative, whereas in an artist or a poet, it is a self-imposed task. It is only hard workers who can hold their own. Spasmodic genius is soon forgotten. Impromptus die as they are born. The artist must take some trouble about it, if he wants his fruit to ripen. . . .

Yours,

M. H.

104.

Leipzig, *December 4th*, 1847.

. . . Talking the other day, with a friend, about Becher's compositions, I remarked that you could always hear the advocate in the music; this was repeated to Mendelssohn, and he was much tickled by it—he caught at my meaning. It seems as if Becher were for ever labouring to make that appear right, which most people consider to be wrong. Of course it does not sound well, but there being such a thing as the chord of the thirteenth (which was not invented by

him), he must be allowed to use it. There was a Jew who said:
" What do false oaths exist for, if you are not to be allowed
to take them ? " . . . We were in Berlin from the 3rd to
the 12th October, and had a very good time there. We saw
a fine portrait of Jenny Lind by Magnus, belonging to
Professor Wichmann, with whom she lived for a time. I
should like you to see it. It is being engraved, and Magnus
has promised us a copy. I shall be glad to have it, though
the engraving is sure to fall far short of the picture, and still
more of the original, as you will say. . . . We heard
Viardot Garcia at the Königstädter Theatre in *Norma* and
L'Elisir d'Amore. People say that she and Lind are as
different as day and night, in the character of Norma. That
I can well believe, but Donna Anna could not be altered at
will in this manner. Viardot, however, it must be owned,
is an intellectual artist, and knows how to carry one along
with her. Much of Norma was too ugly for me—herself
amongst other things. The charm of beauty is utterly
wanting in her, but she is full of animation, and her virtu-
osity is of the highest order. The other parts were wretchedly
filled, yet I assure you that they all sang better together, and
more musically too, than the whole lot of their colleagues at
the Royal Opera-House. They had good voices, and understood their business ; anyhow, they had learnt it, even if
they did not understand it. I was interested in two other
institutions, the *Singakademie* and the Cathedral Choir ; fine
voices there too ! The *Singakademie* has a splendid concert-
room, but the music we heard there was a dreary funeral
Cantata by Schulz, and it seemed a pity, to see such fine
material thrown away on such poor music. The Cathedral
Choir is first-rate, and I liked some parts of the service,
though I thought the whole thing rather artificial; what
modern music is not ? A good bonfire of the Motets we have
here, would relieve us of piles of trash, which has come down
to us from the prosaic age of wigs, and the few good things
remaining would have a better chance. We should be much
better off with nothing than with all this rubbish. The
Cathedral Choir is composed of the best voices, from all parts
of the country. If the voice goes, the owner of the voice has to

go also, to make room for a new-comer, so the Choir is always fresh and in good order. Tenors and basses are well paid. . . . The second part of our yesterday's programme at the *Gewandhaus* consisted of the Overture and Introduction to Gluck's *Alceste*. Contrasted with the other music, it produced a good effect, particularly the Introduction, which is effective from the very first bar. I thought the Herald's mounted trumpeter an anachronism, and the Aria of *Alcestis* is *wiggy*. No one escapes the influence of his age ; when ages have past, it doesn't take much to find that out. But a staccato rendering seems to me utterly unlike Gluck; to change the music and the time with every new phrase of the text, to represent not the transition but the revulsion of feeling, as if it had nothing to do with what had gone before, that is musically untrue—*i.e.*, unmusical. Gluck says, in one of his prefaces, I think, that he tried above all things to forget that he was a *musician*, whenever he had to write an opera. His meaning is plain enough, but in a certain sense, he had not so very much to forget ; had there been more, he need not, indeed he could not have forgotten it. I do not know whether Raphael tried to forget that he was a painter, when he set to work upon a picture ; I doubt if the thought ever occurred to him. A man that can see does not think of his eyes. There is a sort of loftiness in Gluck. and it is his weak side too. Let a man be ever so great, he is more or less of a fool, if he lets his vanity run away with him. Handel was a bit of a coxcomb, Vogler as great a coxcomb as ever lived, S. Bach, Haydn, Mozart, the very reverse. We don't want anecdotes and sayings to confirm this ; their music shows it clearly enough. . . .

Yours,

M. H.

105.

LEIPZIG, *January 22nd*, 1848.

. . . I am sorry you have so much to worry you ; it is a bad look out, when one sees no prospect of ever being able to live the life one would have chosen. There is less and less time for reflection, as the years go by. I always sympathised with those old kings and warriors—old artists too—who retired from their professional life, because they wanted to spend the few years that remained to them in a cloister, waiting peacefully for their last moment, safe from the bustle of the world. Why should there not be cloisters for people like you and me, our wives and children ? though I couldn't quarrel with the latter, if they preferred to stay at home !

. . .

The only originality I look for in any author, is the actual experience of the emotion that he describes ; barring what he makes out of this, he will never be able to achieve anything positive. All other originality is artificial, and makes itself felt as such. Take the very best music that we have, and you will find no such special originality as shall distinguish it, outwardly, from music of the same date. It is so with Palestrina, Bach, Haydn and Mozart. Beethoven, of course, does not take the straight road, he plunges aside into the thicket ; but this is an exception which corresponds with the peculiar circumstances of the man ; it is the expression of his loneliness, of his solitary position in life,—and then I daresay he did prefer meadows and woods to the well-worn ruts of the high road. He could find his way out of them whenever he chose. The unusual passages in his music are not mere curiosities, like those which occur in the work of many a more modern writer, who must needs be different from everyone else, though he has nothing of his own to start with, and reckons his every fancy an idea. Now, ideas are intelligent and intelligible, however unusual they may be. They have something positive about them, something that is true all the world over ; but fancies are mere accidents, brilliant one

day, absurd the next, sometimes nothing but ridiculous vanity.
They are utterly inartistic. Not but what there are many
people, who never get far enough to be artists, though their
intentions are excellent, and they are quite free from vanity.
A person of this kind stands in the same relation to a
conceited man, as stupidity does to wickedness; all wickedness
is stupidity, but not *vice versâ*. To be a real artist, you must
combine the harmlessness of the dove with the wisdom of the
serpent. . . . The theory of repetition is misunderstood
by the modern school. They want to get rid of it; they think
it superfluous and burdensome. They might as well say, that
the left eye was a superfluous repetition of the right. In point
of fact, I know they often omit nothing less than the half of
their subject. They draw a left eye and put a right ear to
match it—or even a left ear, as the case may be; it's all one
to them. I could give you startling examples, but music is
always going forward; it won't stand still, systematically, like
architecture, and so its defects are less apparent. There is a
certain height and depth in music, space as well as time, and
though metre and rhythm, from the very nature of the thing,
exist only in time, we have a sort of conception of space in
time, by which we understand fixity in a state of progression,
and without which, it is impossible to think of any melody as
a whole. So too with metre and rhythm in poetry; they have
the symmetry of time, they are firmly defined beforehand,
independently of the logical contents of the poem, which, in
the narrower sense, supply the artistic as distinct from the
poetic element of art. This separate existence, which is at
the same time co-existence, is not to be grasped by the under
standing alone, nor can the understanding grasp the essence
of combination; it can only divide and classify. The understanding is the true chemist, who can resolve blood into
lymph, white of egg, and a few other things, but cannot make
them into blood again when he has done it—nor should he
wish to, if he means to understand his own business. With
all the ingredients of a man, he could only produce an
homunculus, a thing that struggles for birth, but cannot attain
to it, having no life, no *actuality*. The understanding,
however, is always comprehended in actual truth, not as the

power of division, but in union with its other half, feeling. It is these two in conjunction, which make up actual truth. An incorrect writer is never correct in feeling, and can never express truth perfectly, nor with satisfaction to others. "God understands me," says the man who does not know how to express his feelings clearly; or "God only sees the heart." Well and good! but just for that very reason, take care that we, who cannot see the heart, should not see a distorted reflection! . . .

We have just got a fine engraving of Mendelssohn's portrait, by Hensel of Berlin. Have you seen it? It is well done, and a faithful copy of the original, and that is the very reason why it does not quite satisfy me, for it has nothing of Mendelssohn's nature in it. The portrait by Magnus is far better, and though not entirely satisfactory, it ought to be engraved or lithographed. Knauer, our sculptor here, has a creditable bust of Mendelssohn, but it wants dignity. Riet-schel of Dresden is at work on another. Wagner has had the Order of the Red Eagle conferred upon him in Berlin, for his *Rienzi*, though it seems the opera did not please the public. Oddly enough, Wagner himself speaks very disparagingly of this work, as well as of his *Flying Dutchman*, and yet he prints them, and has them performed! . . .

Yours,

M. HAUPTMANN.

106.

LEIPZIG, *May* 20th, 1848.

. . . I am glad you have not abandoned your plan of making a catalogue of Seb. Bach's works, though I could wish it had been printed a few months earlier, for the book and picture trade is at a miserably low ebb; twopenny pamphlets, and caricatures more loathesome still, are all the fashion. A pretty kind of musical department in the advertisement sheet, are those songs *To the German Parliament!* To-day, I see two more of them are advertised. Some of them were performed in Frankfurt the other day, at a *fête* given by the *Liederkranz*, and it is said that they *inflamed* the audience, that it was a memorable day in the annals of the *Liederkranz*, &c. The whole thing makes me wretched. Are they desperately young, or are they tipsy? In such an intoxicated company, one sober person would be about as comfortable as the one tipsy man at a sober evening party. . . .

I can't say I care much about daguerreotypes, though I never weary of looking at one we have just had done of our little girl; it is as good as a highly finished drawing. But properly speaking, daguerreotype ought only to be used for pictures and works of art. The plaster cast of the loveliest hand in the world—what is it but an image of death? All we catch is but a chance moment of real life, on the point of extinction; and therefore all daguerreotype is disappointing, because it is so limited. The healthiest subject looks sickly, and it is unnatural to fix and to isolate a passing moment, the vitality and truth of which depend solely upon its continuance. Artistic expression, therefore, need not dispense with individuality—*i.e.*, the likeness, but this will be given in and with the idea of the whole, just as when you express yourself algebraically, the particular proposition defined must be included in the general, as the most truthful definition of all, since it expresses everything on which the minor proposition rests, and everything in which it is contained. Of course, the portraits of Rembrandt and Vandyke are, in the highest sense, accurate likenesses; it could hardly have been otherwise, and independently of that fact, they are recognised as historical all the world over, by virtue of a certain well-defined ideal expression, true to all time, to this very day, because it is part of our common humanity. A false conception of the word *Ideal* leads to no end of senseless squabbles and misunderstandings, if it be understood to mean *beautifying a thing*, when all that it ought to mean is—That we should not look at nor represent a thing in its unreal isolation, but in its living entirety, the individual in its genus. Of course, this is a kind of beautifying, but not through the medium of flattery, only through the medium of truth to Nature. The work of a good painter, which gives us the whole character of

a man, is truer than daguerreotype, which pretends to give a
picture of the whole man, but only fixes the expression of a
sitter, during a single moment, the conditions of which are
entirely accidental. By accident, we may hit upon a favourable
moment for the likeness, though never for the revelation of the
higher qualities; it is a mere lottery, one big prize among a
lot of little ones, and heaps of blanks! How often we fail to
recognise our most intimate friend! Children are better
subjects than their parents, little children are better than
older children, dogs are better than both ; the less self-conscious
life there is, the easier it is to recognise universal Nature,
and the type of the whole in the individual. . . .

Yours,

M. H.

107.

Leipzig, August 24th, 1848.

. . . I had rather you were Director of the Cathedral
Choir in Berlin than of the Thomaner Choir here, for at
Berlin the Soprani and Alti are constantly being reinforced,
whereas here we drag on with the same members of the
chorus, whatever their voices may be, from the age of eleven
to that of nineteen. Every one of the sixty members has to
take part in the Choruses (and a curious part it is too),
directly he is received into the school. Besides preparing
for the Sunday music, there are the Saturday Motets, which
take up all the rest of the time allotted to music. With only
an hour daily, how is it possible to give the boys a general
idea of the science, and at the same time to produce their
voices, so that practice may become second nature ? We are
always talking about rehearsals. The Quæstor comes every
morning, to ask whether we are to have a half rehearsal or a
whole one—i.e., with Soprani and Alti, or with the whole
chorus. We never dream of singing-lessons ; we do as our
fathers did before us. Of course, I can change the whole
thing in a moment, if I choose. I am my own master, not a

soul interferes with me about the disposal of my time, but every minute of it is taken up in preparing for the performances, and if I have a few days free, and devote an hour to some particular phrase, which I want them to sing decently, it is over, before even a few have understood. Of an evening, the Prefects conduct the Motet rehearsals, and everything that I have tried to drum into their heads is lost ; not a word properly pronounced, breath taken at every bar, &c. I wonder it sounds so well as it does in Church ; it must give people some sort of pleasure to hear it, for the Motet performances are always crowded. It is the same with an orchestra ; let the individual members do what they will, the general effect is always good. Even the Chorale singing, in a full church, sounds well ; there are any amount of wrong notes, but the right ones get the best of it. . . .

I think sometimes, the people must be tired of a Cantor, who was unable to do anything for nearly six weeks before he went to Dresden, and had to begin by sparing himself all he could, directly he came back. The very idea, that they are tired of me, does more to reduce my strength than the work itself. . . . It irritates me to feel that I am hindered from doing my duty by weakness, and then again, the irritation hinders me from doing it still more effectually. I run round and round in a circle, like a cat in pursuit of her own tail. . . .

Have you no friend, to say a good word for you in Härtel's paper ? The letters of Schiller and Goethe, Merck and many others, all show that they took care to secure the favourable criticism of intelligent men, who would not praise their weak points, but call attention to all that was good. This is quite a different thing, from the extravagant mutual glorification of Weber and Meyerbeer. Meyerbeer's first opera was puffed to any extent, but no good came of it, until he wrote some others, which pleased the people (myself not included) directly. I have no words, to express my loathing of the insolence of penny-a-liners in daily papers, with or without the defence of "Anonymous." Anyone may have dirt thrown at him, at any moment, by one of these literary *gamins*, and there is nothing to be done but to shake it off one's cloak, as the King of

Prussia did at Düsseldorf. To pitch it back again, or shout
" Police ! " would only make matters worse. . . . I came
by chance, the other day, on Shakespeare's *Coriolanus*, and
I am greatly interested, to see that it throws light on the
present condition of politics among the lower orders. I should
like to see the play acted in some low theatre ; it would be
curious, to watch the effect of the hero's outbursts of wrath
against the people and their tribunes ! I can't imagine
Mendelssohn back in the present state of things ; it seems to
me, that he was taken away in time ; it would have stirred him to
the depths of his soul. So it does me, but I must stick to my
post. . . . I feel so sick of a morning, when I go early
to the *Conservatoire*, and hear every room resounding with
unmusical music, for that's what the compositions of the
modern *virtuosi* really are—tears and despair for ever, and yet
it leaves one quite unmoved ! I had much rather make my
escape, and leave them all lamenting. In the whole of *Don
Juan*, there are but two numbers in a minor key, the first
Duet, and the scene with the *Commendatore*. I should like to
see, how that libretto would have been treated, by one of our
composers. We should want a lantern to hunt for D major,
and the C major of the first *Finale* would be changed into C
flat minor at least, that being more discordant than B minor,
and therefore more despondent. I remember, when we were
at Vienna, how Spohr objected to passages being played in
unison by clarinets and hautboys, and Meyerbeer said, that
in certain situations, he liked the effect very much : " It
sounds so splendidly false ! " It is easy to see what he meant
by that. There is something poisonous in the impurity, but
the impurity consists in the wish to make use of the poison.
In saying this, I do not mean that clarinets and hautboys
should never be played together ; the effect may be good,
in spite of the impurity, but not because of it.

Robert Schumann has just finished an opera which he
calls *Genoveva*, the libretto of which is based upon the
tragedies of Tieck and Hebbel. I do not know the latter, but
there is very little of Tieck in the book, which I read when I was
at Dresden. I detest Golo, who in Tieck excites my sympathy.
Here, he is made out to be a coarse sensualist from the very

first, whereas Tieck lets him down gradually, and very effectively too. There is a wicked woman, like the fortune-teller in the *Ballnacht*, a truly repulsive creature, and a scene in which the populace force their way into Genoveva's bedroom, as in the *Sonnambula*. The mischief of it is, that poor Genoveva is left quite alone in the Castle, with the rabble rout all round her. Of course Schmerzenreich and the doe are omitted, though they have always been inseparable from the heroine. In short, it seems like the libretto of most German operas, destined to live only a night or two. I can't imagine, how the music will turn out; beautiful, ingenious, and full of feeling, it is sure to be; but as for style,—well, we must wait! The Opera will probably be brought out here in the first instance, hardly at Dresden. We have entirely given up going to the theatre; perhaps, if we went oftener, we should feel keener about it. *Prinz Eugen* is the only new Opera I have seen; these experiments are always so stupid, and I grudge the two *gulden*, especially just now, because I get nothing for them. . . .

Yours,

M. H.

108.

LEIPZIG, *October* 28*th*, 1848.

DEAR HAUSER,—

. . . For the last three or four weeks, I have been writing on Musical Theory. I will have a few sheets copied and sent to you. I fancy it is easier to write than to read that kind of thing, now-a-days, and I daresay your mind is too much occupied with other matters, and you will never have time for it. The horrors that are going on are all absorbing; they penetrate into every nook and corner. We are still quiet enough here, and if people could keep away from newspapers, and go as little into society as I do, they might at any rate save the time that is left, before the storm actually breaks over their heads. But this is just what we cannot do. It is not mere curiosity, it is the connection of mind with mind which prevents isolation, and I cannot imagine, where we are

to find rest. Up in the mountains, alone and quiet, amongst
men of peace ? Even less than here perhaps, for here at all
events, we have moments of exhaustion, and as we cannot
alter matters, we let them go. How peaceful the old days
seem to have been, as compared with our own, even in times of
war ! It was all so transitory,—but now, what earthly prospect
is there of our living to see a better state of things ? We read,
in yesterday's paper, a report of the bombardment of Vienna,
but it was mere hearsay ; nothing official has reached us, and
to-day the report was contradicted again. . . .

At this very moment the *Singakademie*, with a full orchestra,
is performing Handel's *Judas Maccabæus*. I only stayed for
the first part. I don't care to listen to anything just now. I
often wish I had nothing to do with music *ex officio*, and need
only go to a concert, when I liked. I never care to stay the
whole time. It is almost always too long, and the music
never seems to be in tune. I always used to rank *Judas
Maccabæus* very high, but to-day I thought the airs so formal
and old-fashioned, that it was quite impossible to fancy they
could give anyone any pleasure. The soloists too left much
to be desired, though they were supposed te be first-rate.
But it was just the mood I was in. A certain amount of
sympathy, or rather a great deal of it, becomes essential, if music
is to please. How comes it, that children are fascinated by a
good deal that we think stupid, unless it be, that they read
more poetry into the thing, whereas we look for poetry in the
thing itself, and expect it to attract us ? No wonder we are
often disappointed ! We live surrounded by a crust of prose,
which it is hard to break through. . . . Modern works are
conspicuous for want of rhythmical perfection, though people
are content with them, and get satisfaction—nay, in many
instances, pleasure out of them. Much of the latest musical
composition sounds as if some unskilful hand had dabbled
with the score. There are many conductors and composers,
who, as they cannot succeed in keeping their own operas on
the boards, have a passion for cutting out bits of other
people's, that they may figure as negative composers, at any
rate. When listening to a work by Haydn, Mozart, or the
Italian writers, we are never reminded of rhythmical

regularity, for it is an essential part of the structure. A healthy man is only conscious of his legs and arms, when something goes wrong with them. Even in Beethoven, we are occasionally reminded of the anatomy, and in some instances, he goes even farther than this. There is indeed such a thing as cloying perfection, which makes one wish that it were less perfect. Mozart's manner, if perpetuated continuously, tends towards this, for the skeleton of form, pre-determined and finished beforehand, peeps through the flesh, whereas, you know, it ought to be nothing more than the receptacle of the soft substance, in which is the life. This is Nature's way, and the artist will always do well to bear in mind the structure of the body. . . .

If Mephistopheles had not some disagreeable points about him, I should not mind letting him strike thirty years off my reckoning; he would be a very pleasant guide through the world. The only hopeful thing is, that children are always bringing fresh life and enjoyment into it. Next year is the hundredth anniversary of Goethe's birthday. How he would abhor the present state of affairs! he, who even in 1813, took refuge in "the pure East," and brought back thence his *Divan.* Such men could not exist, as the world is now. I was relieved to hear, that Jacob Grimm had left Frank·furt again for Berlin. Why should a man like that waste his time in idleness, or in a vain fight with vulgarity? . . .

109.

LEIPZIG, *February* 3rd, 1849.

DEAREST HAUSER,—

. . . To-day we are to have Mendelssohn's music to *Athalie;* I was greatly pleased with it at the rehearsal, and liked it even better than *Antigone,* as being a more solid piece of work. The fact that *Athalie* is a more modern play, may have made it easier for him to avoid aiming at strange, old-fashioned effects, which cannot be properly developed, and when perceptible, do not conduce to the success of the music, which, under all circumstances, should be the outcome of individual feeling. The music to *Athalie* is, like that of *Egmont,*

F 2

intended for the concert-room, and the words have been
arranged for recital by Edward Devrient. I think the combination will be very telling. For a long time past, Schulz's
choruses to *Athalie* have enjoyed a classical reputation, but I
should think that no one living has ever heard them, and if anyone did hear them, he would be puzzled to account for their fame.
Goethe himself was much edified with the music written to his
Egmont by Wolf or Schweizer, I forget which; but were it to be
given now-a-days, it would merely disfigure the play. It is always
so with this art of the soul; it cannot do without the
temporal and external, when it wants to express its
meaning, and so it becomes temporal itself; although, considered from the point of view of the soul, it should be always
and everywhere the same. Assume a first-rate poem, and
new music may be adapted to it every fiftieth year, just as
fresh garlands may be hung over an old stone monument.
Music, like a flower, depends on sap for its life, and we know
only too well, how soon the sap dries up. Cut flowers, and
nothing more, are what we get, for the most part; but even
that which has roots will die—for what are a few miserable
centuries! Most perishable of all, is the music purposely
constructed to astonish the age in which it was written;
the only things that last were the best of their own time,
but they contained no special novelty. Order in freedom,
and freedom in order—but if you dissociate them, one is as
Philistine as the other. . . . Whilst working at my
Harmonica, many things about which I was in doubt have
gradually become plain to me; there is really nothing to *do*,
there is a great deal to *find out*. That which is felt to be
good or bad, false or true, must be traceable from simple,
human, natural reasons, as intelligible to a young chorister
as to Sebastian Bach. I am not inventing, I am not conventional, I merely point out the organism, the inner law of
every form of expression; I prove, that with the utmost freedom
there is no caprice. I have lately looked through Chladni's
and D'Alembert's Essays on Rameau's *Tonsystem*. What
clever people, to be sure! Two first-rate mathematicians and
one good composer, perfectly satisfied with theories so
insufficient and untenable, that the first argument that came

to hand would scatter them to the winds. When talking of intervals, no one ever gets beyond the question, of how much or how little pleasure we derive, from the more or less simple proportions. Next comes the calculation of Temperament, and interminable logarithms, intended to adapt Nature to Art,—a subject which has not the least theoretical or practical interest; since one can no more tune a piano by logarithms, or by anything else except the ear, than one can imagine a sharp fifth or third, instead of the pure interval, or assign to such a perversion any musical significance. When one of Sebastian Bach's eight-part Motets is sung, is it possible to think of tempering his fifths or thirds, to make the performance feasible? Spohr indeed thinks that we have been accustomed from childhood to tempered intervals, and we can't fancy any others. But starting with such assumptions, it is just as easy as it is impossible to get at a musical system, and it is fortunate that in the production of a work, feeling is a better guide than arguments so ill-founded as these.

Capellmeister R. Wagner has a scheme for transplanting the *Conservatoire* to Dresden, and he is said to have expressed himself to the effect, that in process of time they might get rid of their expensive orchestra, and depend on the gratuitous service of our pupils—on whom he probably reckons for taking operatic parts as well. As a reward for this brilliant idea, I should like him to hear one of his own operas, executed by such people! An execution it would be in every sense—nay, a capital punishment. In the *Vaterlandsverein*, he is strongly in favour of arming the nation and getting rid of the soldiers; I suppose he would extend the same doctrine to music. He himself, however, is too much of a *dilettante*, to know the amount of wearisome, mechanical drudgery, that is necessary in a composer who cannot depend on the humour of the moment, and whose inspiration has been choked off by a surfeit of music. I doubt if *one* of Wagner's compositions will survive him. Even now, he is obliged to attend in person, if any of his operas are to be given. There have been several performances of *Der Fliegende Holländer* in Cassel, but with this exception, not one of his operas has been in demand elsewhere. It is poetical justice, which will not allow egotism to dominate Art. Meyerbeer's case is not quite analogous, for he is not ambitious of an isolated position. All that he aims at is popularity; he *will* be popular; he *will* create an effect. This he does with the most commonplace stuff, so long as it serves his ends; he showers handfuls of pepper over the thinnest broth, and makes people believe, that they are swallowing good strong soup. It burns and bites, but there is no nourishment in it. . . .

I have had more than enough of the papers, and am soon nauseated, as I have no turn for gossip. I remember once, how I went to that unspeakably tedious opera of Morlacchi's, *I Danaidi*, how I left the house after a few minutes, and how, returning two hours later, to speak to someone in the theatre, I wondered to find those unhappy women still lamenting, and the audience still in their seats and able to listen. The same astonishment possesses me, when I take up a newspaper. The same people are always talking, and the Frankfurt Parliament is always discussing the eternal question of German Unity. I should have said my say, long ago. Once out of the world of politics, it is a hard matter to get back again. I really cannot study them now; I am disgracefully unpolitical. As my personal comfort is not likely to be interfered with, I live and let live, though I have my qualms now and then. I am like a volunteer; he will stand fire for once in a way, but after that, he prefers to go back to his work, and leave all the fighting to the regular soldier, whose work it is. . . . A fund is about to be started, for the free education of musical students, and the scholarship is to bear the name of Mendelssohn; it will bring more students to the *Conservatoire*. A performance of the *Elijah*, in London, realised a considerable sum, but to my mind,—a good deal of the scheme is not exactly what Mendelssohn would have liked. You can find the statutes in the last number of the now extinct *Allgemeine Musikalische Zeitung;* Schleinitz is the sole responsible author. Not a farthing will I give, if I can help it. It is no great hardship for a student, to have to slave to win his position as an artist. If Art be not his vocation and he fails, let him throw it up; the elect are sure to come to the front.

Schröder-Devrient and Clara Schumann gave a Concert here, a few days ago. Schröder only sang a few songs, but subsequently, at a Subscription Concert, she gave a scene from Gluck's *Orpheus*. I was not there to hear it. You cannot say that she has lost her voice. The tone is still fine, and she sings in the old style, but it is less spontaneous, and she occasionally drags her *Tempi*—an old fault of hers, that has grown upon her. She was cheered to the echo each time. . . . Spohr's *Last Judgment* was performed at the annual Thomaner Concert in December. I cannot think that these oratorios of ours, when we have once discarded them, will live again, after a hundred years, like those of Handel. Their colours are pretty sure to fade. They have admitted into the Dresden Gallery, pictures by Kügelgen, Grassi, and the landscape-painter, Friedrich. As these are to the old masters, or as Canova's statues in the Munich *Glypthothek* are to the antique, so will our music be to the music of Handel and Bach. In fact the comparison holds good even now, but the modern composers are *our* composers still—which makes us overrate them. What I do love and admire in Spohr is his straightforward honesty; he never wishes to appear other than what he is. If the world were full of Berliozs, he would never have been misguided enough, to wish to be anything but Ludwig Spohr. Quite right too! But don't let us have any more *Historical Symphonies*, with imitations of Handel and Beethoven and the new School; Mozart was the best, but still— . . .

Yours,
M. H.

110.

LEIPZIG, *January* 18*th*, 1850.

. . . I wish they would let me have, as assistant for the Choral Class, a regular singing master, capable of teaching the young people how to open their mouths properly, to sing in a natural manner, to get a certain amount of tone, to enunciate their words clearly, &c. If they only learnt these things

when they first came, we should soon have a well educated choir.
.   .   .   But what is the good of talking about singing lessons,
when I cannot so much as raise my voice ?   How I envy J.
Schneider of Dresden his power of always hitting the right note,
with that harsh, grating, metallic voice of his !   Nothing can
be done, unless you sing the passage yourself.   Wild told me,
that when he was a chorister boy, he learnt nothing, except by
listening and having his ears boxed.   I get on much better
with my composition lessons ; there I am a practitioner to a
certain extent.   .   .   .   I am at this moment teaching the
two young Labitzkys, who have had three years in the
Conservatoire at Prague.   They are good, hard-working lads,
who have learnt absolutely nothing ; I should have had a far
better chance of getting them on, if they had never been
taught anything at all, for anyhow, they would not be so cock-
sure, that " the major Seventh is always resolved upwards ";
that, for instance, when a and b are sounded together, the b must
rise to c.   This, and plenty more such stuff, was what they
got from Kittl's teaching.   To be sure, I very seldom bring
theory before them *explicite*, except in special and rare
instances, where pupils show a wish for it.   This is not
invariably the case with the most musically gifted.   But
theory is *implicite* a part of my teaching.   I wish them to
feel the ground beneath their feet, however careless they may
be about the nature of mother earth.   Everything in the
organism of harmony is so natural, that a child is quite able
to grasp the meaning.   But as it often happens, that we cannot see the wood for the trees, it may be that we cannot see
the trees for the wood—*i.e.*, we cannot distinguish between
what is unity in the whole and variety in the several parts.
The trees *are* the wood, yet each tree has its own distinct
nature.   Therein lies the possibility and actuality of its
existence and of its individuality.   The chord of the Seventh is
amongst others a harmony of sevenths ; but then again, it
is something very distinct in itself.   Instinct and rules allow
the seventh in this chord (of the dominant Seventh) to be
freely taken, without preparation, upon the keynote held on,
while in the case of the other sevenths, only the keynote can
enter upon the seventh held on.   The chord of the dominant

Seventh, however, is the only one, whose seventh is a fundamental note, for in G, h, D, F, the seventh is F, the root of
the subdominant harmony. The other sevenths, F, a, C, e ;
a, C, e, G ; C, e, G, h ; e, G, h, D, are each composed of two
perfect fifths (as indicated by the curved lines in the book),
only one of them (*i.e.*, the interval b to f) is a secondary (or imperfect) fifth. In metre, this seventh must fall upon the
secondary place in the bar, the so-called up beat, and thus
must either be struck immediately after the octave, or be
suspended in the harmony in this part of the bar, if the keynote is taken on the strong part of the bar (*auf dem guten*) as
a fundamental note. If otherwise, it is, as a general rule,
contrary to the natural course of things. . . .

Rietz has contrived to finish an Opera, in the intervals of
his duties as director of the Theatre, the Concert Hall, the
Conservatoire, and the *Singakademie*. I have never observed,
that the quantity of a composer's work depends on the quantum
of time at his disposal, at least not in the same proportion.
If a man be in the right humour, his hours of work are only
broken outwardly, the continuity of the whole is unimpaired,
and the only difference is, that it takes a little longer to finish.
I have never been able to console or to excuse myself for my
idleness, with the reflection that I had no time ; conversely,
with little time at my disposal, I have done something. The
truth is, that a strong mental effort is necessary, if we are to
woo the Muse successfully, and not *bemuse* or merely *amuse*
ourselves. Few succeed like Mendelssohn. He never was
idle, even in playtime, and, with all his engagements, he still
found time to work. Some of his biggest things were finished
here, and yet he was no hermit, and no one thought he
worked particularly hard. If he wanted to be alone, he
would suddenly break away from business, and go to
Switzerland, or the Rhine country ; but there he did more
with his pencil than with his pen. Do you know his three
Psalms, recently published by Härtel ? From a purely
musical or technical point of view, they are nothing out of
the way, and not beyond the reach of other composers ; but
admitting that, what other modern music is to be compared
with them for beauty ? Now-a-days, anyone can imitate, but

Mendelssohn had no one to copy from.   He took the Psalm itself, and nothing but the Psalm; he never thought of Bach, Handel, Palestrina, nor anyone else, nor did he adapt it to any particular style; consequently, his music is neither old-fashioned nor new-fangled, it is simply a fine setting of the Psalm.   Three thousand years have not made the words sound strange to us, and I think time will not affect the music either; it has no artistic pretension, nor is it anything apart from the words; it is just the element of feeling, which gives them life.   These Psalms, like most of Mendelssohn's later compositions, notably the *Lauda Zion* and *Athalie*, are grander than their predecessors, which, *beautiful* as they are, rarely approach the *sublimity* of Beethoven, even in one of his minor works, where it often startles rather than pleases one. In this respect, Mozart is far behind not only Mendelssohn, but many an inferior composer, and, unlike Beethoven, he always keeps within the bounds of artistic symmetry.   Music restrained by the laws and limitations of Art, according to a definite plan, is not sublime.   It takes something colossal to overpower us—witness a movement of Beethoven's Second Symphony, which seems to launch us into Infinity, though we know the whole thing will be over in ten minutes.   Still, this too has its limitations, its definite plan, though on a proportionately grand scale; else it would be outside the world of Art.   It all comes back to this: is the composer in the right frame of mind? can his art follow the flights of his imagination?   He must guard against over-ambition, for that is felt at once.   It is as if a little boy, who looked well enough in a jacket that fitted him, were to put on a big suit of armour. . . .

Yours,

M. HAUPTMANN.

111.

LEIPZIG, *December 7th,* 1850.

DEAR HAUSER,—

. . . The bare idea of the Catalogue makes me shudder! Such a heap of Cantatas and Organ pieces!   If they are *all* by Bach, what a lot of Bach there will be,—to say nothing of those which are unmistakable ! Genius cannot invariably have kept pace with the unvarying technical activity of the composers of that time. Handel's Coronation Anthems are, to a great extent, mere Handelian ware. The merits and defects of such pieces, written off in a moment, and for special occasions, depend upon the moment itself, apart from the occasion. The same thing applies to the Fugues. With the subject for warp, and the counter-subject for woof, Fugues were turned off the loom almost mechanically. I fancy, it was as difficult in those days to help writing a Fugue, as it is for us to write one at all. Most of the schoolmasters then could have beaten most of our *Kapellmeister* now. An odd doctrine, you will say, coming from a member of the *Bach Society*, the object of which is the publication of the *entire* works of Bach. Nevertheless, I am in favour of this. There is room enough in the sky for the lesser stars and the *nebulæ*, as well as for stars of the first and second magnitude, and these owe all their brightness to the former. Deep thought and feeling breathe through the architectural ornaments, and the outlandish *rococo* illustrations, which disfigure the drawings of Albert Dürer, and they are all the more fascinating, from the contrast they offer to the prevailing bad taste of the time. Though not strictly analogous, Bach's art suffers from the fashion of his day—witness those intricate arpeggios and elaborate passages, running over the whole keyboard, in a style utterly unsuited to the organ. The other day, I heard one of these Fantasias, full of such figuration for one part; it began, it went on, it ended with it. It is very effective, if introduced occasionally, as a contrast to the full and sonorous parts of the same work, but here there was nothing else. Therefore, I think it is not uninteresting, to bind together in the same volume those great works of the master, which are destined to endure for all time, and those little works, his also, in which we recognise the passing fashion of the day. The dear good old fellow himself would laugh at it; why, no-one could imitate a single bar of him ! Surely, there can be little difficulty in weeding out what is not genuine ; whenever another man could have written it, you may safely say Bach did not. Similarly, a real critic should detect a forgery in

Shakespeare; and who can mistake Mozart, even in his
lightest moments? It seems incredible to us now, that
compositions by Eberl and others could have been printed
with Mozart's name attached to them.

This is not an answer to your letter, but just a few scratches
to prevent the white paper from dazzling you, and to get my
money's worth out of the post. For the same reason, I send
you this riddle: Canon à 4—

the solution of which I beg you to send me in my next, if I
am to retain any respect for the Orlando Lasso School of
Music. My love to you.

Yours,

M. HAUPTMANN.

112.

LEIPZIG, May 13th, 1851.

DEAR HAUSER,—

. . . A rose with a hundred petals is not a bouquet of
roses; it is just as much a rose as onꞓ ꞏth five. Speaking
generally, every song, be it what it may, has some sort of
connection with the *Volkslied*, and you have no right to set
lyrical strophes to an independent musical narrative of your
own. The composer should take a lesson from the poet, who
adapts his many thoughts to the form of a single strophe.
Franz Schubert's *Erlkönig* is absolutely different from Goethe's.
It is like Homer in prose, entitled *Tales from the Ancient
World*, which still continue to interest, though Homer is
conspicuous by his absence. We only get the historical
element, and possibly the poetical as well; the artistic is
gone. . . .

Kistner has just published Mendelssohn's 98th Psalm, for
chorus and orchestra; it is No. 20 of his posthumous works.
It was performed here, a few years ago, in the *Gewandhaus*.
We thought it lovely, and though it is simple, and has nothing
far-fetched about it, it is very effective. The first half is for the
chorus alone; harp, orchestra, and organ follow later on. I

think it was the choruses of *Antigone, Œdipus,* and *Athalie* that induced Mendelssohn to set some of the Psalms to music. In his earlier days, he adopted a fugal rather than a cantata style, and there was more rhythmical variety in the vocal parts ; later on he gets more declamatory, the chorus is more fully employed, and not unfrequently, it passes into unison. The music is much less independent, and greater importance is attached to the words, though the proper balance is always maintained. I do not include the three Motets in this category, they are more in the old Italian style. Though Mendelssohn never missed his mark, and the Greek choruses have their merits, I think them rather wanting in spirit and force. It was merely a royal whim—on the whole, I am sorry he yielded to it. The music is not strong enough to stand of itself, without the tragedy it illustrates, and the plays will not be given. In so far as he allowed it to influence his church music, the result has been, and may still continue to be a happy one, if his successors are men of intellect and genuine feeling. Mere imitation of a man's workmanship is easy enough. Substitute an ordinary four-part for a double chorus, and any novice can do the job. I have seen some Psalms by Neidhardt, the Director of the Cathedral Choir at Berlin, which take their turn with Mendelssohn's there ; they are as bad as bad can be, you cannot call them music at all, and the first composition of this master, that I saw, was marked Op. 140.

Staudigl is starring it here just now. I am waiting for a good opera, before I go to hear him. We have had nothing but Meyerbeer, hitherto. He can sing Sarastro and Tristan, both of which require a large compass. They say his voice is very good still. I never go to the theatre, except on special occasions. The other day, we had Mendelssohn's vaudeville, *Die Heimkehr aus der Fremde*—very pretty, inoffensive music. A pianoforte edition of it has just been published by Härtel. . . .

Yours,

M. H.

113.

LEIPZIG, *July* 10*th,* 1851.

. . . . Susette thinks, that I ought to have supplemented my last letter with a description of the new monument to Frederick II., by Rauch. Were I asked at a party, what I thought of it, of course I should say without a minute's hesitation, "Very fine!" — and yet, between ourselves, it hardly satisfies me. It is a fine thing, the workmanship is first-rate, and we may congratulate ourselves, for Rauch is probably unrivalled. For all that, modern monuments exist for the very purpose of being criticised. Ancient monuments hold their own. No one thinks of finding fault with the Marcus Aurelius on the Capitol, or the Horse Tamers on Monte Cavallo, but everyone has a fling at a modern statue. Here the pedestal is so big and unwieldy, that the eyes weary before they reach the figure itself. Add to this, scenes in high relief and low relief, horses, men, battle-fields, Frederick in the Council Chamber, Frederick at home—then, a whole story full of prominent allegorical figures—and by the time we get to the top, the small amount of space, allotted to the horse and his rider, makes us feel as if they could only just keep their balance. There is no such sensation, if the base of the statue rests on a simple, solid block, unless indeed it be as mean in size as that of Cosmo, in the *piazza* at Florence. A base like that will bear flat bas-reliefs very well, they are no more disturbing than inscriptions. But if the pedestal be adorned with representations of life, which are as life-like as the statue itself, in fact more so, there is no longer any repose about it, and the base loses all visible solidity. We know what happened to Venice in the seventeenth century, when the piles, on which the city stands, were eaten through by worms. I get nervous lest the horses, on the heads of which the hero is riding, should scamper away from under him. However, it is a majestic statue, and the work of an artist, for whom one must feel the greatest respect. It was never intended for Athens, but for Berlin, for the grand folk *unter den Linden,*

and it is a capital idea, to group together at the feet of the
king, as representatives of his handiwork, the various statues
which adorn the other parts of the city. Of course, Quanz
and his flute have not been forgotten. Had it not been for
Frederick II., what should we know about Quanz and his
book, *On the True Way of Playing the Flute?* And yet here
he is, cast in bronze! . . .

Yours,

M. H.

114.

LEIPZIG, *November* 17th, 1852.

DEAR HAUSER,—
 . . . So you think that at sixty years of age, I
may look for a little rest! I am entirely with you on that
point, but how am I to get it? People ought to start in life
with a plan to carry them straight through. Half way, they
should pass to the dominant, then, after a few modulations,
into the more remote keys, and, at the right time, back again
to the tonic. If they have more to say, let them supplement
the Close with a *Coda*, which may be long, and interesting in
its way, like one of Beethoven's, but free from formal limitation.
But we live on and on, from one day to another, adding where
we did not intend to, with no predetermined Close, just like
the period we live in. I am speaking of the externals of life,
rather than of the mind's forecast, and the course it takes,
though the two are intimately connected. You and I have
served a Bavarian and a Saxon King respectively, from our
fiftieth year upwards. What claim have we on them for a
comfortable retiring pension, after our short service, when we
compare ourselves with a man who has devoted fifty of his
best years to them? People say, it is mean and prosaic to
talk about position, income, &c., but you will not misunder-
stand me, when I maintain that these things combine with
the artistic element to form the poetry of life, so that they
ought to assume one shape. If an artistic close be necessary
in one, it is necessary for the other also. Something is

wrong, if we find ourselves, in our last years, compelled to do what younger men do more easily and better, and not able to do, what we should do better than they. . . . Op. 34, a and b, and Op. 36 are Motets, and as they were not worth much, I gave them to H. Siegel, a rather obscure publisher, reckoning thereby on a scanty sale. One of these, however, *Nimm' von uns Herr Gott*, has become rather popular, and I read in the papers, that it has been successfully performed at several places. When they were published, I thought much more about the money than about my reputation, and I still think that the other two will gradually fade out of notice, and sink into the oblivion which they deserve. . . . My *Harmonik und Metrik* would never have reached the printer's hands, if I had been forced to look out for my own publisher; it is all owing to you, that Härtel is bringing it out. . . . Still, it is rather amusing to me, when I look at the recently published works on Theory, and find in them the same old story—the same worn-out rules. Surely, I say to myself, I must be able to throw some ray of light in that direction. . . . Schiller, writing to Goethe, says that he would gladly exchange all his philosophy and æsthetics for a really technical grip of art. Now-a-days, we teachers are ourselves too abstract to teach in this way; we cannot deny ourselves or our scholars more general knowledge—we tell them more than it is good for them to know. Consequently, when they leave school, their heads are full of hazy notions, and they are uncertain even of elementary facts. Such, at least, is my not unfrequent experience of pupils, who have gone through all the classes. . . .

Yours,
M. H.

115.

LEIPZIG, January 5th, 1853.

. . . Peters has recently printed some really excellent vocal exercises by Bertolotti, written *per i putti*, as the Preface has it. The old Italian edition has long been out of print. I doubt if it ever reached Germany. These Exercises date, I

believe, from the latter half of the last century, and they are
serviceable for class teaching, for they are in the good Italian
alla cappella style, and good models of two-part writing.
They are unaccompanied, and I often make my pupils sing
them. Just at this moment, I hear an echo overhead from
the Rehearsal Room, where they are practising Durante's
Misericordias Domini (No. 1, in the Schlesinger Collection).
It sounds effective. It opens well and it ends well, but I
don't call it good music from beginning to end. I have never
quite liked the *alla cappella* music of the Neapolitan School;
it wants depth. Of course I except Alessandro Scarlatti, and
notably his eight-part *Tu es Petrus*, a grand work, cut out of
rock, as it were. How curious it is, that the style of Palestrina
should have co-existed with that of the Cantata for so long
a time! The same composers had diametrically opposite ways
of expressing themselves, until the figured bass got the upper
hand, swamping independent polyphonic harmony, and
transforming the polyphony, formed upon prescribed harmonies, into a mere display of superficial skill, whereas it had
formerly the effect of a natural organism. *Now* the natural
thing was melody with accompanying harmony. . . .

Yours,

M. H.

116.

LEIPZIG, *June 2nd*, 1853.

. . . Our modern professors of singing and composition
talk about a great number of things, that never occurred to
their ancestors; yet singing and composition were better
taught formerly. There are more things in Heaven and
Earth than are dreamt of in this philosophy also. I think
you have too good an opinion either of my book or of the
savans, or of both, if you think they will condescend to waste
their time over it. They won't disturb themselves, they
will take no notice. However little it may hinder the
routine of the ordinary practical teacher, there are points in
the first chapter, to which A. and B. may take exception.

Marx is about to publish the fifth edition of his *Compositions-lehre*, but he must alter his first chapter very considerably, and re-cast the following pages, unless he means to ignore what really is irrefragable truth, and not my invention. But Newton's Theory of the Divided Ray lived on after Goethe's *Farbenlehre*, which was avoided as if it were a dead dog, and similarly, the students of harmony and metre persist in ignoring harmony and metre in their natural state. Because the real man is too big for his clothes, they say the clothes are the real man, and that he whom God created is only the raw material, out of which a work of art has to be formed. If a living heart still finds room to beat below the clothes, we must attribute that to irrepressible vitality, which refuses to be stifled. We mistake a tempered for a pure tone, and often prefer downright failure of intonation to slight deviations from mathematical purity. But when, as in the opening of the *Jessonda* Overture, the horns in E flat and the trumpets in B blare out together, when D sharp sounds as if tuned to E flat, and B is made the third to G on the horn, what a horrid row it always makes! Then they say that the wind instruments are out of tune, the truth being, that they sound out of tune, because they are blown in tune, and indeed it can hardly be otherwise, considering the natural tones of the horn and the trumpet. Why these eternal discussions about Temperament? When once this fiction gains credence, it brings hundreds of other delusions in its train. According to the *Cycle of Fifths*, the most innocent little piece in C major, which does not depart from that key, can only be played with tempered tones. How does this affect the question? We may consider slight deviations in the light of accidents, which hinder the play of individuality, although they do not change its nature, and are not com-prehended in our *idea* of it, because they are not organic, internal conditions. Up to the present time, I have met with but one person who agrees with me, L. Köhler of Königsberg. He found it hard to part with the old trite explanations of theory, but they left *him*, not he them, so that now he joyfully accepts my system of metre, which teaches the principle of self-formation, when freedom is controlled by law. I have not heard a syllable from my Leipzig friends on the subject, but I expected nothing else. There are many who think that they need not trouble themselves about it, because they " do not understand mathematics"; yet all the mathematics in it amount to this—that twice two make four,—and this, I think, they ought to have remembered from old schoolroom days. . . .

I like Moritz's last Songs, which are good music, and vocal too. Most people are all for harsh and crude sounds, as being more expressive. You remember Thümmel, the bard of Cassel, who thought nothing poetical, which was not absolutely unintelligible. Moritz must be a little on his guard, against a very Mendelssohnian modulation, which may soon degenerate into a mannerism; I mean that of the major seventh against the prolonged Prime in the bass—

It has its charm, but just because of this, the repetition of it strikes one more than a less piquant harmony would. . . .

How strange, that we get so little music from Dresden! Notwithstanding its 80,000 inhabitants, it cannot boast of one single composer, who is known beyond the walls. They are like people shut into a fortress, into which nothing comes, and out of which nothing goes. One never-changing Symphony, from one Palm Sunday to the next—that, of course, shuts out numbers of others. The race of Klengel has not died out; they affect to be classical, but there they stick; they never hear an opera, nothing but an occasional piece by Schuster, or a Seidelmann Mass, or a concert now and then on the Brühl Terrace. And with it all, they inherit the musical arrogance of their forefathers, though they hear nothing themselves, and can write nothing which anyone else cares to hear. Reissiger and Julius Otto are the only stars which shine far and wide. The music trade, too, has sunk to nothing; there is no music to be got, for nobody knows anything about it. The book trade is nearly as bad. Picture dealers are a little better off, for though the Dresdeners do not trouble themselves about Art, there are

plenty of visitors. Anyone, who wanted anything out of the
way, was always voted an outsider. I still remember how,
in my childish days, people ran down the Körner family, for
affecting to be more poetical than others. Tieck, too, stood
alone. Theodor Hell was the representative man of Dresden.
Not a soul knew the Schumanns. Men like Carus and
Bendemann are obliged to hold together, but now there seems
to be another split among the artists. . . . Well, the
Gallery, the Terrace, and Saxon Switzerland are the best of
it, and the last especially is very refreshing for a time,
particularly if one happens to come from such uncountrified
country as that about Leipzig. . . .

Yours,

M. HAUPTMANN.

117.

LEIPZIG, December 14th, 1853.

. . . It is high time that Klengel's Canons should
appear, and now Härtel has published them. I always thought
that there was no chance for them, before Klengel died. It
was all his own fault, he used to ask too much money for
them. What publisher would give him 25,000 *thalers?*
Perhaps he valued himself at 1,000 *thalers* a year, and these
Canons represented twenty-five years' work. Fifteen or twenty
years ago, there was a better chance, his work was then known to
many people of consideration, but they are most of them
dead now. There had been no musical 1848, no Berlioz,
no Wagner, nothing had been said about a complete musical
revolution, no one had discovered that the old school of music
was pedantic and trifling. No firm but that of Breitkopf and
Härtel could risk the publication of a work like Klengel's, the
cost price of which cannot be less than ten *thalers*. In spite
of its early reputation, I daresay it will not sell well. . . .

I believe the Overture to *Tannhäuser* has been given in
Munich. The first time I heard it here, at a *Gewandhaus* concert,
in Mendelssohn's time (though he was not present), I thought
it a misshapen, clumsy production, and I see no reason to

change my opinion now. Yet I am told that it is a masterpiece, unapproachable, full of poetry and high art. The flattered Wagnerites, however, must not plume themselves too soon on their flatterers, much as they may like to inhale the fragrant incense, for there is always a set of people in existence, who have never proved themselves real Art critics. They form a *coterie* like that of the Leipzig *littérateurs* in the Revolutionary time of 1848-9,—blustering, impudent fellows, avoided as if they had been mad dogs, who were ignominiously driven out, and their ideas of freedom scattered to the winds, in the days when comparative law and order were restored. But ours is an age of growth and development, and who shall undertake to describe the course of this bomb, or the flight of that rocket?

. . .

Berlioz has recently given a performance of several of his works, first at the *Gewandhaus*, then at a concert of his own. Oddly enough, the selections were the old stock pieces, which we have known for fifteen or twenty years past—*Romeo, Faust, Harold, &c.* It is all regular barricade music, glittering and sparkling at times, but never warming. But whatever it is or is not, the interminable talk about it is enough to drive one crazy. When he is right, he is as tedious and monotonous as when he is wrong. In the first case, he repeats himself everlastingly, in the second, he talks stupid nonsense. I admit that Berlioz is a highly cultivated Frenchman, full of *esprit*, but how *borné* is this Symphony, concocted out of *Faust*—here a *soupçon* of Goethe, there a *soupçon* of his own—no unity, no taste! Still more aggravating is it, that a large audience, credited with good judgment, is so blind as not to see the absurdity of it. People think it must be sublime, because it is glaringly untrue. It is bad enough that *Brendel's Gazette*, the only musical paper in Leipzig, should be supposed by the outside world to represent the opinion of the town. Liszt was present at both of Berlioz's concerts, with a lot of his Weimar hangers-on. These, coupled with the hangers-on *here*, made a pretty considerable party of *claqueurs*, strong enough to overawe and carry away the *plebs* with them. So we were complimented on our progress by the *Gazette*, in consequence of this complete victory, the good cause having failed here ten years ago, when Berlioz came to us for the first time, and Mendelssohn was at his zenith.   . . .

Yours,

M. HAUPTMANN.

118.

LEIPZIG, *March 7th*, 1854.

DEAR HAUSER,—

. . . We were delighted with Jenny Lind Goldschmidt's singing. There is still the old abiding charm, and the voice is good enough to sustain her in her highest flights. I don't like to hear people always talking about her *voice*. Whether Spohr plays on a Stradivarius, a Guarneri, or a Mazzini, is not the main question. No doubt, we get the *sound* from the instrument, but the *tone* is the speciality of the player, and relatively it is the same, whatever instrument he uses. The same thing may be said of singers. In Moscow, I once heard an old Frenchman sing some French romances ; he had hardly a note left in his voice, but to this day, I have never forgotten the impression he made on me. In the spirituality and beauty of his singing, one forgot to criticise the strength or weakness of his powers. What a good thing it would be, if we were less fastidious in our search for the beautiful, if we were just knowing enough to discriminate between the good and the bad, and to delight in the good. Why must the bad always serve as a foil for the good, or as a touchstone by which to recognise it ? The best would only be just good enough for an ignoramus, that is self-evident, but criticism of all imperfect work implies real knowledge, if a proper estimate is to be made.

You are sure to have read Jahn's essay on *Wagner and Berlioz*, in the *Grenzboten*. Our new critics have got their work cut out for them, I expect. The *Niederrheinische Zeitung* has some sensible articles, and by degrees, we shall hear other notes which are not blown by that trumpet. *Lohengrin* may become more widely known, but I have my doubts about the *Niebelungen*, else they would decide the matter. Four evenings, one after the other, in such an atmosphere, would be too much for anyone but Brendel and Hoplit, who are paid to endure it. The third and fourth time *Lohengrin* was given, the house was empty, though on the last night they lowered the prices, and many people had been waiting for that. The opera is now shelved, until the fair is over. A failure here and there is venial enough, but the absurd and stupid arrogance with which some people uphold, as the one true thing, what is radically defective, cramming this doctrine down the throats of others too, is irritating and contemptible. I hear you are going to have a performance of *Tannhäuser* in Munich. Do go twice or thrice, and listen to it the first time *without prejudice*. I am afraid, by the second night, this will have become impossible. How many hard-boiled eggs can a fasting man eat? Answer: One; for by the time he eats the second, he is a fasting man no longer. . . .

Yours,

M. HAUPTMANN.

119.

LEIPZIG, *April 24th*, 1854.

. . . There is another review of my *Harmonik und Metrik* in the *Signale*, and if it does not go very deeply into the matter, anyhow it is very complimentary. I find the book now and then referred to, as a standing authority, in reviews of other theoretical works, and that sort of thing is not a mere advertisement, and may certainly be considered gratifying. I can well understand (*si parva licet componere magnis*) Goethe's lively gratitude for the faintest recognition of his *Farbenlehre* and *Metamorphose der Pflanzen*, profoundly indifferent as he always was to any criticism of his poetry. The two things are quite distinct. Every work of Art is a perfect circle, existing in and for itself; it does not interfere with any other, it co-exists peaceably with those of the most opposite character. Schubert writes a song, and side by side with it, Mendelssohn writes another. A. writes Fugues, B. writes Songs without Words and *Morceaux de Salon*—there is fair play for all. If the *Prophet* and *Tannhäuser* command full houses, *Don Juan* and *Figaro* do not mean empty benches. With scientific works, it is quite different; no two opposite theories can be equally recognised. Newton or Goethe! The Newtonian must wage war with the Goetheian, or become one himself; but it would be rather hard, to ask a professor, who has lectured for years on colourless light composed of seven colours, to pitch his notes into the fire, and use his holiday time for re-constructing a new set of lectures. And that would be the only plan, for he cannot change his views gradually. I certainly have done my best, to avoid adopting a hostile attitude towards theorists of the old school, but of course you may read between the lines and come now and then upon matter which ruffles some Sir Oracle, whose position seemed to him impregnable. Take such a passage as this : " No rational person can talk about conventional definitions of chords, arrangements of a key or scale, arbitrary changes, raising or lowering the degrees of sounds given by Nature, &c., though these are common terms, in the mouths of people who are sane upon other subjects." I wonder how Marx, G. Weber, A. André will appreciate such a compliment. What rubbish is their stereotyped talk about the circle of fifths, and about Temperament being indispensable to our music! Kiesewetter, a so-called Aristoxenian, is deliciously *naïf*, when he maintains that it is downright false, to say that two-thirds of the string define a fifth, since twelve such fifths, consisting of two-thirds of the length of a string, would not lead back to the starting point, but a trifle beyond it, and consequently that as the twelfth fifth of C—*i.e.*, b sharp, would have to be C exactly, which it is not, so the pure fifth, for these reasons, cannot be two-thirds of the string's length, but must be a trifle less! When such things are said, one can hardly believe one is listening to a grown-up man, much less a man of science. This is Mr. Schmidt, of Munich, writing to me about his *Gesangschule :* " No one ought to be a singing-master in a public institution, unless he teaches from some standard book of authority, or unless he has worked out some system of his own, which has met with the approbation of those who know." Why, Socrates would have to write Plato and Aristotle, or

Christ a Gospel, before they were qualified to act as public teachers! I like the answer made by Kant's servant to a painter, who was staying in the house to paint the philosopher's portrait. Complaining of *ennui* one evening, he asked for a book. Answer: "We have no books. When we want them, we write them ourselves." . . .

I am an honorary member of the Royal Academy of Arts, not of the *Singakademie*, and my privileges consist in a statutory permission to copy pictures in the Royal Palace at Berlin, as also in the Palaces at Potsdam and Sans Souci! I have a further right to a seat in a box at the Opera. That I don't care about, but think of the copying! . . .

Yours,

M. H.

120.

LEIPZIG, *September* 14th, 1854.

DEAR HAUSER,—

. . . Your cheerful letter brought me a whiff of mountain air. We settled down at Dresden, and made a good many expeditions, but it is never a real *dolce far niente*. It's very nice to feel that we can get there with the children, and they are well looked after, and one sees one's sisters and a few friends, &c., but there's no real refreshment in it. For the most part, it's just like being at home, only one is not so free and not so comfortable, and often one would like to do something and one can't, because there's no study and no writing-table. What is Man without ink? How can there have been any men at all, before ink was invented? Goethe says: "It is the feeling for weights and measures that makes men of us." That's all wrong. For *weights and measures* read *pen and ink*. Why, but for pen and ink, his dictum would have been unrecorded, he would have spoken to the winds. Apart from the question of ink, the heat was so oppressive, that one could hardly do anything in comfort. Reissiger had promised us the *Idomeneo*, the only opera I should have cared to hear, but nothing came of it—*pensate a questi tromboni!* First of all, Fräulein Ney was away, then Vogelwiese, so time slipped by, and the thing became impossible. When Ney returned, Vogelwiese disappeared, so again it fell through. Perhaps *with* Vogelwiese it might have been done *without* Ney, but that combination never came off. The sad news of the King's death, in consequence of that disgraceful accident, reached us during our last days in Dresden. What must be, must be. Had a postillion died in the same way, no one would have thought it remarkable, but if a poet had invented such a catastrophe, to change the succession, how people would have laughed! History does it with the kick of a horse. Poetry cannot do it without complicated State transactions. But it's all in the order of things, for when accident, or what seems to be accident, prevails, Art is out of it. . . .

121.

Leipzig, *December 2nd,* 1854.

. . . Thank God, you are quit of that dreadful cholera at last ! We were in constant panic ourselves, for with every precaution, nobody is safe. Four years ago, when we thought ourselves quite free from danger, the scourge was upon us in our own house, a dear child was suddenly carried off in a few hours, and we, who had nursed it and carried it in our arms, escaped. This fearful Crimean expedition is another scourge. I can hardly draw breath, when I think of what those poor fellows are going through. Plays, balls, concerts, dinner parties go on, just the same. I could almost despair of civilisation. We belong to a time, when men *ex officio* kill one another by thousands, when might is right. I really shudder, when I read of 5,000 or 10,000 slain, and the question of settlement is still farther off than ever. They talk of relays of men, as if they were so many bags of sand, yet every man there has a heart that beats like one's own. If this be the way to settle who is in the right, we are sunk in barbarism, and seem likely enough to stay there. It is the old club law that obtained in savage times, more refined, but all the more cruel from its wide extension. Why doesn't Czar Nicholas fight it out with Napoleon and Victoria, with the King of Prussia and the Emperor of Austria acting as seconds? . . . Cherubini's *Lodoiska* has been given twice. I hardly think that there will be a third performance; the house was empty, the public apathetic. How did poor Cherubini get hold of such bad librettos? in Paris too, where they usually do such things well! Badly translated into German, it is as silly and childish as a German original—a mere commonplace story about a Polish Knight, no better than a fifth-rate novel from a circulating library. Yet, with it all, Cherubini has treated the work, from first to last, as if he were in love with it. Though it was given now and then in Cassel, my memory for music is so treacherous, that it sounded quite new to me. I was interested from beginning to end. It was refreshing, once in a way, to get rid of that disgusting, boneless pulp of emotion, out of which modern operas are made. Every other Art requires something more than this; why should poor wretched Music have to depend on nothing else? The odd part of it is, that these young composers look upon themselves as artists who have burst the bonds of tradition, and are actually upon the road to truth! Cherubini feels every subject deeply, but his emotion is so chastened, so beautifully subdued by artistic form, that we never suffer the pain of oppressive realism, which it is the aim of modern musicians to inflict. They do all they can to torture and torment us as naturally as possible, and with great success, as far as their Art is concerned, for after submitting to one operation, we get so flabby, that another one is impossible. In spite of the utter absurdity of the libretto, I listened with unflagging spirits and complete enjoyment to every note of *Lodoiska*. The *Cantilena* is never prominent, though the music, as we should expect of an Italian, is vocal throughout; but the orchestration supporting it is marvellous. The harmony is not lumped in chords, it hovers about, it is woven of various and consonant figurations, each of which seems to exist solely for itself; it never becomes an inert mass, there are no clammy, thorough-bass accompaniments, filling the middle parts, and stuffing and developing the chords into "those interesting harmonic progressions." "Interesting harmonic progressions"

there are, however, and plenty of them, the fact being, that
the most interesting of such things date from Cherubini,
their virtual founder.

But to be able to write like Cherubini, is equivalent to
saying, that one can play with the most difficult tasks, as
he did. It is not born in a man to do this; it takes any
amount of hard work to acquire the capability. How to aspire
to such knowledge, how to set about acquiring it, is a task
our composers never set themselves ; it never occurs to
them, to make any effort in that direction. A painter cannot
get on without first learning how to draw, but our composers
and singers think that any cultivation of God's gifts is a
desecration of them. " What need of knowledge," say they,
"when feeling and inspiration are always at hand to guide
us ? "

I wonder if you have read Hanslick's little book, *Ueber
das Schöne in der Musik.* There are many good things in it,
especially his definitions of what Music is *not*, which are better
than his constructive definitions of what it *is*—a hard matter
to define at all, by the way ! The book is more assertive in
negation than in assertion, but he has said many things one
is glad to hear said, for originality of thought is too often
sacrificed to a mere repetition of other people's opinions.
The Third Part of Sechter's *Compositionslehre* is just out. I
don't know whether it is to conclude the work. There is
nothing as yet about Fugues ; he devotes all his attention to
possible and impossible counterpoint. It is a highly instructive work. Sechter is no more theoretical than other
theorists. On many points, he adheres obstinately to principles laid down by himself. Reality is with him a deduction
from a self-created idea, the idea is not an abstraction from
reality. But anyhow, his arguments are better and more
advanced than all the philosophical jargon of those dabblers
in literature, who betray their artistic impotence, whenever
they have to give the shortest practical illustration, for the
benefit of some eager student. And yet this useless rubbish
goes through edition after edition ! . . .

Yours,

M. H.

122.

LEIPZIG, *May* 29*th*, 1855.

DEAREST HAUSER,—

. . . *A propos* of your son's Opera ! In the old Italian school, every opera was intended to be a mere framework for the introduction of Arias. We cannot stand that now; it delays the action too much. However, Arias can easily be left out, when they are in the way, and there are not so many of them in this opera. It is less easy to get over single phrases and clumsy repetitions of the text, in which he rides the libretto to death, by further insisting on statements that need no reiteration. This is what makes the opera too long, and even if it were much shorter, it would have the same effect, because there is a want of movement in it. I remember that when my *Mathilde* was given in Cassel, though I had made any number of cuts in it, I only longed to make more, to break off abruptly in the Dominant or anywhere else, simply to get forward. It is hard to say theoretically *a priori*, where one should put the drag on by repetition, and where one should go ahead. But once launch the piece on the stage, all that is easy enough. The study of first-rate operas will scarcely help us in this particular, for where everything is exactly as it should be, one cannot learn the character of a fault. I always think that a dramatic work, which has been cut about, runs a better chance of pleasing the public than a more complete one, which is too long. *Le secret d'ennuyer est celui de tout dire* comes in usefully here. If mere chipping and cutting can never make bad music good, they may make it bearable, anyhow. So much for the faults, now for the merits, which are considérable. . . . The orchestration is effective, never overloaded, never too thin, and one would say it was the work of an experienced hand. The orchestra is a stumbling-block to many; it requires a special aptitude, such as Gade showed in his early works. Here he was more at home than Mendelssohn himself, whose orchestration is not seldom instrumentation. Still more praiseworthy, because it is a rarity now-a-days, is the vocal character of the solos and *ensembles*. This propitiates the singers, and their likes and dislikes make all the difference to a composer. No one on the stage, no one in the band, works merely for love of him; we didn't do it ourselves, in old days. Maria Weber used to say: " One must write so as to produce the intended effect, let each man do his d——d duty, and nothing more." Surely a good principle, for what more can one expect at a performance? Were everyone concerned to make it an opportunity for displaying his own gifts, what a chaos would follow—cellos, horns, chorus-singers, drums, prompter, all pulling different ways! . . .

We had a pretty *Offertorium* by Salieri, in the *Thomaskirche*, the other day; it took exactly three minutes. When I first came here, I chose rather long works for the first few Sundays, and when I changed them for shorter, David said to me : " Solid music will gain you the respect of every member of your orchestra, *short* music his affection." Addio. . . .

Yours,
M. H.

123.

LEIPZIG, *November 4th*, 1855.

. . . I should like to hear how Moritz is getting on at Düsseldorf, where I am told they are still in want of good singers. That's a very old story. As long as they have a good ophicleid, never mind the rest ! Do you remember, what the comic man in a farce said to the director, when the impresario was at his wit's end, because all his singers were down with illness ?—" Let's give the *Prophet*—I've an old pair of skates at home—never mind the rest ! " . . .

Yours,
M. H.

124.

LEIPZIG, *January 25th*, 1856.

. . . A few days since, our quartet party played Mozart's Serenata (written in 1780); it is for two oboes, two clarinets, two basset-horns, two bassoons, four horns, violoncello, and double bass. It is a lovely work, and deeply interesting; the harmonies are so full, that I fancy it might sound still finer in the open air. The music which Mozart wrote during the last ten years of his life, shows how rapidly he advanced in the formation of his style. One year with him is equivalent to ten with an ordinary man. Order, not eccentricity, was his motive power, from the very first. I think *that* a safer criterion of genius than the ferment of storm and stress; the latter has to be cleared off altogether, the former has only got to be developed. It shows a well-organised nature, instinctively rejoicing in appropriate expression. What a man *does* always depends upon what he *is*. . . . Once upon a time, the French King Louis XII., commissioned Josquin des Prés to compose a Canon in which he might take part, or rather, to adapt one of his favourite songs to that form. Josquin found that the song could be made into a two-part Canon, and he arranged it for two boys' voices, adding a bass part for himself, and a fourth part for the King, in which even a King could not go wrong, for it was only one note. Here it is—

Vox regis.

(N.B.—It might have been sung as a three-part Canon).

The King was so enchanted to find, that he could sing in four-part music, that he handsomely rewarded the composer for his trouble. . . . Do you know the story of the Countess Hessenstein, who, after a performance of the *Zauberflöte*, went on raving to Spohr about the glorious *Triangle* (Trio) in the second Act. She also talked about *camels* (camelias) flourishing in the open air, in North Italy. She said she should like Switzerland, if it were not for the *Chrétiens* (Crétins). "My son, Louis, plays violin duets with *Concertmeister* Barnbeck," she used to say, "but Barnbeck can't keep up with him, for he has got to the bottom of the page, before Barnbeck is half-way down it."

The selections for the Mozart Festival are from the *Re Pastore* and *Idomeneo*, and they are going to do a Violin and Cello *Concertante* besides the Isis Choruses from the *Zauberflöte*. There is to be a play at the theatre, with Mozart as one of the characters, not the old Schikaneder thing, but a drama, probably of the tearful order, with allusions to the hardships of his life, and I daresay the story of the *Requiem* woven into it. . . .

Yours,

M. H.

125.

LEIPZIG, *February* 18*th*, 1856.

. . . Härtel has sent me Maier's Latin Motets; they are very vocal, and I am charmed with the pure counterpoint. One might quote Hamlet's words about the honest man : " To be honest, as this world goes, is to be one man picked out of ten thousand." Most musicians scarcely know what pure harmony is—they hardly feel the need of it. The pianoforte is now made the starting-point of all musical education, and no doubt the student gets from it a certain feeling for a compact sequence of harmonies, though not for the concordance of melodies, the human and personal element in harmony, failing which, we get nothing anywhere but an aggregate of materials,—an inert mass, not a living body. But the pianoforte will always be valuable to a teacher of composition, if he is of the right sort. He can help his pupils solely in the mechanical part of their work, he cannot endow them with musical and poetical sensibility and invention. But it takes a specialist to teach harmony. I wonder whether, in old days, the teachers, like the Guilds of Architects, had secrets of *technique*. Certain it is, that formerly the merest dabbler in composition was a better hand at it than any of our masters, however hardworking he may be. . . . Even Klengel, as a rule, succeeds better with his Canons than with his Fugues. Anyone can keep his individuality in a Canon, but when it comes to Fugues, we cannot help comparing them with the whole of *Das temperirte Clavier*, and there the choicest of modern work is dwarfed by the meanest music of the Bach period. Ours is an exotic—the other, a healthy plant, springing straight out of mother earth. . . .

Yours,

M. H.

126.

ALEXANDERBAD BEI WUNSIEDEL,
July 23rd—*August* 10th, 1856.

DEAREST HAUSER,—

. . . We were ten days in Dresden, and have been nearly a week at Alexanderbad. We are within a quarter of an hour from Jean Paul's Wunsiedel. The town authorities have placed a bust of him, in front of his house. It is the work of a Munich sculptor, and there is something Beethovenish about the face, that I never observed before. . . . I take pine baths here, and drink the waters. I am no better, and no worse. . . . A few days before we left Leipzig, Spohr paid us a visit, on his way back from Prague and Dresden. He is hale and hearty as ever ; not so the wife and sister-in-law, who have aged considerably. If the old fellow had his own teeth, or anybody else's, I should see no difference in him whatever. He is just as keen about music, and he never changes his opinions ; it's the old, old story. " Perfection of form !—Interesting harmonic progressions ! "—Never mind ; long may he be spared to us ! For he is still a strong pillar, and the mere fact of his existence furnishes a connecting link with the good, quiet old days. Where is there such another ? I know of none. There are plenty of people who have grown old ; he is the only one that is always young. . . .

Before we left Leipzig, I wrote two more pieces of sacred music for orchestra, and I was busy with the third, when I had to leave. I will finish it when I get home, and then try them all three. I am longing for some sacred music, without those infernal trumpets and kettledrums. Why is the Almighty to be thundered at perpetually ? A great deal of it is mere tradition. Why should " Praise be to Thee ! " or " Great is the Lord ! " invariably suggest a deafening crash ? Mendelssohn's Hundredth Psalm, " O be joyful in the Lord ! " one of his three Motets, is exactly what it should be, and yet there is nothing of the *fanfare* about it.

I have again taken my text from *Oser's Kreuz-und Trost-lieder*, where I have also found the words for a four-part choral Hymn, which may perhaps be inserted in some future collection. The first six hymns have been engraved, and I am to have the proof-sheets here. Siegel absolutely refuses to look at the four-part songs you recommended; young publishers are very shy of dealing with unknown names. Even well-known men have their work cut out for them. Reissiger lately set the 114th Psalm, " Out of the deep," and I, thinking it eminently suitable for Cathedral music, asked him if it would soon be printed. " Printed ! " said he, " Sacred music by me ! Who would agree to print it? No one—even if I were to make him a present of it. As for payment, I never dream of such a thing." If this happens with dry wood, the green wood cannot complain. Reissiger's Masses are considered amongst the best in the Catholic Church at Dresden, and some of his best work is to be found in them ; they sound well, and have more character than most. . . .

Yours,
M. H.

127.

ALEXANDERBAD BEI WUNSIEDEL, *August 5th*, 1856.

. . . I agree with you about Mozart's instrumentation of *The Messiah*. It resembles elegant stucco-work upon an old marble temple, which might easily be chipped off again by the weather. But in that case, an organ accompaniment is quite necessary, for Handel is not content with music in two parts, except in particular instances. I have often heard, in the *Gewandhaus*, Cadenzas to Handel's Arias, such as this—

i.e., in two parts, without $\frac{6}{4}$. How stupid and unreason-able ! Even S. Bach is guilty. Look at his organ and cembalo parts, with the figured basses ! A regular forest of figures, which would puzzle many a modern organist, as he so frequently figures the passing notes, even with figures which do not express them, such as chords of the seventh and their inversions. I don't know what will become of this edition of Handel. Gervinus is the only enthusiast, and the fact that it is Gervinus does not seem to inspire others. It is now six weeks, since I heard anything about it. . . .

Yours,

M. HAUPTMANN.

128.

LEIPZIG, *March* 15th, 1857.

DEAR HAUSER,—

. . . I daresay you heard that Liszt gave a Concert here, with the Weimar Company, a few weeks since. One half of it was partially, and the second wholly devoted to " The Music of the Future." Happy they who, like ourselves, will not live to see it ! . . . The selections from the *Symphonic Poems* were the *Préludes* and *Mazeppa;* these were followed by a Liszt Concerto for the piano, played by Bülow, and a Romance sung by Milde. Milde and his wife are very good artists. Then we had a Duet from Wagner's *Flying Dutchman,* and a *Preghiera* from Schumann's *Genoveva.* Of course the *Brendel-Zeitung* speaks of the Concert, as if it had made an epoch. What rubbish ! The *Brockhaus* and the *Leipziger-Zeitung,* and even the *Signale* are much nearer the real truth. Liszt also conducted *Tannhäuser,* at a perform-ance given by the Weimar Company, for Behr's benefit. Behr's voice, however, began to fail him, before the end of the opera. They took a lot of money at the doors, on both occasions. The Concert was for the *Pensionsfond,* there was no Subscription Concert. . . .

Yours,

M. H.

129.

LEIPZIG, *July 5th*, 1857.

DEAR HAUSER,—

. . . It is such a bore, to have to pass the night in our own home at Leipzig, on the way back from Alexanderbad to Dresden! In the modulation of the second part of a Sonata, the fugitive recurrence of the principal key may occur in passing, and in a place where it appears strange, which is always rather gruesome, and sometimes even wrong. Why should we go farther, when we have found the place we belong to, and the place we love best? Good composers avoid this fault, which is more commonly found in works that are not written by rule. I don't call this passage out of the Overture to *Oberon* strictly pure, when the tonic has unexpectedly turned

up, and one has to begin again with the Dominant, so as to start afresh. I blame Weber for being casual, not for being capricious; both these qualities are false in Art. There, in a series of keys, that of D major appears casually. "Hallo! Why, here we are at home again! Who'd have thought it? Anyhow, now we have got here, here let us stay!" The course of modulation would just as well have allowed us to stay in the preceding key of F sharp major, and how are we to know that D major is the leading key, unless it makes itself necessary all along? There is always a touch of dilettanteism about Weber; it is silly, therefore, to rank him amongst the foremost composers. I do not think that Gluck stands in the first rank, either. His art is not thorough. I do not allude to his ignorance of counterpoint, I think him wanting in the sound principles of musical construction, the grasp of which constitutes a real composer, a thorough artist. After all, it is mankind in general, and not *connoisseurs* in particular, who finally pronounce upon Art, and it is a good sign, that the supremacy of such names as Haydn, Mozart, Handel, and Bach is indisputably and universally acknowledged. It is not the *connoisseurs* who sustain a work of Art, especially in music; it is the fact that, when it is performed, it pleases not A. or B., but the normal Man, who exists in us all. A choral melody, well sung in a big church, by a large number of voices, sounds all right, though were we to pick out one here and one there, we should find they were out of tune. If two people sing in tune, it is merely one voice doubled; if they sing out of tune, each sings out of tune in a different way. Large choruses always sound better than small. Nothing is so bad as two to a part. I have just come back from an open-air concert, where I heard some music of Wagner's, arranged for an orchestra; listening to it from a musical point of view, it seems a mere straining after vulgar effect. He spares no pains, as long as he can carry his audience away with him, yet we are always hearing about the purity of his expression, the directness and spontaneity of it all! He wears his crinoline, just like any other exaggerated French or Italian musician. . . .

Yours,

M. HAUPTMANN.

130.

LEIPZIG, *December 6th*, 1857.

DEAREST HAUSER,—

   . . . I am fresh from the great representative meeting of the delegates of the Bach Society—a huge gathering from all the four quarters of the globe:

> "The walls of Rheims could hardly hold
> The many guests that came."

Yet we were quite amongst ourselves as usual, even without our Becker, who, summer in, summer out, makes a Tusculum of Plagwitz. Proske, Prebendary of Ratisbon, was elected member of the Committee, by a majority of votes. Of course, he may refuse to act with an evangelical Society that edits Cantatas, one of which contains the petition: "From Turk and Pope, good Lord deliver us!" If he does, we shall have Joachim, who was next on the list. On Sunday, Spohr conducted *Jessonda*, for the last time. His desk and chair were covered with flowers, and as soon as the opera was over, he appeared on the stage, surrounded by all the members of the company, and was presented with an address and a laurel wreath. Then the band played the March from *Die Weihe der Töne*, and there was a regular ovation. Lately, he has not been up to the mark, they tell me, and Reiss had to do duty for him, even at the rehearsals of *Jessonda*. I hope Spohr will get reconciled to this ; he did not like it at first. He saw no difference in himself—perhaps that was one of the worst signs.

Yesterday, I received the last few sheets of the third volume of Mozart, including some of the Dresden letters (April, 1789), and the famous letter to Baron——, contributed by Rochlitz, sending him back a composition with his own criticisms upon it, and some remarks on his own method of composing. It is once more quite obvious, that the whole letter cannot have been written by Mozart ; it is a fabrication of the worthy Herr Rochlitz himself, patched up from casual reminiscences, and purporting to be strictly genuine, word for word. Rochlitz is a very old hand at this sort of thing, but he assumes such a pious air of truthfulness, that people are scandalised when the forgery is proved. He says his Essays are intended for " quiet hours "—the world is too dissipated to understand him. As soon as one has got " a quiet hour," one finds him out. He says he wanted to write a History of Music, and spent half his life in preparation for the task, ransacking all the libraries in Europe ; but he gave up the work, because the world was not quiet enough. Then he took to printing his collection of ancient music, beginning with that of the Flemish school, choosing from amongst cartloads of MSS. all that he thought most important, most beautiful, and most characteristic. How about all these European libraries and cartloads of MSS. ? They dwindle down to Becker's library, a well-furnished one, no doubt, but easily stowed away in one small room—and even then, Rochlitz comes to all sorts of grief, for he supposes that the single piece, taken by Becker from the *Tablature*, and set to music by him in three different ways, was made of three different pieces. Had he observed the 2/2 in one place, and the 3/2 in another, he would have seen that it was the same thing tried in different *Tempi*. And there he sits, with the divine tranquillity of Zeus, as if he were perfectly omniscient and all-seeing!

I have just heard, that Jenny Lind is *not* going to sing at Halle. I hope the fact will be announced, as many people who wished to go will not care to do so now. I have it from a private source, but " on good authority," as the papers say. I wonder whether it is true, that she wanted to have the church warmed, and that they refused, because of the trouble and expense. . . .

Yours,

M. HAUPTMANN.

131.

LEIPZIG, *February 22nd*, 1858.

. . . At Frau Frege's, the other day, we heard a private performance of Handel's Oratorio, *Jephtha*. There are such precious things in it, and such a lot of them too, that he would be a bold man, who should attack that subject again. And indeed I cannot at present think of any great music, be it Opera, Oratorio, or Symphony, with anything like calmness or freedom from distraction. It is the musical '48. . . . How Mendelssohn would have suffered, had he lived! He would be forty-seven now. They reckon him an obsolete Philistine, and treat him like a dead dog—contemptible creatures that they are! . . .

Yours,

M. HAUPTMANN.

132.

LEIPZIG, 21st March, 1858.

. . . There are many sins of omission, which I regret exceedingly, but one cannot always arrange these things beforehand. Life gives the material—we have got to shape it as best we may. Some make a much better affair of it than others. Raphael, at home with the Farnesina, creates the loveliest pictures in the world, whereas another person, in the same circumstances, would feel himself hopelessly cramped and quite incapable of good work.

End of the introductory observations.

The second part of Köhler's book on Pianoforte Playing is complete; it will be forwarded at Easter. The first part, which deals with the mechanism, was finished long ago. The second treats of Metre and Harmony. His work is founded on mine; he attempts to be more practical, though he follows me step by step. I have had the proof-sheets, but I only dipped into them here and there. They seem to me too abstract and theoretical, and I doubt the success of his efforts to popularise the system; he has the idea of an organism, but it is a skeleton, without flesh and blood. I think my way of putting it the simpler one, though it presupposes, and must inevitably presuppose abstract thought. Perhaps the work, as a whole, may have a different effect, and I hope it may be so, considering all the trouble that Köhler has taken. He may not have grasped everything and each thing, so that principle makes an error in any part impossible—still, I doubt whether anyone else has taken so much trouble to master the subject. . . .

I daresay you have heard something about the *Riedel Gesangverein*. It was founded some years since; they practise nothing but ancient music. No doubt their zeal and enterprise are highly commendable; but the newspapers, not content with giving them credit for energy and for moderate success, make so much of their concerts, and of everyone who takes part in them, that to read the critiques, one would suppose that the *Riedelsche Verein* was the centre of gravity, on which the musical life of the town depended. Of course, the *Singakademie* and the *Thomanerchor* are old worn-out institutions, with no life nor go in them! As regards the latter, this is no news to me. I have been told quite lately, that it is no longer what it was in the days of Calvisius, Hermann Schein, and Sebastian Bach. He must have very long ears, who can hear things so far back as that. They prefer to ignore Weinlig; if it were a question of Schicht, perhaps they might know what they were talking about, but it is impossible for anyone to go further than Hiller and Doles. Bach himself complained of having so many pupils "incapable of forming a *quarta* in their throat," and I fancy that the difficult and sustained parts of Bach's *Oboi d'Amore*, played by the apprentices of the *Stadtmusikus*, cannot always have sounded *con amore*. Oh, for some musical photographs of our time, to hand down to those that come after us! Oh, that we had some pictures of the Past! They would have taught us, among other things, how to understand Greek music, which we know, or rather do not know, only through unmusical philologists. I think it quite right, that every important town should have its Association for Ancient Music. Even though it be not always enjoyable from a musical point of view, still it is historically interesting. But these antiquarians are as bad as the musicians of the Future; they immediately become so bigoted and illiberal, that they look upon the Present, and everything connected with it, as quite beneath them. Such exclusiveness may have its good side, but then exclusiveness is in itself an evil.

Three thousand tickets are to be issued gratis, for the Riedel performances in the church. You hear a great deal about the universal sympathy of the public, and people infer from this, that the music and the performance are equally good. But what a hollow sham it is! They take H. Schütz's *Passion,* which is really made up of "the finest passages" of all four, and when they have transmogrified it, and turned it inside out, so as to make it practicable for amateurs, they advertise it in their programmes, and produce it in public as a really beautiful thing. Most of it—*i.e.*, all the words of the Evangelist, excepting those which Schütz, like Bach, had already set to choruses, has been recast, by an affected imitator of the old masters. Surely, it cannot touch the hearts of the audience, and yet they think themselves obliged to say, "How beautiful!" The Association is supported by well-to-do people who, inasmuch as they take no part in the singing, are nicknamed the *tin* instruments.

Yours,

M. H.

133.

LEIPZIG, May 18th, 1858.

. . . Strange, is it not, that so ardent an apostle of the music of the Future as Louis Köhler, should trouble himself about my book? His confederates dare not give him up altogether. They are in a regular fix, and I can't help laughing at them. Wonders will never cease. Liszt's *Graner Messe* is actually making a *furore* in Austria. I don't know a note of it, but I fancy we should loathe it as sacred music. Nothing but Liszt, the Almighty quite out of it! Everyone is raving about the composer. If things were as they should be, he ought to be clean forgotten. . . .

Yours,

M. H.

134.

LEIPZIG, September 11th, 1858.

DEAR HAUSER,—

. . . Herr Berger is anxious to be introduced to you. He is a professional musician, a Londoner by birth, though his parents are German. He studied composition with Ricci, in Italy, for four years, then he was my pupil for a short time, and during the last three years, he has followed his profession in London, as a pianist, a teacher, and the conductor of a choir. His compositions have something of the Italian grace and smoothness, which is almost unknown to our students of thorough-bass. I have lost my old belief in Italian *Conservatoires* and Italian music. It is past and gone. Cimarosa and Paesiello, that was what I enjoyed in former days. The modern Italians never gave me the same pleasure. . . . The Spohrs and Frau von Malsburg dropped in upon us at Alexanderbad, on their way back from Prague, where Spohr had a very flattering reception. Nobody grudges him these triumphs in the evening of his life, and there is no fear of his being over-excited; he is not nervous, he takes these things quietly, they do him good. But since his visit to Leipzig two years ago, he certainly has aged considerably; he is less active, he is deafer, and less inclined to join in general conversation. Happily, he seems unconscious of these infirmities, but it grieves me to think of the contrast offered by former days. I always prophesied a vigorous old age for him, like that of Haydn, whose *Seasons* and "Come, gentle spring!" were written when he was seventy. Spohr had begun a Requiem, but he got out of heart with it, and so it remains unfinished. Fräulein Pfeiffer told me at Alexanderbad, that he had taken up his Autobiography again, but I can't imagine how he gets through his day, without composing and attending rehearsals. . . . He certainly does enjoy one privilege. If he wants a holiday, he can take it without asking leave. We expect him here for our third or fourth *Gewandhaus Concert,* when a Symphony and some other pieces of his will be given. He conducted *Jessonda,* at Prague, and considering the means he had at his disposal, they say it was a good performance. The singers were second-rate. I don't hear much good of the concerts, except as regards the solos by Laub and Dreyschock. . . .

Yours,

M. H.

135.

LEIPZIG, *October 5th*, 1858.

DEAREST HAUSER,—

. . . Herewith, my boy Louis's lottery ticket for the Industrial Exhibition at Munich. Will you please find out, whether he has got anything, when the winning numbers are declared, and take charge of it for him? If he gets a loco- motive, you might drive it yourself to Leipzig, only mind you don't get off the rails! We resumed our concerts yesterday; summer will be upon us, before we know where we are. Wiele used to complain that he felt the first breath of winter, as soon as the chestnuts began to bud. We were at Dresden for a week or two, and met Reissiger. He is much altered. He was a fine, stately looking fellow, when he was the King of Saxony's first *Capellmeister*. All that has gone; he has had a stroke, and he never will be again the man he was. People complain about the Theatre, and the Committee of Manage- ment in particular. Since the death of the wife of *Intendant* L., Reissiger has grown quite apathetic. Farewell! I must be off to the *Conservatoire*, to examine the new recruits and tame the young barbarians. . . .

Yours,

M. H.

136.

LEIPZIG, *January 3rd*, 1859.

DEAREST HAUSER,—

. . . I ought to have earned your congratulations, by telling you about the Munich Order. Maier brought the news here, but it was no news to me, for David had read it out to me in the *Augsburger*, of the 28th, and next day it was in the *Leipziger* and the *Tageblatt*. The Order was sent through the Dresden Embassy. It is a pretty thing—a little too big, I fancy though. I have not yet tried it on. Why should I make a guy of myself, like the ox at Whitsuntide? The

Cantor would always be seen behind it, and it is not only *one* of his predecessors who puts him to shame ! The expression " eminent services " occurs in the patent—lithographed—the words, not the services ; the Chapter would be in a fix, were they called upon to specify the latter. There is a Pegasus on the reverse side of the Cross; that means Art. Science is represented by an owl. I have the Pegasus. Our little Ernest, when he shows off the Order, says, " Look at the *Pecus* on the back of it ! " and when he brings in a letter addressed *Dr. phil.*, he reads it out *Doctor Philister*. Zelter once wrote to Goethe : " They have made me a Doctor of Philosophy, Heaven forgive them ! " I rather plume myself on my knowledge of Harmony and Metre, and that living nature of theirs which makes them human, but this kind of thing, alas ! one cannot communicate to others. . . . Modern Counterpoint is an abomination to me—notably, the Fugues of these days ; they are like periwigs on a modern costume. Everything polyphonically conceived and invented becomes fugal of itself, witness even Mendelssohn's choruses, which are so full of animation, and sound so natural, that we never think about their construction. It is only when he takes to writing actual Fugues, that their weakness, as music, becomes patent ; they are mere bits of mechanism, the composer is trying to show what he can do. I talked with Mendelssohn himself about the B flat major Fugue in *St. Paul*, and he said that people always looked out for a regular Fugue in Oratorios, and if it were omitted, they would think it was because he could not do it. I would far rather he had proved his knowledge in some other place. We have more than enough of Fugues in Oratorios ; it's a mere concession to fashion, a formality that had best be avoided. The Fugue was much more natural, when as yet there were no Fugues—in the days of the old Italian masters, for instance. You will find not a single Fugue in all the Passion Music of St. Matthew and St. John, though every note, dramatically conceived, is animated with the spirit of the Fugue. The pattern Fugue owes its first development to the organ—a pedal point is another name for it ; in vocal music it is a sheer anomaly, we don't want to hear a bass singer struggling with the lockjaw.

Mendelssohn has granted a fresh lease of life to the Oratorio, but excepting *St. Paul* and *Elijah*, there is not much yet that is fireproof. Spohr is out of the reckoning : he was a writer of Oratorios before Mendelssohn, and looking neither to the right nor to the left, he never aimed at being another Handel nor Beethoven, he simply sat before a mirror, which reflected his own face ; hence there is very little variety, but we must respect him, for he is true to himself. Hiller, in his *Jerusalem*, took Mendelssohn for his pattern. I heard it twelve years ago, and thought it the best thing of its kind.

Yours,

M. HAUPTMANN.

137.

LEIPZIG, *January* 19th, 1859.

DEAREST HAUSER,—
        If you want to know how old I am, I had better tell you at once, before I get any older.   Older than you are I certainly must be, your wife is quite right there.   I saw light for the first time on the 13th October, 1792 ; whether it was radiant Apollo or My Lady Moon, I can't say, but the Dresden registers know all about that.   It is possible that they had both of them hidden their faces on the joyful occasion, and were surprised and delighted by the sight of me, later on.   You say you feel " so old, and yet so young ! " Well, it is just the same with me !   It's not quite so easy to get about as it used to be, and one may not be quite so enterprising, but there is little change, intellectually.   If trifles no longer absorb one as they did, more substantial interests are not wanting, and I look upon that as so much gain. Of course, it makes one long for a little more time. . . .
        Why has Gade so long ceased to be original ? His first Symphony, which was beautifully scored, had good stuff in it, but it was rather strained.   Two less effective Symphonies followed ; then came the fourth and lovely one in B, a perfect thing for a drawing-room, neat and crisp—but his subsequent works, graceful and melodious as they are, cannot hold a

candle to the first; they are rather flabby, no real bone in them, more nerve than muscle. Construction, however, is always his weak point, and yet all music, that is intended to last, must have a solid basis; failing this, it runs off into water. By a solid basis, I do not mean a scaffolding outside the music, for the skeleton of the animal does not exist before its flesh, nor the crystal before the drop of water. One particle of salt takes a different form from another, and yet, beforehand, each was simply and solely a drop of water, which could have made its escape through the thickest filter. A thing which has no form always precedes a definite object, but then it has the laws of form within itself. This formal part, I should like to term the metrical, as distinguished from the rhythmical, but you ignore this when you say " a rhythm has four beats." The powers above may know what you mean by it, but it's a nonsensical expression.

We are now practising a pretty little Motet by Gade, well written for the voices, but a mere mollusc,—a kind of embryo. All very well in a short composition, but in a longer one you lose the ground under your feet, it gets pulpy. Goethe says in his *Italienische Reise*, à *propos* of his remodelling of *Tasso*, which, like the *Iphigenie*, was originally written in prose : " These pieces wanted defining, they were all in a pulp. In accordance with more recent experiences, *I have allowed form to predominate*." Passion, as the subject of a work of art, becomes oppressive, unless the burden of it is borne by form. To satisfy the literal truth, by introducing one bar more or less than the metre requires, is as little in harmony with artistic truth, as real tears and real laughter would be in singing.

The *Brendelsche Zeitung* has offered a prize, for an Essay on " The Extension of Harmony in the New School." Liszt, Weitzmann, and I have been asked to act as judges. I am rather amused, for I cannot conceive of any extension of things, the laws of which are in themselves infinite, nor, on the other hand, can I think that harmony,—so-called " enharmonic,"—which is by nature confined to the key-board, is capable of life. In a post office in Carinthia, I once saw a picture of the Trinity — *i.e.*, a face with three noses and four eyes $^\circ|^\circ|^\circ|^\circ$ in which the two eyes nearest the centre had to do duty "enharmonically" for two noses. It was a repulsive monstrosity, though the division of the head was rather cleverly managed. The Trinity is contained in all things human, divine, and natural, and he who seeks to represent it in a particular form, has not yet understood it. The Trinity is the unity of opposites; every phenomenon of life contains the Trinity, and is the Trinity. . . .

The eighth volume of Bach, comprising four Masses, is now complete, and I am going to send it to you. The Masses are those in F and A, G minor and G major; all four are published by Simrock. They are, for the most part, compiled from the Cantatas, and it is rather curious, that the same music should be equally well adapted to perfectly different words. Most curious of all is the Kyrie of the G minor Mass, where the introductory chorus of the Cantata, "Lord, Thine eyes," is made to do duty for "Thou smitest them," and "Their face is harder than the rock," with its rock-like harshness and severity, is adapted to the *Kyrie* and the *Christe eleison.* One can't help thinking of fists and black eyes. One other passage

I have always looked upon as a blunder of the copyist, the bars after the † having been introduced accidentally, instead of later on, where they are in their right place. In the Cantata too, the passage is utterly at variance with a phrase, which ought to come in later on, with its own *motif*. Now all this stands in the MS. of the Cantata, in Bach's most unmistakable handwriting, also in the Altnicol copy of the Mass, so that one is fairly puzzled. I cannot commend it. . . .

Yours,

M. HAUPTMANN.

---

* Where the tenor part is absolutely impossible, there being no bridge to the a flat after the A major chord.

I

138.

LEIPZIG, *January* 21*st*, 1859.

DEAREST HAUSER,—

I forgot to answer a point raised in your last letter. It concerns the *Tempus*, regarding which you agree with Frankinus Gafor, who declares it perfect, when it consists in 3 × 3. Gafor has both *tempus* and *prolatio*, either perfect or imperfect. The dual with him is imperfect, the triple perfect, thus he arrives at—

prolatio perfecta in tempore perfecto   (3 × 3) 𝅘𝅥. 𝅘𝅥. 𝅘𝅥.

- imperfecta -   -   -   (2 × 3) 𝅗𝅥. 𝅗𝅥.

prolatio perfecta in tempore imperfecto (3 × 2) 𝅗𝅥 𝅗𝅥 𝅗𝅥

- imperfecta -   -   -   (2 × 2) 𝅗𝅥 𝅗𝅥

Now, if this triple arrangement is declared perfect, my view of Harmony and Metre will not only appear imperfect—it will be an absolute nonentity, entirely without foundation. Of course, this is no argument and no proof that duality represents perfection.

Once upon a time, somebody recorded in print his opinion that the Abbé Vogler was a blockhead, whereupon Vogler printed a long list of his titles, saying that he was an Imperial Councillor, a *Capellmeister*, and lots of things besides, so that it was out of the question he could be a blockhead. But apart from Fr. Gafor and my theory, with its illustrations, we have only to look at music from a historical point of view, to get an answer to the question, whether triple arrangements of rhythmical units are preferable to dual, or rather quadruple. With the early Netherlanders and old Italians, it is the almost universal custom, to begin a piece of music with a rhythm of four beats, or a rhythm of twice two beats. A distinction must be made here. Then, in the middle of the piece, there is a section in triple time (𝅗𝅥 𝅗𝅥 𝅗𝅥), and for the close, there is a return to square rhythm.*

---

* Compare the opening of vocal and instrumental Canzoni, 𝅗𝅥 𝅗𝅥 𝅗𝅥 | 𝅗𝅥 *circa* 1600.—*Note by Tr.*

Now, isn't it odd, that a piece should begin "imperfect," then pass to a little bit of "perfect," and when that becomes tedious, return to "imperfect," and then fail to reach a satisfactory close? One is reminded of *Tannhäuser*, who having done no good at Rome, finally prefers to return to the Venusberg. But this is not the case in ancient music only. Consult a thousand Symphonies, Sonatas, Quartets, as to whether or not it is the rule, that they begin and end in triple time, leaving the dual and quadruple time as a vital contradiction (*als Lebensdissonanz*) to be ultimately resolved! The ordinary course of things, on the contrary, is that a piece shall begin and end in square time, having a division in triple time near the middle. What we all feel to be true and right should stand at the beginning—then a deviation, a doubt, may find expression—finally, there must be a return to that which is right and true. Just as though you were to set up I, V7. I, (Tonic, Dominant Seventh, Tonic). The last I is an equivalent of the first I, yet it is a separate entity.

This sort of thing may find expression in various other ways, and the metrical scheme may be different, or even reversed: the first and last movement of a fine Symphony may be in $\frac{3}{4}$ time, and the Andante in $\frac{4}{4}$ or $\frac{2}{4}$. Yet in the abstract, the former arrangement is the most spontaneous and natural. Gafor was mislead, I think, by his desire to connect a three-fold metrical arrangement with the idea of the Trinity. But this is a confusion of the number 3 with the conception of three in one—which conception does not consist of three separate things standing next to one another, but rather in the combination and unification of two opposites; the Roman figures I, II, III, illustrate the matter to some extent—to the eye at least—but I don't think this particularly significant. The fine face with the three noses and four eyes, which I described in my last letter, represents the sort of Trinity which is contained in the idea of three combined entities. The human face, as *le bon dieu* created it, is a true Trinity, and accords with the conception of the unity of opposites—a self-evident truth which needs no comment. A nose and two eyes as opposed to two eyes and a nose! A true opposite arises only, when a thing forms the antithesis to itself. Thus, to return to my example of the red ball : we understand the distinction between red roundness and round redness, yet, in reality, both exist together and simultaneously. I refrain, for the present, from showing how this applies to the nature of metrical rules. It is all set forth in my book, where I have also shown, how a measure of four beats (not that which results from the repetition of two beats, but rather that which has passed from dual to triple and thence to quadruple beats) pertains to the same conception, and comes under the head of the same idea as the *Third* in Harmony ; we cannot go *beyond* the Third in harmony, just as we cannot metrically go beyond that which is *quadruple*. It is equally impossible, to add a note to a consonant Triad, or to add a fifth beat to a metrical unity of four—unless indeed some harmonic or metrical dissonance be intended. These are proved truths, which any-body may understand and elucidate in his own way. They appear in everything that appeals to our eyes and ears. We can hardly talk so positively about the mouth and the nose—taste and smell are material senses ; they have nothing to do with Art, which addresses us through intelligible Form ; they deal only with that which is fluid and formless. Thus, a hard crust of bread is tasteless, until it has been chewed and become pap ; and we smell nothing, until it is turned into vapour. Did I ever tell you of my System of the Senses,— a six-rayed star ?

A good many short, detached Essays of mine are still in existence. They are not quite so disconnected as they appear, but I hardly know what to do with them. Several might serve as illustrations to and comments on my Harmony, for they elucidate single points, and contain a good deal that is con-crete and readily intelligible. There is one on Temperament, another on Solmisation, on the Hexachord, &c.

Jean Paul tells us, that he was so often asked by young authors, to write prefaces to their books, that he gave up some of his spare hours to compiling them, so as to have a number on hand. This done, however, the applications ceased, so there was nothing for it but to print and publish the whole batch in one volume, and now any youngster, in want of such an article, can pick and choose for himself. I mean to do the same with my Essays. They will be like notes to a text that has been lost—like Arnim's ambassador of a Court that has ceased to exist. But these novelists (I don't reckon Jean Paul among them) are themselves, to some extent, ambassadors of such a Court. With all their great gifts, depth of intellect, and poetical views of life and truth, they are not good enough for the people; their cultivation was one-sided, they kept aloof; as far as the common cause was concerned, they might as well never have lived at all. Whereas greater writers, such as Schiller and Goethe, live and will continue to live amongst all classes. They lived in Court circles too, but they were never aristocratic poets, they were real men both to prince and to people—men that did not mind hard work, when it led to great achievements.

. . .

Yours,
M. H.

139.

LEIPZIG, April 11th, 1859.

DEAR HAUSER,—

. . . Dr. Schwarz is advertising himself tremendously in Berlin, by giving anatomical lectures on the windpipe; I hear, too, that he sticks a mirror into a pupil's throat, that he may watch the formation of the tone. We are getting on anyhow, for they didn't learn that from the old Italians, from Bernacchi and his system, though they know it by heart. Yesterday, the Riedelsche Verein gave a performance of Bach's B minor Mass, with full orchestra and chorus. The work was well rehearsed, for though the Society is full of amateurs, Riedel takes the greatest pains in drilling them. . . . Many numbers of the Mass are sublime, but in several parts of it in the solos especially, Bach never rises to a higher than his most ordinary level. Here, too, we see that curious adaptation of pieces from the various Cantatas; this you will have observed elsewhere, in the last volume I sent you, where the intercalated numbers are specified. Many of these are

so altered to meet the new frame, that the re-modelling would
have been more troublesome than re-writing to any other
man, but in the majority of instances, they are only so far
altered, as to meet the exigencies of the text. As for the
solos, you go through a period of aversion, and another of
blind enthusiasm, before you settle down to them as they
really are, and form a just estimate. It is impossible to
think them really vocal, except during the second period, when
the whole thing seems divine. To my mind, they are orchids—
mere parasites, twisting and twining round themselves and
round each other,—no stems nor branches. How different from
the growth of an Italian song!—developing itself out of the
metre of words, and the melodious intonation of them, the
singer passing from one point to another, in a chain of causes
and effects that are independent of everything but each other,
engaging the full attention of the listener, while all the rest,
however varied, is mere accompaniment! Here, everything is
conceived and carried out instrumentally. I would often
gladly exchange the orchid-house for the garden, where plants
grow straight out of Mother Earth, and put forth boughs and
stems, as Nature bids them. Has the voice nothing else to do
with the words, but to run on in canonical imitation with the
Oboe di Caccia or d'Amore? If there are words enough for
the instrument, there are too many for the voice; the voice,
with a few notes set to words, does more than all the
obbligato instruments put together. All vocal music should
be a kind of development of the *Volkslied*, for that is of the
nature of Song itself. In Bach's songs, one cannot get rid of
the polyphonic instrumentation that accompanies them. One
is never quite comfortable in listening to them, however well
they are sung; when they are badly sung (as is usually the
case) it is sheer misery. And how few singers there are, that
can even sing these melodies smoothly! I only know of you
and Schelble,—and it is more than we have a right to expect
from the average singer. There are choruses specially written
for the B minor Mass, which are of surpassing depth and
grandeur, quite unequalled in music: equally grand, too, are
some of those adapted from the Cantatas—*e.g.*, the Crucifixus,
taken from the Cantata *Weinen, klagen*, with a different

ending. Such numbers as these, even with a large orchestra
and chorus, are wonderfully effective. A large orchestra
and chorus do not enhance the beauty of Bach, as a general
rule, unless your one aim is material effect; who would care
to hear *Figaro* in the Crystal Palace? You can never overdo
the thing with Handel; he wrote in London, and knowing he
was sure of any amount of resources, wrote accordingly. His
composition is transparent; it can be supplemented by any
number of voices and instruments. . . .

Have you seen Mozart's autograph copy of the *Zauberflöte*
at André's? In the Duet *Bei Männern welche*, he first
wrote—

Then he struck out the bar lines, and wrote—

though as far as the text was concerned, the first setting was
certainly the best, as the accents, which now fall on *welche* and
fühlen, then fell on *Männer* and *Liebe*. Mozart, however, felt
as a musician, that he had no alternative but to make the
change. . . .

I wish we could meet in the summer holidays, but
Alexanderbad and Carlsbad are too far apart. I spare you
my views of politics, which are a terrible nightmare to me.
Happily for us, our daily and hourly anxieties at home
relieve us from other thoughts. Petty cares shield us from
great ones. The axe may be at the root of the tree, but the
insect goes on building his house on the leaf. . . .

Yours,

M. H.

140.

LEIPZIG, *June* 18*th*, 1859.

DEAREST HAUSER,—

. . . A week ago, we had the grand *Zukunftsfestmessen-wochenmusikerzusammenkunft!* You may break up the word into as many fragments as you please, like the music itself, every bit of which is independent. They say that the last Mass we had at Easter was the worst ever known, barring Liszt's. That Mass so utterly depressed me, and so ruined my digestion, that next day I got very little enjoyment out of Bach's B minor. You must have a clean tongue to taste good wine. Those were my only dissipations during the week. I avoided all the speechifying and the lectures, but a good many people came to see me, and amongst them twenty-one samples of musicians from all quarters of the globe. . . . The newspapers will burst with accounts of the great results of this concourse of musicians, and their performances —not a word of truth in them! There were no tickets to be paid for at the church, so the church was full; they had to pay at the theatre, and so it was empty. The Mass produced an irritating effect, even upon persons rather inclined to the new musical creed; such an outrage in God's house is thought unpardonable. Of course it will all pass off, but meantime these clouds of mephitic vapour are hard to bear, and when they have cleared off, what then? A new genius would stay our fears, but what are we to expect from persons who halt between Mozart and Liszt? . . .

The B minor Mass is full of sublimity, especially in the Choruses, yet I don't exactly know its *raison d'être*. The Passion Music is a different matter, but the Mass is too long to be used as a Church Service, or indeed for anything but a Concert in Church—and for this, the words of the Catholic Mass seem to me unsuitable. Besides, there is no economy of form, and it is most wearisome, to see every tittle of the text conscientiously taken in hand and turned into a separate piece, an Air with a repetition of the first part. It rather amuses me, to pick holes in a work so extravagantly and indiscriminately praised, alike by the understanding and by the ignorant. If Spohr's vocal music always betrays the violinist, we invariably detect the organist in Bach's. Not the grandly rolling eight-part Motets alone, but the Airs, intertwined as they are with the instruments, seem to be the direct outcome of his organ music. Such compositions as *Der Geist hilft*, or the *Kyrie* theme in the B minor, would never have occurred to the mind of anyone, whose whole intention was to write for the voice. The Motet, *Ich lasse dich nicht*, is far more vocal than the other five, and it is well known that this, although the most popular of the set, is wrongly ascribed to Bach. Too often he is wanting in sympathy for the voice. I once inveighed strongly, enough single-handed, against the Passion Music, but withdrew my opposition afterwards. It was that silly, indiscriminate *Wunderschön!* that drove me to it. If people only knew how to criticise a thing *in its own place*, they might praise it as much as they liked, but this unqualified flattery, extended even to the Recitatives, is absurd. . . .

Yours,

M. H.

141.

LEIPZIG, *August 26th*, 1859.

. . . I have finished twelve Duets, which can be sung without pianoforte accompaniment, in the open air—though the occasion is not likely to arise, especially on the dusty Promenade here. I was led into writing them, by the fact that there was a poet at Alexanderbad, and that I had two singers—Susette and Fräulein Friderici—besides which, there was the open air. It is my whim to print these Duets simply in two lines, without pianoforte accompaniment, whereas others, though meant to be sung in this way, are published with some sort of keyboard arrangement underneath. This often perplexes a composer, who is in doubt whether he should put a bass to it, as that should be included already in a two-part composition, if it is well written, and if it is badly written, the words "To be sung without accompaniment" are super- fluous. Spohr was three weeks at Alexanderbad, and would have stayed longer, had he not been obliged to go to Würzburg, for a performance of his *Last Judgment*. He has lost much ground since last summer, and has become more feeble. He complains of sleeplessness and restlessness, and he is so unwieldy, that it is very difficult to move him. . . . A sad old age! I had hoped it would be happy and painless, and that he would be able to compose up to the last, "sweetly wandering towards a self-appointed goal." Such activity would have kept him unchanged, but helplessness, and the feeling that he is unable to do anything more, utterly depresses him. He has been obliged to give up the violin too, so his whole life has become a blank. The one amusement now left him is to listen to his own music, and he is constantly on the move to different places, to hear performances of his larger works. Last year, for instance, he went to Bremen, Magdeburg, Meiningen, Detmold, and Würzburg, where he was honoured and *fêted*, just as in old days. He declined to go to Vienna. However, he still interests himself in other people's music, and is bent on a journey to Hanover, to hear *Lohengrin*, which is new to him. The other day, we got up a quartet for men's voices, and he sang the second bass part capitally. Susette has made a very good sketch of him, an outline slightly shaded; he wears his little cap. Koch, the Cassel litho- grapher, is going to engrave it, and if it turns out well, it will be the best likeness we have of Spohr, though that is not saying much, where all are bad. He never sat to any good artist except Grünbaum, and that portrait was taken when he was a young man. We have only the portrait by Krauskopf in his *Violinschule*, well drawn, and a good likeness—not of Spohr, but as it happens, of Wilhelm Grund of Hamburg. Now it is too late, though Susette has succeeded admirably in concentrating the life that is still left in him, and giving a faithful representation of him in his best moments. It is now-a-days the fashion with painters, to represent men who have been great in their day, in the last stage of decrepitude. I will not reckon Laroche among these, though his Napoleon is a painfully depressing picture, but Hübner of Dresden has painted Charles V. in a condition when he was more fit for a coffin than a picture, and his Frederick II. is much the same. I have come across many other mummy-like portraits of this kind, always of monstrous size; one can't think where they will find a home, for they are not good enough for a gallery, and they are too ugly for a private collection. They can but emigrate from one *Kunstverein* to another—wandering Jews!

I suppose you have heard that Bendemann is going to Düsseldorf, as Director of the Academy. He is sorry to leave Dresden, but they did little or nothing to keep him there. The late King would not have let him go, but the present one takes no interest whatever in Art. Science and Literature are more in his line. Bendemann is certainly the noblest representative of the Düsseldorf school, but going back there after an absence of more than twenty years, I expect he will feel out of his element. It is long since I have seen anything of that school, but several of the younger Düsseldorfers were making vigorous efforts to work their way out of it. The landscapes and *genre* pictures were rather Dutch and Belgian in character than German. . . .

Yours,
M. HAUPTMANN.

142.

LEIPZIG, September 20th, 1859.

DEAREST HAUSER,—

To-morrow we are off to Dresden for Julia's birthday, and as the Härtels have been good enough to get my two four-part Songs out of hand, in honour of the occasion, I send you a copy. You will find that several of them might have been written by anyone who knew how to make crotchets and quavers, but often—I might say always—the very essence of music is, not to sound artificial. You know what I mean; I have no time to explain. . . . I want to have your opinion of my new doctrine of Harmony. I have got some way on with it, but I doubt whether it will be practicable. It really is a repetition of my *Harmonik*, only less abstract, and with musical notes for illustrations. I question whether it is not rather beyond those who cannot think for themselves, and must have rules before them; pupils with heads on their shoulders will find it superfluous, my *Harmonik* is enough for them, and the new Essay treats only of the logic of Harmony. Last week, I wrote five four-part Songs; the first was written years ago, so these came in to make up the half-dozen. The words are taken from Klaus Groth, and from Bodenstedt's *Mirza Schaffy*. I don't mean to print them, till I have heard them rehearsed. When I try country lads for the *Thomasschule*, I often profit by the occasion, to confirm my ideas of the nature of Harmony. They stumble at passages which are easy to a town-bred boy. To-day, for instance, a lad couldn't manage—

but oddly enough, always sang—

which, one would have thought, was the more difficult of the two. But that was because the minor third is not a direct interval; the lads hover about with the e flat and c, lacking proper support. So for tuning—if the piano is to set the pitch for the A string of the violins, it is customary to play the chord of D minor instead of D major; the same thing is done in church, when the organ sets the pitch. It is the universal custom, yet nobody asks why. The a in the chord of D minor stands in a double sense as fifth and third. D f a—

in the D major chord, D is more prominent; D f sharp A.

To tune D, the chord of D major or of G minor would serve better than that of D minor. In a similar way, the distinction between the note forming the third in the harmony and the note forming the fourth big fifth in the harmony, C e, C G D A E

practically plays a more important *rôle* than people generally
think.* I don't mean those folks who deny the whole
story. . . .

Yours,
M. HAUPTMANN.

143.

LEIPZIG, October 1st, 1859.

. . . Last Sunday, we heard *Lohengrin* at Dresden.
Glowing reports of it had reached Leipzig; we were assured
by people who were presumably good judges, that we could not
criticise the music, till we had heard it there. It might be unfair,
to hear it done in a hole-and-corner theatre, with a second-rate
orchestra, but it makes no difference whatever to me, whether
I hear it in Leipzig or in Dresden. I am not to be blinded by
dresses and scenery, which are poor substitutes for the real
thing. We sat it out with difficulty till the end, and then we
found that we were all of one mind, never to hear such a
work again, wherever or however it might be done. The
Dresden performance has been exaggerated ; we understand
the few musical passages of the opera better at Leipzig,
notably the Introduction and the Finale of the First Act,
which sounded much better in the *Gewandhaus.* The
Nibelungen are so interminably long, that I should never
survive the fourth evening, so I must console myself with
what I have heard already. I fancy that *Tristan und Isolde*
will come out before the Trilogy, the text was printed long
ago ; it is just as conceited and foolish as all the rest. When
you are reading the poetry, he says you're to think of the
music—when you are hearing the music, he wants you to
think of the poetry—there is nothing to lay hold of anywhere.
Did you hear what Schnyder said, when he was asked his
opinion of *Tannhäuser?* "I put Richard Wagner before Goethe
and before Beethoven." This was a floorer to his questioners,
who couldn't believe he was speaking seriously. "Yes," he
continued, " Wagner composes better than Goethe, and he is

---

* The comparison is between the small e, C e, and the capital E, which forms
the fourth fifth, starting from the initial C.—*Note by Tr.*

more of a poet than Beethoven." This last is no great matter, when one thinks of Beethoven's

> " Not these tones, O my friends,
> But others and more agreeable ! "

I am not acquainted with Goethe's compositions. Writing to somebody about his *Rhein und Main-Reise*, he says : " You will find all sorts of things discussed in it, except music, which I know nothing about." What a pity other people are not so reasonable ! We can talk much more easily about things which we see and feel. Music is the most difficult of all Arts except Poetry, yet everybody thinks he has a right to have his say about it. Old Concertmeister Wiele hit the point, when Spohr asked him what he thought of Cherubini's Violin Quartets, in which he had been playing second violin at Paris : " I found several very pretty passages in my part," said he. That was something positive anyhow. . . .

Yours,

M. H.

144.

LEIPZIG, *October 22nd*, 1859.

DEAR HAUSER,—

. . . Veit is Chief Magistrate at Eger, but at Leipzig he's a composer. Last Thursday, a Symphony of his was played at the *Gewandhaus*, a graceful thing, and very well written ; unpretentious as the music is, no one grudged the applause which greeted it. Perhaps you know the composer, for he used to live in Prague ; I daresay he comes from there. Music seems to agree with the lawyers of Bohemia, *vide* Kittl, Wolfram, Kleinwächter minor, yourself, and many others. . . . We have sad news of Spohr, though only at second hand. All last week, the Wolffs were very anxious about him. The bare idea of his death used to be terrible to me. I felt as if I should be left an orphan. But for the last two years, his condition has been such, that he himself had hardly any pleasure in life, and it was getting worse and worse. There was nothing left but to pity him, he seldom had a bright moment, and took but little interest in anything,—only occasionally in music,—and even then he soon fell asleep over

it. The whole course of things has prepared us for the end.
Pray Heaven it be a painless one for him !

Here, as elsewhere, I suppose, they are making great
preparations for the Schiller Jubilee. The Goethe celebration,
ten years ago, was far less popular; obviously, the people
like Schiller best. He himself says : " Man reflects himself
in his gods." I think it is quite in the nature of things, that he
should be, to the people, a more imposing figure than Goethe,
who is too natural and downright, too much given to express
all that is highest and deepest in the homeliest language—

> " Who never ate with tears his bread,
> Who never through the weary nights
> Hath sat and wept upon his bed "—

Bread and *bed*—ordinary words enough, yet they go deeper
into one's soul than all the high-flown figures of speech.
What could be more beautiful than his, " Again thou fillest
wood and valley," than *Werther* and *Götz von Berlichingen*—
poems which, contrasted with the bombast of the time, are
like dewy roses growing up out of a heap of rubbish. Even
though there be a *Grosskophta*, and plenty more of that
description, it was written less for effect than because he felt
obliged to get rid of the stuff. His love of Schiller, and the
high estimation in which he held his friend, make him even
more loveable. Schiller, in his letters, does not always speak
so loyally of Goethe, as Goethe, under all circumstances, does
of him. Schiller is now and then two people in one, Goethe
never. . . .

Yours,

M. H.

145.

LEIPZIG, October 26th, 1859.

So dear Spohr is gone, and there is really no one left to
take his place ! One-sided he was no doubt, but his was the
right side ; all we have now is the left, and that too the
extreme left, and a rabble rout they are ! It is just like
Frankfurt in '48. The recent revolution in Art made Spohr
so angry, that I think it lessened his pleasure in life, though

of course the real misery was his inability to compose.
Composition was as necessary to him as the air he breathed.
Happily, his end was comparatively painless. You and I
enjoyed his friendship for many years. I knew him as far
back as 1811. I lived near him for a year in Gotha, for six
months in Vienna, for some little time in Dresden, for twenty
years in Cassel. All that time, he was the same indefati-
gable worker. I saw no change after we came to Leipzig,
and it was only during the last two years that he began to
fail. . . . Leipzig was not represented at the funeral. I
did not feel up to it. . . .

Dr. Ambros, probably known to you as a native of Prague,
has published a little book called *Ueber das Quintverbot, eine
Studie*, with a motto from the *Harmonik* (p. 70, " For the
master," &c.), and dedicated it to me. I am constantly
being made aware, that I am not explicit enough. If people
will only read out of the book, if they will not read themselves
into it, they will invariably come to grief; it must be taken all
together from A to Z, and there are very few people who get
to Z. If the constructive principle is as clearly at the
bottom of all metrical definitions, as it is at the bottom of
harmonic definitions, all meaningless acoustic figures ought
to be eliminated as a matter of course, for they are void
of significance as part of a metrical code. Metre supports
harmony, and *vice versâ*. So says Ambros. It would be
much better to ignore my principle utterly, than to try
and take up a position midway between it and the
acoustic theories of former days; it is nonsense, at one time
to commend what I have said as true, and at another, to
stick to the old doctrine, for they are often in direct contradiction. This may also be said of Carriere, who speaks of
" the great service " I have rendered, in applying to music
the discovery of Pythagoras about the relation of tones, so as
to make it clear to musicians. No one has taken the trouble
to understand the matter properly, nor to let it develop in his
own mind. One need only listen to another person repeating
what one has said, to see how rarely one is understood ; and
if this is our constant experience in everyday life, how much
more often must it occur in abstract things. In his *Quinten-*

Studie, Ambros muddles everything up together, making no distinction between the fifths of the thirteenth century, in real parts and actual harmonic progression, and such fifths as occur in the passing notes of modern music. Now it would have been something to have distinguished these, and to have discoursed on the qualities of each ; but, as a fact, such men as he are not sufficiently well grounded, they can only write. Words and opinions, no knowledge ! Good writing has become such a common accomplishment, that science, in its serious aspect, suffers grievously ; it is become too much an affair of *belles lettres,* and the work gets scamped.

I suppose you saw in the papers, that I was to figure as one of the examiners for the Prize Essay *On the Extension of Harmony in Modern Times,* but I have withdrawn my name. At first, I thought it would be good fun to say No to everything the others praised, but after all, no one would have known of it outside the jury-box, the verdict would only have been " Successful " or the reverse, and neither the Essays nor the discussions would have been made public. So I told them they had better do without me, and choose a believer in my stead, as I should only stand in their way. I read one of the Essays, and glanced at a second—wretched, shallow stuff, but what could one expect ? Let them praise it among themselves, and bamboozle people as much as they please, what is not firm by nature will never last. . . . Brendel, however, must announce my resignation, if for no other reason than to get a substitute, unless they arrange matters with Liszt and Weitzmann ; those two will bo sure to agree. They may, if they choose, print my correspondence with them, but I expect they will let well alone. . . . So *Tristan und Isolde* is really to bo given in Carlsruhe ! ? Liszt has set the "Sermon on the Mount" to music, also "St. Elizabeth "!!!

Yours,

M. HAUPTMANN.

146.

LEIPZIG, *November 3rd,* 1859.

. . . At any rate, my *Harmonik* has made me a member of the Berlin Academy of Arts, and, I daresay, a Doctor of Göttingen into the bargain. *Rousseau* says, *à propos* of Rameau's *Traité de l'Harmonie:* "Everybody praises it, nobody reads it." The second remark applies to my book, if the first does not. However, d'Alembert re-wrote Rameau, and then everybody read him. I wish I could find a d'Alembert.

Spohr's widow has written a very pretty letter to Susette, describing his last days. They were quiet and peaceful—no pain, no struggle. He was out for the last time six days before his death, when he went to the Reading-room; he came home very tired, took to his bed, and never left it again. His Autobiography goes up to the time of his residence in Frankfurt. We are hoping that the widow will finish it; she is quite capable of doing so, and it would be a pity to leave it a fragment.

As for the new Architecture, Semper also has declared, that if anyone will give him a new idea, he will *carry it out architecturally;* in Dresden he could not get quit of Roccoco and Renaissance. When people rack their brains to produce something new, nothing ever comes of it; if they will only work out something they have themselves felt, the novelty will come spontaneously, for no one ever feels the same thing twice, exactly in the same way, and no two persons ever feel things precisely alike. Nevertheless, what one man has felt is the common property of all, and will find an echo in every heart that is not ossified. Great works were never undertaken for the sake of novelty. Novelty must be backed by sterling excellence; only he that can do well in the old, is capable of giving us a new thing. . . .

Yours,

M. H.

147.

LEIPZIG, *December 14th,* 1859.

DEAR HAUSER,—

. . . You remember my telling you, that I had given up my examinership for the Harmony Extension Prize? I now see in the *Rheinische Musikzeitung,* that there is a candidate for the post. He sends, as a proof of his capacity, a most delightful article, full of ironical praise of Liszt's Mass; do look it up, and read it. . . . Ferdinand Hiller has dedicated to me a canonical Suite in eight movements, for pianoforte and violin; we are to hear it played this evening. Why this long delay with my Symphony in Munich? I call it *mine*—really it is Rietz's—but you used to call Mendelssohn's *Overture to the Hebrides* yours, because he dedicated it to you. That Symphony, which certainly is among the best things in modern music, ranks as his most popular work, after the A major Overture. Spohr, who heard it here, was much pleased with it, and reproduced it soon afterwards in Cassel, with great success. I recommended it to the Philharmonic Society in London, when they asked me for a Symphony or an Overture, and they were delighted. To-day, I am not at all in the humour for critical subjects, but I enclose a few remarks on the *Quintverbot*—mere scribbling. The thing is as clear to me as noonday, so why should I waste my time, writing or talking about it? However, it is not clear to Ambros; he takes no pains to classify nor discriminate, so that from beginning to end, he never touches the real point. Otto Jahn's *Mozart,* complete in four stately volumes, is on my table; the first and fourth ought to have been compressed, but the work was originally published in parts, and the difficulty was not foreseen. There is too much of it, and it is too dear—still, it is an admirable work in every respect. It will be the standard authority henceforward. Not only has he collected every particle of evidence, but wherever it was possible, he has supported it with proofs.

. . .

If Rietz goes to Dresden, it will be a blow to the Handel and Bach Societies, but nothing is decided, and they talk of Vincenz Lachner as a possible candidate.   Probably too, there will be a vacancy in Cassel, for Reiss may go to Vienna as Proch's successor.   Lots of favourite song-writers have lately become conductors—Proch at the Kärthner Thor, Krebs at Dresden, Kücken at Stuttgart, Abt at Brunswick.   People were rather taken aback in every case, and I don't think the results have been particularly good.   Fischer, our famous old choir-master, is dead.   Lipinsky, now quite done for, is pensioned off.   One after the other of the old lot disappears. Already, I could make up a numerous orchestra of my dead friends.   I doubt if one of my colleagues in the Dresden band is left, except old Kummer, the violoncellist, whom I recommended to Morlacchi, ages ago ; he became a member of the orchestra, after I left.   They wanted a hautboy, so he blew away at that, until there was a vacant post for the cello. He must be the oldest surviving relic of those days.   Every Kummer was a born musician.   Everyone of them could do something, even in composition—nothing very important perhaps, but still it was always instinctively correct, and had a certain go about it. . . .

Yours,

M. H.

As regards forbidden fifths, we have to distinguish between the parallel progress of fifths in skips, and of fifths progressing by seconds.   The former do not sound well, inasmuch as a nearer and more obvious progression is avoided; for example—

Here the natural succession of the parts would be—

Then again, such fifths may occur as so-called covered fifths— which are even more repulsive than a progression of fifths, in which the *Remplissage*

does not itself progress in fifths—

In a succession of fifths, in which both parts move by seconds, the difficulty is of another sort— inasmuch as the succession of chords here lacks connection. This succession starts from the triad on F and proceeds to the triad on G taking the triad D F a (D F a c forming the link from ^C_F). Now D here supports. Thus the triad on G will retain this D as its lowest degree; if the D forms the upper step, then the C will, all the same, proceed to b natural, as in every case where there is a D in juxtaposition with a C, or where it is supposed to be in such a position—

It is unreasonable to say, that fifths are admissible and good, when they are not audible as consecutives. First, it is a question as to *who* fails to hear them, and whether such persons have any business to speak in the matter of the nature and purity of harmony; secondly, we do not write parts so that they shall not be heard.

Ambros does not sufficiently distinguish the various occasions, upon which successions of fifths occur: passages such as—

are not to be lumped together with fifths such as occur in the works of the Netherlanders of the fourteenth century.

Ambros also thinks that the resolution of the chord— as it is said to occur in Beethoven's Mass in C major, is quite correct; but that resolution is entirely wrong.

If I play such a succession on the piano, I am clearly unable
to render the progress of the parts, and it does not sound
wrong, because the progression may be—

In the separate parts, however, the progression—

is as incorrect as anywhere else, and no good composer would
so put it; if some authority has been guilty of putting
forward an untruth, that does not make it true; and if said
consciously and willingly, it becomes a pure lie.

148.

LEIPZIG, *January 3rd,* 1860.

DEAREST HAUSER,—

. . . I hear that the performance of *Tristan und Isolde*
at Carlsruhe will have to be given up. The singers are dead
against it, and even Schnorr, who was enthusiastic at first,
declared later on, that they could never get through such a
work in one evening. Human nature cannot go beyond a
certain point of endurance; a pity for the advance of music,
isn't it? Commend me to the pianoforte! that musical
instrument *par excellence,* as regards Temperament. It is
curious that these musicians—lovers of Temperament—always
return to the assertion, that Temperament changes intervals
so very little, that they can be taken as pure intervals—as
though that were the essence of the question! *Per contra,* one
might say that intonation, which is mathematically pure, is
insufficient for animated execution; we desire to have the
leading note higher, the Dominant and diminished Seventh
lower than would result from mathematical calculation. In—

D flat is surely to be sung lower than C sharp, and yet c – d flat is as 15 : 16, c — c sharp is only as 24 : 25, that is, the first difference greater than the latter. This is the psychical aspect of intonation, of which the pianoforte of course knows nothing. After all, whatever may be said against a Tone System based upon Temperament is nothing else, than that a pear tree cannot naturally be expected to bear apples or nuts. They will do wisely, to abstain from publishing my correspondence with Weitzmann and Brendel, on the subject of the examinership. So far, they have confined themselves to a simple announcement of the fact of my withdrawal, and of Prof. Lobe's appointment, in the same number of the *Neue Zeitschrift*, which contained the name of the Prizeman, and the beginning of his Essay. It was I myself who advised Brendel to do this, for he came to me in trouble about it, not knowing how to make the thing public. The winner of the Prize is Weitzmann himself; he abstained from adjudicating, on the pretext that the Essay was by a friend. I can well believe that his was the best, for he is a sound musician. Some will say, that he has exchanged Saul for Paul; *we* affirm that instead of a tolerable Paul, he has become a first-rate Saul. There is more of Saul about him. Enharmonics too are a form of godlessness—a hither and thither, that does not start from one point, that has no middle, and no medium.

We always have some sacred music at our New Year's Concert; this time, they did a chorus of mine, *Ehre sei Gott*, for men's voices and wind instruments. It is my one composition in that line. I wrote it for a wedding, and it has often been done since; a few years ago, it was performed at a Rhine festival, with 700 voices. In the abstract, I dislike four-part songs for men's voices, though I admire some of them, Mendelssohn's *Wald*, for instance. It sounds so unnatural to ram four-part harmony into *one* (Octave?), it wants a contrast such as that which exists between a 4-ft. or 8-ft. organ stop. The rule in the *Philister* would apply—Tragedy is the law, Comedy the possibility of evading it. . . .

Yours,

M. HAUPTMANN.

149.

LEIPZIG, *January 12th*, 1860.

. . . You did not write to me about *Tristan;* that
cowhorn business is most amusing. Wagner has a similar
curiosity in *Tannhäuser*, where he introduces us to a Shepherd,
sitting on a rock, and piping away all out of tune. It is odd
that he should think it characteristic of Nature in the open
air to be totally unnatural. These 16 horns of his
remind me of the play with the 7 girls in uniform!
The second time it was done, they had 14. Now, I hear, they've
got 24. How lovely it must be! In old days at Cassel,
we had a Torch-Dance in honour of the wedding of the Duchess
of Meiningen; Spohr wrote two parts, and I wrote the other
two, for 53 trumpets, in 5 or 6 different parts. It really
sounded very well, and wonderfully *soft*. All the harsh tones
of the trumpet were deadened in the mass of sound. Sound
bears no relation to the number of instruments employed.
It seems a paradox, but it is true nevertheless, that small
choirs and orchestras do not sing and play with the same
purity of intonation as those that are larger. Right prevails
over might, and forms the contour of the whole. This by
the way! I don't mean it in favour of the 16 horns. I have
only seen the book of *Tristan*. The music was introduced
here during the grand week of the Future, but the people of
the Present didn't like it. I was not there. Wagner is in
Paris, where he hopes to get a footing, and to bring out all
his operas at the *Théâtre des Italiens*, though none but
German singers, specially engaged, are to take part in them!
Can you tell me, where he gets the needful, for energy alone
could not enable him to carry out these schemes? I'm sure
I don't know. Liszt cannot afford it. There must be a
regular Company for the Music of the Future. . . .

Yours,

M. HAUPTMANN.

150.

LEIPZIG, *January* 24*th,* 1860.

DEAR HAUSER,—

. . . I suppose you have heard, that Rietz has decided to leave us ; he is to conduct the next Palm Sunday Concert at Dresden. He is a great loss to us. . . . Paul Mendelssohn was here, a little time since. There was an extra rehearsal of the A minor Symphony at the *Gewandhaus* in his honour. That is one of his brother's finest works. Is it his judgment, informed by genius, or is it his genius, controlled by judgment, that we admire the most ? He never lets himself be run away with, and yet every note is penetrated with genius. Spohr disliked the Finale, a sort of hunting-piece, which is not in keeping with what goes before. It reminds me of young Fortinbras at the end of *Hamlet*, when the general smash takes place, when the new life appears, and a new *régime* begins, which would have been utterly impossible in the old state of things. 1 am a great admirer of Mendelssohn's later compositions. Though the rest of the music to *A Midsummer Night's Dream* does not bristle with genius like the Overture, which was written at a much earlier date, yet it is riper and more reposeful, and it stands on a higher artistic level. I think I prefer *St. Paul* to the *Elijah;* there is more inspiration about it, and it is more original. The noble orchestral style of the A minor Symphony does not distinguish all his instrumental compositions. Sometimes, in the Overtures to his Oratorios, and in his concert pieces, the instrumentation is too evident ; they are hardly native to the orchestra. I never could feel quite at home with his String Quartets. Hauptmann used to call them, " The Battles of the Ants," though later on he had nothing but good words for Mendelssohn, particularly after he wrote the Overture to the *Midsummer Night's Dream*. There is plenty of slight work in that too, but it is in keeping with the nature of the subject. One of the finest of his earliest works is the Motet, *Mitten wir im Leben sind*, which was performed here last Saturday. Someone observed that it did not sound so Mendelssohnian as usual ; its early date

would account for that. What we call *Mendelssohnian,*
Spohrian, Cherubinian, is mere mannerism, and it would be a
pity, if anyone were to begin straight off with a manner of his
own. Spohr's Opera, *Alruna,* of which only the Overture is
known, contains a great deal that is not at all *Spohrian;*
even *Der Zweikampf mit der Geliebten,* a later work, is much
more musical, in the larger sense of the word, much less like
Spohr in his own limited sphere, than what he did afterwards.
Now and then, there is more of Mozart in it. The "choice
harmonies" of Cherubini, I expect, had the most potent
influence over him. To such a mind as his, the opening of
the Overture to the *Wasserträger* must have been most con-
genial, and doubtless it fostered many a latent germ. He told
me himself what I can well believe, that he remembered the
day when he valued Cherubini more than Mozart. There
was a time with me, too, when Spohr stood very high; when
I preferred the charming chromatic harmonies of his operas
to the transparent, diatonic style I had been accustomed to
at the theatre. I thought that even Mozart's harmonies
were not substantial enough. Spontini's *Vestalin,* when
played in Dresden, made a kind of epoch. I, too, revelled
in it, for as a pupil of Morlacchi's, I was not yet competent
to feel the impurity of his harmonies; it was Spohr, who subsequently drew my attention to this, but then again he insisted
too much on the details, and thus he missed the grander
conception, the action, gradation, and development of a whole
scene in its breadth,—though I daresay he learnt to respect it
more, when he had stood for some years at the conductor's
desk, in front of the stage itself. The second Act of *Die
Vestalin* is well enough in this respect. It is difficult to
say, how such works as *The Huguenots* would have pleased the
audiences of those days. There is a time for all things.
My time for *Lohengrin* has not come yet. When some one,
talking about a very complicated piece of music, remarked,
"It may be very beautiful, but I do not understand it," I
heard Mendelssohn say, "I *do* understand it, and I think
it detestable." But enough of this gossip. . . .

Yours,

M. HAUPTMANN.

151.

LEIPZIG, *February 6th*, 1860.

DEAR HAUSER,—

. . . Malibran's biography of Spohr is a silly, shallow book, that ought never to have been translated into German. The author, however, is such a worshipper of Spohr, that one cannot exactly quarrel with him, not even when he says that *The Last Judgment* is a musical version of Michael Angelo's. Resemblance apart, he really means *Das Jüngste Gericht*, an Oratorio written by Spohr for Erfurth in 1811, and conducted by him, for the second time, in 1813; at Vienna. It was never given again, so that Malibran knows no more about it than we do. I heard it in Erfurth, on Napoleon's birthday, the 14th August, 1812. I suppose the story of this *fête* came to Malibran's ears, and he enlarges upon the great impression the music made on Napoleon, and the fact that he, a man of genius, appreciated the genius of Spohr. Now whether Napoleon was at that time in Russia, I can't say, but he certainly was not in Erfurth. Crowned heads, in those days, had other things than Bischoff's Concerts to attend to. After that, he lands Spohr in Vienna, whither he is supposed to have been summoned as *Capellmeister*. I quote his own words : " Vienna, at that time (1813), had her Albrechtsberger, Mozart, and Haydn ; Beethoven and Hummel were among her guests ; but Spohr had no need to be afraid of them," &c. He goes on to say, that when Spohr was travelling in Italy (1816—1817), his *Faust* was performed at all the great theatres, exciting indescribable enthusiasm ! The whole story is a tissue of lies.

Berlioz is said to have taken great pains with the recent revival of Gluck's *Orpheus* in Paris. He drilled the conductor in his business so assiduously, that the lady who was to sing the part of Eurydice, asked whether the gentleman who was arranging everything, was Gluck. Years ago, when *Don Juan* was given in Paris, someone said of the composer, " C'est un jeune homme qui promet." . . .

Yours,

M. HAUPTMANN.

152.

DEAR HAUSER,—

It is a colossal undertaking to copy Mendelssohn's letters yourself, unless you are doing it, because there are bits of them which you would not like others to see. Paul Mendelssohn has plenty of people to transcribe for him. Reckoning on his prudence and discretion, I sent him all the letters and notes his brother had ever written to me, and they were returned two days afterwards. I have no patience for copying, and cannot give my mind to it; my head is too full of other things. Surely, it is not worth your while to copy my correspondence with Weitzmann and Brendel. The Prize Essay is in print, it came out first in the *Neue Zeitschrift*. I did not follow it. From what I saw of it, I had no desire to. An opponent of Weber's, with whom he had waged a long newspaper war, proposed to come and meet him one day, with a view to arranging terms. Weber published his answer in the same newspaper : " Having had plenty of opportunity of seeing my neighbour's *inside*, I have no curiosity about his *outside*." . . .

Susette, Helene, and I spent the first fortnight of March in Hanover, by special invitation of the blind King, who for a long time has wanted to know me personally. He likes some of my compositions, which are often sung to him by his new Cathedral Choir, and it so happens, that my songs (the later songs, written for Susette, I expect) suit the Queen's voice exactly. Their Majesties were very gracious. One evening, Joachim and Wehner played my G minor Sonata, Op. 5, and Frau Platzhoff sang the Violin Songs. His Majesty complimented me highly on the Sonata, which he thought very poetical, and he encored the Andante; the whole Sonata was repeated at a second *Soirée*. They were most friendly. We were at a Concert one evening, before I went to Court, and the Queen, seeing Helene was with us, sent her an invitation. Imagine her delight! She has been

nothing but " Your Royal Highness " ever since. . . . We
were just about to leave, when the King begged me to put off
my journey for a day or two, as he wished me to hear his first
tenor, Niemann, in *Lohengrin.* Niemann was at loggerheads
with the Director just then, and was not singing, but he
consented for this once, to please the King. It came to nothing,
however, for the *Intendant* took good care to make *Lohengrin*
impossible on that particular evening. Fräulein von Malsburg
was telegraphed for, and telegraphed off again. A first tenor
like Niemann consults himself, not his King. I was pleased
with the new choir. The soprani, though rather young, and
wanting in tone, sing the simple liturgical service with great
purity. The choir is the King's special hobby, and it is
trained by Liedhuld, of Düsseldorf, who studied singing in Paris.
He must not overdo it with his theories; otherwise, by the time
they have learnt how to produce their voices, they will have no
voices to produce. I attended a private rehearsal, and they
said they would like me to conduct my *Salve Regina ;* they
had sung it once, and it would go better the second time. The
King thanked me for paying his choir this compliment.
Nothing could be kinder than he was, altogether. It happened
to be Susette's birthday, when we went to Court for the second
time, and the first thing the King and Queen did, was to
congratulate her. All this sounds rather boastful, but you
know me too well to think that.

The *Riedelsche Verein* performs Beethoven's Grand Mass
in D this evening. It seems to me too grandiose, too sonorous,
too much overcharged with Beethoven's personality. So few
words, so little humility ! It is more appropriate to a Concert
than to Divine Service. Less would mean more. It is just
like Clärchen's songs in *Egmont ;* Reichardt and Zelter are
much more suitable, because, insignificant as they are, they
don't devour Clärchen with their music. A "composition "
is the last thing we want there. Good gracious ! Has Clärchen
got a composer for a lover as well as Egmont ? As music
however, the Mass is stupendous. Rietz is conducting the
Ninth Symphony at Dresden to-day. That work is twin-
sister to the Mass. There is the same straining after power,
which, in a work of art, repels rather than attracts me. It is

impossible to be fond of Michael Angelo's *Last Judgment,*
astonishing though it be. . . . I saw Marschner in
Hanover—youthful as ever, more youthful than most! He
has been pensioned off, though he is far and away their best
man, I expect. He has just finished another big opera. They
still allow him to conduct his own works, and he always
receives an ovation, when he appears at the desk. The
Intendants manage these things very cleverly. I heard *Don
Juan* the other night, the *Tempi* were hopelessly wrong. They
pension off their good singers, and take up with raw
recruits. . . .

The Beethoven Mass is over. I can retract nothing, except
the expression : " So few words ! " I ought rather to have
said, " Too many "—*i.e.*, too much made of particular words,
too little in their collective sense. On the whole, the effect of
such music is rather nauseating ; in that respect, and in no
other, it partially resembles Liszt's Mass. . . . Such
music, with all its 'overwhelming force, has an element of
weakness, because it is guided by feeling alone, but more of
that hereafter ! . . .

Yours,
M. HAUPTMANN.

153.

LEIPZIG, *Whitsun-Day*, 1860.

. . . Hiller has just published a little book, called
Uebungen in der Harmonie, or some such name ; I can
recommend it highly. After a short dissertation on harmony,
he introduces melodies, which the pupils are to supply with
basses, and, *vice versâ*, filling up the other parts as well.
Capital practice ! Fenaroli, Sala, and other Italian teachers
did the same thing in former times, leaving the basses to be
filled in ; but as no one studies them now, it is well that there
should be something of the kind. I am at issue with everyone who runs down Counterpoint and Fugue, and calls them
useless ; we may just as well ignore Latin and Greek in our
Gymnasia, because they are of no use to us in after life. To
be sure, they may be forgotten, but there they are, though

unseen; they are the scaffolding, the mainstay of all other
knowledge. So too, Counterpoint and Fugue are the very life
of Harmony, making a compact mass supple, and the parts
articulate. It may be, that we are as little likely to be called
upon to write Fugues as to speak Latin, but a song or a dance
tune is enough to show, whether the composer could, if he
chose, do something else. If he can, his music will be
bright and spontaneous, with none of that morbid egotism
and sham sentiment, which are so painfully oppressive in
modern music. The Bach volume is out at last; I suppose
you have seen it. . . . The Härtels have any number of
big things on hand, including a score of *Tristan und Isolde*, a
regular Leviathan or Mammoth. Handel is to follow, and
Hofrath Gervinus, who is never satisfied, is making a great
fuss about it. I wanted to back out of it long ago, but though
my services are really nominal, the Härtels say that if I go,
they will wash their hands of the whole concern. Rietz, now
that he is a fixture in Dresden, retires as a matter of course.
Spohr's widow has recently sent me a volume, containing four
huge scores of Handel's Italian operas; she wants to know, if
they are in Handel's handwriting, which is not the case. Is
it worth while to print such things, for the sake of a few
fanatical Handelians ? Think of the enormous waste of time
and money, on music which will never be used at all ! There is a
terrible amount of rubbish. It is another thing, if they mean
to hunt for Airs that can still be used. But veneration goes
too far, if every note of Handel, who wrote a great deal that
was very uninteresting, is to be religiously preserved ; we
should never get to the end of it. In spite of the 1,000 *thalers*
which the King of Hanover subscribes every year, a great
deal more is wanted, to make up the sum required for the
intended issue of three volumes every year, at ten
thalers. . . . The three Sonnets, *Solo e pensoso*, &c., are
now being engraved. . . . I suppose you have received
from the Härtels a copy of my four-part Songs, which, I
believe, have been recently issued. My last work is a
short, unaccompanied Psalm, written for our Rector's
Jubilee. . . .   Yours,
                                                    M. H.

154.

ALEXANDERBAD BEI WUNSIEDEL, *July* 18*th*, 1860.

DEAR HAUSER,—

. . . I had already anticipated your advice, before I got your letter, and instead of tearing up one of the original seven, I am writing five additional Songs for male voices; three are ready, and I am at work on the fourth. As Rückert has been my librettist all along, I must go to him again, and at a pinch, I daresay I shall find something. His two thick volumes abound in lyrics, no doubt, but to what extent these are suitable for a chorus of men's voices, is another matter. There is a great deal too much kissing for a *Liedertafel;* it would be better to treat it humorously; but I always cancel such passages, if the rest of the poem suits me. I consider a slight transposition of words quite permissible with Rückert, who often omits the lyrical cæsura, and I had rather make a small alteration here and there, than emphasise some unimportant word in a strophe. I know how poets resent this— but they have themselves to blame for it. . . . We always meet plenty of good company here, so that we manage to tide over the bad weather. The best part of Alexanderbad is, that all the patients are in rude health. . . .

Yours,

M. HAUPTMANN.

155.

LEIPZIG, *September* 5*th*, 1860.

. . . We go to Dresden on Julia's birthday, for a little while. Rietz tells me that my Mass is to be performed in the *Katholische Kirche* on the 23rd. It is just thirty-four years since I took that Mass to Morlacchi. *Pensate a questi tromboni!* said he, and would not perform it—and now it is to be given without my having anything to do with the matter! . . . I cannot but think that a good deal of the Mass will be ineffective, there is such an echo in the Church. Of course things could be written to suit it, but they would have to be quite different. Well, Rietz is responsible, and he knows something about the Church too! The great fault of the choir is its numerical weakness—twenty-four voices, all told. As the *Sanctus* requires a large body of voices, of course it sounds poor enough. Rietz allows the soloists to join. . . . He finds no authority for the supposed law, which forbids the performance of music other than that of *Maestri*, who hold or held appointments in the *Katholische Kirche*. The custom probably arose from convenience, or from the inclination of these gentlemen to listen to nothing but their own music. Rietz also proposes to do Cherubini's *Requiem*, before the close of the year. . . . I suppose you have heard of the hailstorm here. The hailstones were as big as hens' eggs, that's no exaggeration—you could have shovelled together a heap of them. One report says, that they were the size of glass letter-weights, which seems to me as lucid a description as Lichtenberg's "About the size of an ordinary blot." I am not responsible for the calculation, that in the space of five minutes, Leipzig was damaged to the extent of two and a half million. The school buildings, and the houses in our neighbourhood were so much injured, that glaziers and masons were in requisition, far and near. The storm happened on the 27th of August, and even now the damage is only partially repaired; two thousand houses are still roofless. Great havoc was done to the skylights of the Museum. Laroche's Napoleon, Schrader's Frederick II., and the regicide Cromwell all have holes in their heads; anyhow, the hailstorm was an impartial politician. . . .

Yours,
M. H.

156.

LEIPZIG, *October 1st*, 1860.

. . . My Mass was very well performed, under Rietz's direction, in the *Katholische Kirche*, on Sunday, the 23rd. . . . It sounded much clearer than I expected, and those who took part in it said plenty of pretty things to me.

There is a complete change in Dresden since my day; a new generation of musicians has sprung up, full of energy and enterprise, and they attend Concerts, Lectures, &c., for the pure love of Art—not because they must do it. In my day, none but the old fogies dared say a word; the young ones simply did as they were bid. I remember that when La Grua was going to sing at a Concert got up by Krägen, the orchestra, after half-promising to play, declined in a body to do so; I, however, stuck to my post, whereupon *Concertmeister* Dietze, a snappish *intrigant*, a regular typical, courtier-like *Kammermusikus* of those days, summoned me before him, and harangued me for daring, as a younger member, to take my own line. I, very impudently, stuck up to him, and said that off parade I should do as I pleased, a remark which he never forgot to the end of his life. But the Mass was a real success. . . .

Yours,

M. H.

157.

Leipzig, *November 1st*, 1860.

Dear Hauser,—

. . . I entirely agree with you, as to the method of teaching singing. At the preliminary examination in the *Conservatoire*, the other day, a girl sang Schubert's *Erl-King* quite delightfully, Reinecke accompanying her very well. She is now continuing her studies here, and I said to Schleinitz: "I only hope she will sing as well, a year hence, as she does now." Hitherto, she has only been instructed in the pianoforte, and she plays charmingly. Now she will have to turn her attention to "the opening of the mouth," and "the formation of the voice." Years pass—the voice goes—and it becomes a spiritless thing. The many teachers who know nothing of singing are not the worst, I think; they leave the voice alone, treating it as an unmethodical pianoforte master treats the piano. Anyone who can sing a song without being taught, need not unlearn so much, at any rate. But then comes a man like Sch., who sets to work to form a voice, and songs are out of the question, for years to come. It is just as if the pupil had a broken limb; he must not move till he is perfectly sound. By the time that the lessons cease, Art has not yet been acquired, and Nature is gone. . . .

Your opinion of the Holmeses squares with what I said of them long ago. They certainly did not play my Duets in a very finished style, it was more like clever reading at sight, and as they had not studied the things very minutely, the performance was interesting from its vigour, though at times it lacked refinement. It was another thing at the *Gewandhaus*, or rather it was *not* another thing; the public missed the neatness and smoothness to which they are accustomed. An artist with a white neckcloth on, must not play slippers and dressing-gown. Four years have passed since they were here last; I daresay they may have learnt a good deal in the interval. That slipshod performance spoiled their chance at the *Gewandhaus*. I cannot blame the Directors for refusing to let them play again. . . .

Michael Haydn's music, so far as I know it, never inclines me to regard him as greater in church compositions than Joseph. He is more old-fashioned than his brother, and his reputation is hazy, because people know less about him; unquestionably he was a clever fellow. I once conducted a Requiem, the two first movements of which, the *Requiem æternam* and the fugal Kyrie, were his. He certainly might have learnt better instrumentation from Joseph. The work is dated 1806, and from its orchestration, you would suppose that Mozart and Haydn had never existed. . . .

Yours,

M. H.

158.

LEIPZIG, *January 3rd*, 1860.

. . . The Holmeses left us the day before yesterday, when the thermometer stood at 15 degrees; they are on their way to Amsterdam, to appear on the 4th at a Concert in *Felix meritis*. They had a bad time of it, being detained for ten days at Cassel, where they got a letter from the Leipzig

authorities, refusing to allow them to give a Concert.   .   .   .
We have heard them twice, and they played several of my
Duets very finely, though their *Tempi* were too restless to
please me; there is no balance—they hurry too much,
especially in the Adagio and Andante—else, they have got
the real stuff in them. They constantly talked of you
and your household, in terms of genuine regard, and
with gratitude for your kind reception. Travelling hither
and thither, to give concerts, is expensive work; what
they want is some permanent post, in a place where they
could live together. I do not think they could bear to be
separated.   .   .   .

The last thing I desire is a paper war with young Osterley.
When once you have rushed into print, you must expect your
work to fall into unwashed hands—and why am I to provide
the soap?   .   .   .   He is so *borné*, he cannot see that
he is not the man to clear up all the problems of the old method
of teaching. They have no Conception of a Conception, they
offer us notions and ideas. Truth has a Conception and an Idea,
they feel the constraint and narrowness of this doctrine, they
think it too simple, so they adopt the more convenient way of
mythology, and have a special idol for everything that comes
to pass, in imitation of the Romans, who, not content
with the twelve Greek divinities, added yet another dozen, after
the example of the Greeks themselves, when they specialised
all the Nine Muses out of one. This last arrangement was a
pity, eight would have been much better, for then Apollo
might have stood as King in the midst of the ninepins.
Köhler's book on Harmony is not bad, for it leaves the way
open to those simple propositions, which underlie all the
rest. It will make no very great stir, for the market is
glutted with such things. In old days, the *Gradus ad Par-
nassum* was accepted so universally, that no one thought of
questioning its authority. The quarrelsome and disputatious
Mattheson did it no harm. It was, as Johann von Paris says,
the best inn in the world, because there was no other, far or
near. It was a text-book in the Italian *Conservatoires*, and
anyone who wanted to learn his trade went to Italy, and not
to Hamburg to seek out Mattheson.

When I get your big letter paper, I shall plunge into Classics, Romanticism, and the Academy; just now, I have not paper enough, nor brains either. . . .

Yours,

M. HAUPTMANN.

159.

LEIPZIG, *May* 31*st*, 1861.

. . . If I ask a pupil to write a short four-part Hymn, he can hardly get through a single bar correctly—it all stands on end, and is such a mass of faults, that I can scarcely believe he has ever studied harmony. They may have called on the Virgin once or twice, but they always go back again to the Venusberg, as steadily as Tannhäuser himself, and I cannot exactly blame the Pope for refusing absolution to a half-repentant sinner, who is never consistent for a moment together. He ought to give signs of real amendment first. I don't blame the Parisians either; it seems they don't think much of him. You complain of the Academical ways of the Painters; music is free from this anyhow; we have rather too little of the Academy. Our fault is hideous, uncouth, distorted, egotistically sentimental Naturalism. "What would I give for a Berlin *gendarme !* I hated him when I was there—here I should embrace him as my best friend !" So said Bogumil Goltz, when sailing on the Nile, with a crew of ignorant, treacherous negroes, amongst whom he could not feel safe for a moment. Again, "Oh for a Berlin tea-party ! Oh, for white kid gloves ! Oh, for a slice of their thin bread-and-butter, and a cup of tea !" When I hear the grotesque productions of young composers, I sigh for the dreary *soirées* consisting of the so-called *Capellmeistermusik ;* ordinary music, unexciting though it may be, is better than such extraordinary music as that. Of course, symmetry is not the subject itself—nor is it the rind which surrounds the kernel ; it is only the form of the subject, arising from the nature of the subject itself—the means by which the subject becomes artistic. A good photograph of a congress of *savants* and

artists, grouped together in a lecture-room, is still far from
being a *School of Athens,* quite apart from the dress-coats and
the cold, professional faces. The photograph itself is not a
picture ; it gives but a momentary view of Nature, and Nature
is not worthy to be represented in Art, before it has gone
through the reasoning process, by which man absorbs it—in
fact, it cannot become natural again before this stage, for
Nature is not the phenomenon of the moment, it is the
transition from what is Past to what is Future, and an artistic
mind alone is capable of representing the phenomenon of the
moment in this light. The Dutch masters paint tipsy
boors, Jews, and beggars, in all their native ugliness, yet their
pictures, so far from being repulsive, are often delightful.
Our second-rate, modern German *genre* painters deal with
kindred subjects, such as fairs, shooting matches, &c., where
people behave more decently than they do in a Dutch pot-
house, but they are disgustingly common, and one would
rather be in the vulgar company itself, than in that of the
vulgar painter, or his vulgar picture. His Jews are ideal to
Rembrandt, so admirably has he caught the idea of the old
usurers ; a single living specimen would never have shown all
the characteristics of the race in such perfection ; even if
living models did sit to him, these portraits are none the less
ideal. The inferior painter is content with merely copying
his model, but the real artist adds something of his own, not
garnish, not embellishment, in the ordinary sense of the word ;
he turns the individual man into a person, he makes
a particular character the echo of humanity in general.
To be sure, I am not very learned in modern pictures, but I
think, on the whole, that the so-called Academic style is less
intrusive, less inclined to predominate now than formerly,—
say in the Napoleonic days, or earlier. Since spirituality has
been revived by Cornelius, Overbeck, and some others, merely
formal, external, Academic arrangement, however skilful, has
ceased to be effective—at all events, with intelligent people.
As to the opposition between *classical* and *romantic,* we may
very well accept Goethe's definition : " To be classical is to be
healthy, to be romantic is to be sickly, and in this sense of
the word, the *Niebelungenlied* is as classical as Homer." Of

course, this does not tell us, how the *Niebelungenlied* differs from Homer. Some years ago, Susette read it aloud to me in the evenings, and when we had come to the end, we took up the Odyssey instead. The former is supposed to be a Christian poem, but it is nothing of the kind. The Christianity was laid on afterwards ; it may be something more than a mere accessory, like the spring in *Louise*, but it cannot go very deep, or it would destroy the foundations of the story. If Chrimhilde were a good Christian, what would become of Chrimhilde's revenge ? The Cathedral is introduced, chiefly in order that the two Queens may quarrel, as to who has the right to go in first, and it is easy to imagine, how peaceful they felt, when they did get in ! There is something barbaric about it all, in spite of the love-poetry, and it is so rough and bloodthirsty, that we were quite glad to get back to the Odyssey, where reverence and religion are not an after-thought, but the foundation of the whole work. We came upon people who were more like ourselves, moving, feeling as we do, in moments of strength and weakness. That, however, has nothing to do with the difference between the Classical and the Romantic School, if we mean to stick to the definition of healthy and sickly, for here both are healthy—even the lust of revenge, after its kind. One difference I do detect. In the *Niebelungen*, the world within is treated with greater detail, and the world without is left indefinite, whereas in Homer, the world without is as clear as possible, and the world within is merely indicated. Feeling is expressed by the deed, which is its effect, rather than by a multiplicity of words. But that is the orthodox Greek way ; they only represent that which admits of clear expression. . . .

Yours,
M. H.

160.

ALEXANDERBAD BEI WUNSIEDEL, *July* 28*th*, 1861.

DEAR HAUSER,—

. . . I see by my diary, that I have not written to you, since the death of our late Rector. . . . I had written a Motet for the ceremony of his inauguration, and was busy over the last notes of it, when the news of his death arrived. The first number began with the words of the 15th Psalm, "Lord, who shall dwell in Thy tabernacle?" I had meant it to refer to the Church of St. Thomas. We sang it at the funeral—but there was no need then, to alter the original signification of the words. The Psalm is now in the engraver's hands, and I have parted with it to Siegel. . . . Yesterday, I sent back to Härtel the proof-sheets of my Canons, but I know from experience, what a long time they take over these things. Kömpel, a pupil of Spohr, and an excellent violinist, came here yesterday, for the water cure. He was a great success in Paris, the winter before last, and he played little else but Spohr's music. He held an appointment in Hanover, but I fancy that in the long run he did not hit it off very well with Joachim, so he went away, and at present he is unemployed. Why don't they take him in Lauterbach's place? He is the owner of Spohr's violin; *Amtsrath* Lüder managed that for him. The Spohr family might have sold it very advantageously to a rich Jew in Cassel, but they preferred to part with it to a pupil he had been fond of. As it is, the price was 1,000 *thalers*—no trifle! . . . I have no fears about Kömpel, he plays so well, that he is sure to get engagements, though of course first-rate violinists are far more common now than formerly. In my young days, Spohr was the only man who could play one of his own Concertos, but now the pupils of the *Conservatoire* play the most difficult. We used to think that the second, in D minor, was the highest flight, but it was never any pleasure to listen to it; sometimes a man would dash at the third in C major, but he never failed to come to grief. Now, we never have an Examination Concert, but we hear one or other of Spohr's hardest Concertos, played with faultless technique; yet every pupil is forced to begin from the beginning, just as we had to, thirty or forty years ago. The standard must be higher than it was then. I wish the same thing could be said for the singing. To be sure, composers do very little to help that. I suppose they think that singers should have fresh valves, specially constructed like trumpets and horns, in order to produce their unreasonable noises. They forget that the human throat is the same now, as it was in the days of Adam and Eve. Here I was asked, whether I was going to the Festival of Song at Nuremberg. "No," I said; "if the Festival of Song were at Alexanderbad, perhaps I might go to Nuremberg, but as it is, I prefer to stay where I am. . . .

Yours,
M. H.

161.

LEIPZIG, August 25th, 1861.

. . . On the 21st of this month, I formed one of a deputation, which went to Dresden, to congratulate Johann Schneider, the organist, on the completion of his fifty years of service. His first appointment was at the University Church in Leipzig, and then he moved to Görlitz, but he has never been out of Saxony. I returned here quite comfortably the same evening. . . . People call the railroad prosaic, but it has its poetical side also; it is delightful to put on seven-leagued boots, and fly from here to there in one day. The poetry of the mail coach is no great loss, and one can always go on foot, if one wants to. . . . Spohr's biography is too large and too expensive; all the last part, which was not written by him, is much too full of family history. The photograph, after a bust by a military clarinet player of Cassel, is really the only good picture of Spohr. . . . The musicians of young Germany have been holding a Parliament at Weimar. Some one who had been there said, that Liszt's compositions were quite classical, as compared with the horrible efforts of his disciples. . . .

Yours,
M. H.

162.

LEIPZIG, *January 4th*, 1862.

. . . Gustav Freytag, the author of a volume entitled *Aus deutscher Vorzeit*, has recently published a second, not exactly a continuation or development, but a further study of the same subject. It is a thoroughly able piece of work—a delightful book to read. The result of a perusal of many of the documents of *Aus alten Archiven* is, that we may fairly congratulate ourselves on living in the nineteenth century. If you look closely into it, you will find that our fathers, generally speaking, were not better off than ourselves, and in some ways, they had an odious time of it. I suppose real men are to be found in every age, but now they leaven the mass more than they did in old days, when they were like raisins in a cake, and could impart no flavour to their surroundings. The requirements of the age and of humanity,—the requirements of humanity as a whole,—are better understood now. That which seemed impracticable in former times, is now made possible by combination ; reciprocity and interchange of thought prevail, and a man who can do something is somebody. It is but quite recently, that we have realised this, and come to think it natural. But in my young days, the ordinary citizen, if he wanted anything, must needs condescend to be a Court toady. He had nothing for it, but to fall on his knees and kiss the royal hand, whatever he might happen to want. It is a very different matter, now-a-days. They just ask the King, as they would ask any other man that could help them. You have only to read Sebastian Bach's cringing letter to the Electoral Prince, when he sent him the B minor Mass, as a token of his inferior skill in music, entreating his Royal Highness to criticise this bad composition with princely forbearance, and that indulgence which the meanest of his subjects was so happy as to enjoy. All this is expressed in far more bombastic language, and it turns out that the present and the dedication are meant to be the price of the little title of " Court Composer," which, says Bach, would protect him from the many annoyances to which he is subject here. He gets the title—but not till six years later. It took all that time, to settle the grievances of the Leipzig Cantor ! . . . But now-a-days, personality is of much greater weight, it is not mere professional work that counts. I do not say that there is much less chicanery and cabal, but notwithstanding this, life on the whole is better and more upright. . . .

I have no patience with the tone adopted by the reviewers. They are little people, for all their big stilts. How silly it is, the way they gird at decent music, because it's not Beethoven—or Schumann, whom they often consider his equal. You never can count upon what they will say; they have special organs and special tastes, which enable them to pronounce upon everything. We have a good word for Michael Angelo, and even for Guido Reni, in his way; we can appreciate a Beethoven, a Handel, and a Spohr, as well as a *morceau* of Gade, if it is good—any honest piece of work by a capable man; but they are down upon us like blood-hounds, if it does not suit their particular creed. . . . They were very high and mighty about the *Wasserträger*, the other day, quite condescending, in fact. The opera was written in 1800, and for sixty years, the best judges have thought it a fine work. Down comes the *Wiener Musik-zeitung*, and says there is nothing in it—or very little, at all events. So the many hundreds of thousands, who have enjoyed it hitherto, were so many donkeys, who knew nothing about it ? Well, it does not much matter ; the opera holds its own, and we shall be glad to hear it again, whereas the best fate that can befall the Review is, to be laid on the shelf, and bound up at the end of the year. It will never be read again, and it will not prevent our enjoying what we know to be good. Making is better than criticising, any day. A little piece of music, with some life in it, is better than any amount of discussion. An insect beats all anatomy ; but anatomy treats the insect fairly, and does not say it is worth nothing, or that it ought to have been made differently. . . .

Yours,

M. H.

163.

LEIPZIG, *April 3rd,* 1862.

DEAR HAUSER,—

. . . Chrysander is bringing out two of my miscellaneous Essays on Sound and Temperament in his *Jahrbücher ;*
you will find them at the beginning. He wants more of the
same kind, so I am going to amplify some of my earlier
sketches. They are quite long enough for me, when once
they have cleared up my mind, but they want filling out for
an ordinary reader. I had rather in each case refer to that
part of my *Harmonik* where the subject is dealt with, but it
seems a little presumptuous to do so, for everything hangs
together, and I should be presupposing a knowledge of the
whole book—which most people would decline with thanks.
There is another article on Counterpoint, which if worked
out, might be useful, to show that its vital essence does not
lie in harmonic subtleties, and which will serve to indicate, how
Counterpoint has not only its due place in Fugue and Canon,
but also in the Sonata, in the Song, in Operatic as well as
in Church music, and, moreover, that its essence lies rather in
rhythmical and metrical conditions than in melodic and
harmonic ; in the widest sense in syncopation, not of single
notes, but of metrical contrasts generally

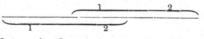

long drawn, determined yet free ; something like the first
Finale in E minor in *Othello,*—

which does not consist of these short syncopations, but is so
contrived, that after the first two beats of the orchestra, the
next two beats are taken up by the voice, and this continued,
consisting of a vocal Thesis to an orchestral Arsis.

Have you had a visit from David ? I am not certain
whether he went to Munich, but he has visited Nuremberg

and Erlangen; we expect him home on Saturday. He is constantly on the move, and wherever he goes, he always meets with a great reception. I think he is quite right to travel about, and show himself off; the impression made by a virtuoso depends on his actual appearance in public, during the best years of his life. It is much the same with our latest composers; their actual presence is almost always a condition of the performance of their works. . . .

Yours,

M. H.

164.

LEIPZIG, January 9th, 1862.

DEAR HAUSER,—

. . . I endorse all you say about methods of singing, notably those which are founded on Bernacchi and similarly mythical people, or the shadows of their shadows. There is worthy Manstein too, a mere *réchauffé* of my old master, Mieksch. He had talked for so long about Bernacchi, always saying the same thing, that in the end, I daresay he fancied he had known him quite well, and had it all at first-hand. I can see him before me as I write, grinning away as he trilled out graceful passages in his thin, falsetto voice. Though they gave him very small parts on the stage, he was sure to amuse the audience, either in light or serious opera. He and Decavanti wore standing dishes, and the public got used to them. You have done well, to overturn all this fetish worship of an obsolete school. I am speaking of the idols only; we shall do no harm to anything else. But in my time, there really was nothing good. We had to edify our selves with the thought of a perfection, which was to be our own work. There was a charm in imagining the sublime, the *ne plus ultra*, though how to set about acquiring it, we did not exactly know. Anyhow, although nothing came of it, it spared us all the trouble of understanding things for ourselves. And what if we did hear the wondrous things, recorded in the *Hildegard von Hohenthal?* Would that give us a feeling of

perfection? I fancy we should think it old-fashioned stuff.
A rhapsodical book, written in the nineties, and Mozart's
name never occurs once in its pages! I can quite believe that
he would not have been at his ease in such company. He insisted
on some human character, whereas the Italians were content
to make their Gods and Demi-gods pipe and tootle like silly
shepherds. The heroic eight-line Arias of Metastasio are
admirably adapted to Canzonets, for they are not characteristic
of individuals or situations, they are merely stock vocal
phrases, which passed muster, and were welcomed everywhere
in those days. I believe that Jomelli himself, the author of
111 operas, set Metastasio's *Olimpiade* three times; it was
thought an admirable book. He wanted nothing but some new
Cantilenas. That is the rubbish, which invariably prepares
the way for revolution, and revolution, in its turn, leads to
the other extreme. In former times, Cantilena was
all the fashion; now, there is no such thing; every
note must have its meaning, its distinct character. If
singers want to sing for singing's sake, they must go to
foreigners, for there never lived but one Mozart, to stand
like the King of the Ninepins, in the midst of the
Muses, all over the world. The Germans write for the voice,
as a violinist would for the clarinet, and *vice versâ*. It is
quite clear, that they have no feeling for its limitations, even
when they deliberately set themselves down to write grateful
music. Spohr, Mendelssohn, and Rietz, not to speak of many
others, have written Concert Arias meant to be vocal, and
intended to show off the best powers of the singer, for whom
they were composed. But who can call them vocal? As for
the vocal part of it, I should not quarrel with any *prima
donna*, who preferred to sing the most commonplace Italian
melody. The interesting passages in our operas are not
generally those which affect the singer. Take that bit of
Marschner's *Templer*—

where all that the singer has to do, is to imitate the notes of
the posthorn—

unless he makes vocal arpeggios of the accompanying harmony. Italian melodies, as well as the *Volkslieder*, would be spoilt, if they were undergirded with abnormal harmonies. That passage of Marschner is supposed to be dignified by the harmony, but in reality it remains the same, whether I hear four accompanying chords, or only one.

The most important things are here said incidentally, and all the "introductory matter" in your book is certainly good, instructive, and to the point, so that I have no fault to find. But in Chapter IV. I take serious objection to this and that, with regard to elementary matters. I am aware that it is impossible always to state all that is true—but I think everything that *is* stated ought to be true—so that there shall be no need of pulling down and carting away that which has been temporarily erected, to make room for purer and deeper knowledge. I don't like the "*half* and *whole* tones" in Chapter II. (there are unfortunately no indications of pages or paragraphs in the proofs before me). When I take the interval e – f, or b – C I have no sense of a *half*—it seems a perfectly clear and *necessary* step from one of the points to the other; it might perhaps appear so on the keyboard of the pianoforte, where a key seems to be missing—but we are not talking of the pianoforte or of any other keyed instrument—and as a matter of feeling and instinct, b natural – C is like C – D. Anyway, what can you mean by a *half* tone ? Can a tone be cut in two ? Two Tetrachords might be so cut : C D e f, G a b natural C, but it would not be a clean cut. If I am looking for a Tetrachord equivalent to C D e f, and if D has been, as is afterwards expressly said, the Fifth remove of the Fifth G—then, in the second Tetrachord G a b natural C, *a* ought again to appear as the Fifth remove of the Fifth D. But it is not so here ; it is so only in the system of Hexachords (solmisation), if it is meant to lead on to b natural ; in our *major* System the succession G a is not an equivalent for C – D, but for D e. A pianoforte player may ignore this : but a singer cannot afford

to do so—at least, if he does, there will be a remnant, and a
knot which some time or other will have to be unravelled. A
singer cannot help noticing the difference, when he has to

intone— 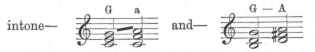 and—

He will find that the *a* of the first example does not chime
with the *a* of the second—and that he will have to raise the
pitch of *a* in the second example, if he happen to have failed in
catching its significance in that position. But the sense for
tonality, as regards the succession—

will not suffice here—for *a* here appears in the sense of a
Third to F. Solmisation only will here give us the true
Fifth—for solmisation will call *sol ut,* and then, starting again
from *ut,* the *re* will be the Fifth *A* we are in search of.

Now, if one cannot and ought not from the outset to touch
upon this sort of thing, Tetrachords and such like matters
should not be mentioned at all. I have made various final
annotations here and there in the book, which can easily be
removed. Amongst them, there is one touching the quotations
from my *Harmonik.* Since the book is mentioned in a general
way, it is of course permissible to make extracts at discretion ;
several excerpts, however, are made from the later sections,
which are not yet published, and I do not wish to see them
anticipated, so that when they come to be printed, they may
look like extracts from your *Singschule.* For instance, the
example—

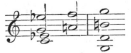

where I treat of the " strained " Triad or chord of the Seventh,
which has the Fourth, Fifth, and the Third $(F-A)$. $^{64\ :\ 81}$ This
harmony appears quite naturally in my *Harmonik*—but the
illustration in type is still in MS. I have just been looking

again at the little treatise, and find that with slight emendations here and there, and a proper conclusion, it will probably be more acceptable than the big, abstract book. In the long run, of course, the big book sets forth the essence of the matter better and more completely than mere hints and indications, which suffer from *lacunæ inter se*. On the other hand, my examples in symbols and letters are difficult to many readers; therefore, granted the big book with all its symbols and all its letters, I can afford to give concrete examples in music notes, without fear of being misunderstood; whereas such notes would have been embarrassing in the book itself. Duffers, great and small, won't see this, because, once for all, they won't take the trouble to read attentively. Therefore, I do not wish that fragments which do not belong to the main work, already printed, should be quoted—unless, indeed, they can be derived from the statements in the main work, and illustrated by examples which do not occur in the smaller treatise.

It might also be possible for you to mention the book rather earlier, without the nomenclature—for example, F a C e G b D, &c., or at least together with this. Attention being thus drawn to the matter, anyone can *look for the reason and the necessity of the capitals and smaller letters, which you omit to state, and which consists in the difference of a tone being considered as a Third, or as a Fifth in its Fourth potentiality*. It is, of course, always difficult to talk of a thing, if the subject cannot be exhausted; still, there should be some indication of the main points—which somehow or other always contrive to turn up and give trouble in practice. Even above, in the letter, when we talk of a Tetrachord G a b natural C, there is an ambiguity; I don't see how we can avoid talking of the difference between the tone which forms the Third, and that which forms the Fifth. Whatever in your work pertains to the mechanism of the voice, and to voice production, is sure to be thorough and based on personal experience. I have no criterion for this, and can only accept it with thanks. . . .

Yours,

M. HAUPTMANN.

165.

LEIPZIG, *August 27th*, 1862.

. . . Our new Rector, Professor Kraner, who was at College here from 1832 to 1835, still remembers with pleasure the Opera-house of those days, which was the constant resort of a certain party of students. Hauser, the baritone, was their prime favourite, and they were fond of Livia Gerhard, and patronised her as a clever *débutante*. Thirty years have passed since then; the baritone is now the Director of a *Conservatoire*, and Livia is the wife of a noble, and much respected. They still enjoy life, although perhaps more soberly. In 1834 I was your guest, for three weeks, in the corner house of Reichel's garden. Now I have been domiciled here for twenty years, but you are in Munich, and we have met about twice, and we don't write as often as we should. . . . I commend you for working so hard at your Hymn Book. My work is still in arrears. Whilst we were at Alexanderbad, I wrote three short Motets, for the beginning of the Service on Sundays. I think I'm rather like the long-haired young German artist, in a charming set of caricatures (water colours they were) that I saw one day in a shop window at Rome. There was a Frenchman, you know, dashing about in a fine fury, in front of his easel, painting a storm, with everything topsy-turvy: "*Il faut faire la nature en ravage.*" And then there was a German, sitting quietly before a forget-me-not, and saying "*Wie gemüthlich!*"

Yours,

M. H.

166.

LEIPZIG, *October 28th*, 1862.
(My Father's birthday in 1755.)

. . . I send you a little poem, which was presented to me on a silk cushion, in honour of my birthday, the 13th. It was a regular *fête* from morning to night. I had regarded it merely as an ordinary anniversary, but my friends made it out to be a Jubilee, as I was appointed a member of the

Dresden orchestra in 1812. Deputations and presents came in from all quarters, there were no end of cards, visits, and letters; and they are still coming in. "Pamina alone is wanting," says Tamino, praising the magic flute that summons all the wild beasts around him. It was a grand day at the *Conservatoire*. They made me sit in a mahogany armchair, covered with garlands, and next morning I found it transferred to my study. The St. Thomas's Orchestra gave me a dinner-service of silver and glass (which I have been very much in want of for some time!) There were a good many other silver things too. I didn't get a cup, but that we can do without. It rained bouquets. Three big pine-apples arrived together; they became as daily bread to the children. . . .

Yours,

M. HAUPTMANN.

167.

LEIPZIG, June 2nd, 1863.

DEAR HAUSER,—

. . . While I was shut up in my room with influenza (from March 12th to April 30th), I was asked to write a Whitsun Hymn for the Deaconesses' Choir in Dresden, as nothing of the kind was to be found in the earlier collection. So I wrote one in three parts, for female voices, with a cough obbligato. This I have sent off, and some other Hymns for Easter, Ascension, and Trinity, not to speak of a Penitential Hymn, and a Chorus for Carmelite nuns, also in three parts, taken from my Opera of *Mathilde*, with a few unimportant abbreviations. These form a collection, ranging from the year 1818 to the year 1863, a term of some forty-five years. Siegel has already got hold of them, and they are being printed. He is a most convenient publisher, for he finds out at once—Heaven knows how, in this instance!—what it is that I am writing, and he gets it into his clutches, and keeps it. I received a formal letter from the *Männergesangverein* of Neisse (Silesia), the other day, enclosing 20 *Neugroschen*, in acknowledgment of a song of mine, *Wunderbar ist mir geschehn*,

which forms part of their *répertoire*. This Association is an
offshoot of the Vienna *Gesangverein*, and is gradually absorbing
all the other Societies. They send the sum of one florin to
the composer, for every new song which they take. Some
time ago, the Duke of Coburg received a *don gratuit* of this
kind, and was immensely pleased with it. It would be a
good thing for us, were every one of the Associations to
send us florins, but it's rather a difficult matter to please
everybody. Barring the beautiful *Grüner Wald*, hardly any
of Mendelssohn's numerous Part-Songs for Male Voices are
favourites with these Societies. It is another kind of music
which flourishes amongst them. Zöllner is the Matador—
the rest are rather inferior to him than otherwise. Perhaps
Julius Otto is the most popular. The buzzing effects, produced by veiling the voice, are very low indeed, but people
like that sort of thing. . . .

Yours,
M. HAUPTMANN.

168.

LEIPZIG, *April 12th*, 1864.

. . . We have just got a new Stutz from Härtel—touch
and tone equally fine. The old Streicher, for which I cannot
find a purchaser, is still on my hands. All Streichers have a
beautiful tone. The machinery got a little out of order ; that's
all that is wrong. But I hate parting with an ancient friend,
and I hope it will fall into good hands. No one likes to see the
old horse, which has carried him faithfully, turned on to the
plough. While the new theatre was being built in Dresden,
before the old one had been taken down, King Frederick
Augustus was asked, what he thought of it all. For some time,
he didn't utter a word, but when he was hard pressed, " I am
considering," said he, " which of the two I had rather were
demolished." The old barn, ugly as it was, was the home of
all his early recollections, and he loved it accordingly. I feel
just the same about my old Streicher.

They are looking out for a Professor of Singing at Cologne, for Böhme is about to resign on the ground of ill-health. I cannot recommend anyone. Can you help them? You have heard of the lady, who wrote to her friend for a steward that was to be a perfect paragon in every way. The friend replied, that she would do her best to find such a man, and if successful, she would marry him! Ideal singing-masters are just the people we all want. . . .

I see from the *Signale* that my *Salve Regina* (written in 1822) was performed at a Concert in London, with great success. It pleased me to read of the *encore*, but one must not make too much of happy accidents. . . .

Yours,
M. HAUPTMANN.

169.

LEIPZIG, October 21st, 1864.

. . . I now learn, for the first time, that you are a free man. . . . I am not inclined to give up teaching yet, so long as I feel up to my work. I like taking beginners who are sensible, and wish to learn. Give me a virgin soil, free of weeds; that is the ground for harvest. It sometimes happens, that a pupil merely wants to learn "instrumentation"; then, indeed, I cannot undertake him. Besides, he is generally a person who cannot write four consecutive bars of pure harmony—who has no idea whatever of the human figure, and wants to be taught how to drape. Away to a tailor with such people! I should like to know if any composer—not Mozart, nor Beethoven, but even one of the most ordinary—ever learnt instrumentation from a master! If they want to know, whether there are such things as A and B horns and clarinets, let them poke their noses into the first score that comes to hand! Of course, everything has to be learnt, but it is not everything that can be taught. Last week we celebrated the Jubilee of Klengel, the violinist, who has been a member of our Orchestra for fifty years, during which time he has never missed a single rehearsal, nor a single performance, and has

never had a day's illness. Even in the depth of winter, I have
never seen him in a cloak or an overcoat ; he rubs his hands,
and is as warm as we are in our furs. It was a pretty *fête*.
The speeches were made, and the presents were given, before
they rehearsed for the Concert; the Council, the Concert
Committee, and the Orchestra were all represented. The
King sent him the Cross of Honour of the Order of Albrecht.
Long may he live to wear it ! . . .

Yours,

M. H.

170.

Leipzig, *December 15th, 1864.*

. . . I read of the great success of *The Flying Dutchman* in Munich. That opera was a favourite with Spohr ;
he liked the later ones much less, though he was well
disposed towards them in the beginning. To be sure, it was
all as anti-Spohrian as possible—but he was very kind to
younger artists, much kinder than he was to contemporaries
like Weber, whose success lay in a different field to his own.
He could not endure Spontini, who was too much in the
habit of doubling his leading notes for Spohr's taste, and he
often complained of Beethoven, on account of his unusual
harmonies, and those which were designed on an abnormally
large scale.

He was carried away by the whole thing, but he was dis-
satisfied with the details. He was easily caught by details
too, and by neat workmanship, which often led him to rank
the *Deos minorum gentium* too high. At the *Gewandhaus*, the
other day, we heard his double Quartet in D minor very well
performed. But of course there starts up a pack of unfledged
critics, who talk about it in the usual high and mighty style,
perhaps bestowing some small amount of praise on one
movement or another, but concluding that all such music is,
on the whole, out of date. And mark you, these are not
music-of-the-future men, nor sticklers for reform ! If we
could but give them an idea, how far above their criticism a
work of Art like this really is !

Beethoven too! It is dreadful for a great man, when stupid people think they understand him. Beethoven and Sebastian Bach—those are their two main supports. They remind me of those sailors, who mistook a huge whale for an island, landed on its back, and proceeded to light a fire, whereupon the creature, finding itself uncomfortable, dived down a bit, and sent them all sprawling into the water. . . .

Yours,

M. H.

171.

LEIPZIG, *February* 20*th*, 1865.

. . . Joachim and his wife were here the other day. She sings very finely, and his playing is quite splendid. Every composer comes alike to him. He is inimitable in Spohr; you forget the *virtuoso*, and hear nothing but a musician of the purest water. He brought a new Concerto with him, but he cannot yet rouse an audience to enthusiasm with his own compositions, as he can with the drawing-room pieces of Spohr. As for Sebastian Bach, no one could play it better, although such music is ungrateful, and not suited to the violin. That instrument is not by nature fit for four parts ; every part beyond two is only wrung from it at the cost of beautiful execution. You may admire the ingenuity, but a far more natural and beautiful effect would be got, by employing a few other instruments as an accompaniment. None but a fanatic would deny this. What beauty is there in chords torn right across the face of the violin ? or in making mincemeat of the *Cantilena*, in order to get hold of a bass, as a polyphonic substitute ? Ingenious of course it is, nothing more, however much we may admire the brilliancy of the player. The almost invariable combination of such music with pianoforte accompaniment has a curious effect. The composer labours to produce polyphony, and they give him, *plus* the violin, a pianist, who, with the ten fingers at his disposal, has nothing further to do than to relieve the violinist of all the trouble, at very small cost to himself. Joachim Raff was here too, a very clever musician, well informed on other subjects besides his own. He conducted an Orchestral Suite at the *Gewandhaus;* it was coldly received at the beginning, but improved as it went on. Raff was the first to revive the Suite form, using it in the first instance for the piano, and after that for the orchestra. He claims to have been in the field before Franz Lachner. The Suite is somewhat contracted in form—a Venice, without a Piazza di San Marco, where one can walk about comfortably and stretch one's legs. Repetitions are avoided in modern music, even where they are required by the construction. Is the left eye to be regarded as a dispensable repetition of the right? No, the two together form "the eye"; one is but the half. And so it is with many movements in music, where the passages may be essentially homophonous. It is another matter with Fugal or polyphonic writings. These grow like plants in *one* direction—not bilaterally, like animal organisms. Yet even here, it is only the visible, or what is destined to become so, that is symmetrical in form. Even with the plant, all that is thought worth consideration is the part that struggles towards the light; the roots lay no claim to it. To-day Wagner gives notice "to his friends," that the reports about him are mere newspaper inventions. Is that so?

But I must return to the subject of Suites, and of compositions akin to them. In so far as they belong to earlier times, to the period of Fugue and polyphony, our modern instrumental colouring is not in accordance with the style. The Fugue produces an effect by its form, by drawing, not by colouring. A Fugue, with effects produced by wind instruments, is rather like a painted statue. I may perhaps say more about this hereafter. . . .

Yours,

M. H.

172.

LEIPZIG, *June 3rd*, 1865.

. . . The performance of *Tristan* at Munich still seems to hang fire. The labour-pains of that opera were so severe, that it is no wonder, if the child does not survive. And whatever may come of it, it is from the first a strange mistake, to suppose that such an experiment could answer. A revolution in dramatic music is nothing new; Gluck's operas are instances in point—but such operas as these were written for mortal men, and they never went beyond mortal nature. Setting all this aside, and admitting that *Tristan* could be sung, acted, and put upon the stage, exactly as the Poet-Composer means it to be, the fact remains, that from its very design, the work is inferior and inartistic; resembling a poem, in which the author, for the sake of being natural, should despise metre, because man does not, as a rule, speak in verse. Three of my pupils here went to Munich for the performance, on the day it was advertised, and they have been snowed up there ever since. I cannot help feeling a mischievous pleasure. Two days would have been enough for their curiosity, but they have waited in vain for three weeks, and there is no prospect of its coming to an end. Here, we have nothing but great gatherings of all sorts ; just now, we are honoured by the presence of 2,000 schoolmasters, for three days. At the same time, we are to inaugurate the Gellert monument—*i.e.*, a marble statue by Knauer, which is to be erected on the edge of the great meadow in the Rosenthal, between Bonorand and Kintschy. A distinguished Austrian lady has contributed 1,500 *thalers* anonymously, Leipzig gives the same amount, and the statue is to be unveiled next Wednesday, with all the honours. The old monument on the Schneckenberg had to be taken down, when they began to build the new theatre, and they did not want to set it up again. Oeser's work was good enough in its day, more than a hundred years ago, but we have changed all that. People are rather too severe on such things. If they are not great enough to last, anyhow they are good solid bits of workmanship, and they illustrate the art of their time. Look at the Zwinger in Dresden; of course you know it? a splendid monument of the Roccoco period, restored over and over again. In spite of the weather-beaten statues and arabesques, the modern work contrasts wretchedly with the old. There is no life, no go in the lines of it, whereas in the old part, they seem indigenous to the building— so much so, that one cannot imagine anything different. However, the restored part proves that they might have been very different indeed. It was a healthy period of Art, which happened to synchronize with a period of perverted taste. Unity of design and clear articulation were the general characteristics, and these we fail to imitate. The common mechanic was a master of secrets, which it takes a finished artist to acquire now-a-days. Music fares the same. Nothing but first-rate music has any claim to be called really artistic— all the rest is dashed with amateurishness; even first-rate men cannot quite shake themselves free of it, or do so only in their very best moments. . . .

Yours,

M. Hauptmann.

173.

Leipzig, *October 3rd*, 1865.

Dear Hauser,—

I entirely agree with you, the organ is a dead-alive instrument; massed with others, it may make an effect, but it makes none musically. The Sixtine Choir, whether the voices are good or bad, dispenses with it, and wisely, in my opinion. The Imperial Choir of St. Petersburg follows suit, for the sake of keeping the right intonation. The temperament of the organ is so artificial, that the tone can never be said to be in vital union with harmony; the intervals, mechanically defined and methodically put out of tune, are made to suit any combination. On the organ, it is one and the same thing, whether a tone be the leading note, or the Dominant seventh—a tone is not dependent for its intonation on the voices alone, but may be taken differently upon all sorts of instruments, whereas on the organ, such a note is mechanically fixed. But without reference to Temperament, mathematically pure intonation is a lifeless thing, such as cannot occur and cannot satisfy anyone in practice. Hence the erroneous opinion, that c c sharp d, the middle note (c sharp) is acoustically higher than the middle note (d flat) in C d flat C, whilst a chromatic interval c c sharp = 24 : 25, the minor second c—d flat = 15 : 16, and therefore is a somewhat greater distance ; but our instincts demand so strongly, that rising and falling intervals shall be differentiated, that we are led to take a changed interval for a pure one.

Yet another defect ; there is no gradation in the strength of the tone of an organ, there is a want of life, which is not compensated for by any number of mechanical *Crescendos.* Once for all, I do not like them. I would rather the organ were a petrefaction, than a channel for the outflow of morbid sentiment, to be indulged in by every bad player. I prefer the plastic side of the organ ; we don't want red cheeks on a statue. To my mind, most of the organ accompaniments to Bach's solos are unsatisfactory. It often happens, that *one* stop is doubtfully in tune, and two veil the solo voices, and here, the failure to graduate the tone is more apparent, than in a greater volume of sound. Musically considered, it can never satisfy ; a substitute it is, and ever will be, obscuring if anything the true sense of the music. Such has been my opinion for a long time, and I am satisfied that I am right. But people now-a-days are getting crazy about organ accompaniment, and we are powerless to stop it, for they look upon a relapse as an advance, and of course, when we find a man like Mendelssohn in favour of it, a good deal may be said on their side of the question. The inherent defects, however, are always the same, and we cannot get rid of them. The purely mechanical character of the organ, *plus* the bad character of most organists, accounts, I think, for the dulness of Organ Recitals. I, for one, can never listen to them for any length of time, I find it so difficult to follow. As the organ cannot give accent, the player, it seems, ought by rights to keep an absolutely strict Tempo, for other-wise, we are at a loss to know, to what part of a bar the

stress pertains.   But you cannot expect a player always
to play in absolutely strict time ; he knows where the
stress belongs, but he can hardly convey it to others; and
thus the hearer is apt to get confused, until some happy
chance sets him right again.   Now this is a defect which the
piano is free from, though it shares all the other imper-
fections of intonation of the organ, for the piano can
accentuate. . . .

I am very glad you liked the *Zauberflöte* drawings—we
thought them beautiful.   They are, as you know, intended for
the decoration of one of the *Loggie* of the new Opera-house at
Vienna.   There was a figure of Papageno, in bas-relief, on the
pediment of the old *Theater an der Wien*.   The *Zauberflöte* had
brought the house so much money, that a monument was due
to it. . . .

Yours,

M. Hauptmann.

174.

Leipzig, *December 8th*, 1865.

Dear Hauser,—

. . . I am a fixture here—I know nothing—I can't get
away—I see nobody.   I wrote out from memory, the other day,
an old pianoforte piece of Spohr's, in the form of a Waltz ; it
would have been utterly forgotten else, for I am convinced
that there is no existing copy of it.   Franz brought it with
him from Gotha, in the year 1809, after he had been staying
there for the first time.   Spohr didn't care much about it ; it
does not close properly in the Tonic, you see—but we liked it
very well, and it made such an impression on me, that I can
still recollect it, though the original copy was lost long ago,
and it must be about fifty years since I last saw it.   I sent it
to Frau Spohr.   Of course, she did not know it either, and she
was quite delighted with it, for it was a new memory of the
old days to her.   It is thoroughly characteristic of him, and
the lapse of more than half-a-century has not taken anything
from its freshness.   There is an early opera of his too,

Alruna, which is not like the rest of his things—Spohr always, and Spohr everywhere—but has turns that remind one of Mozart, like the *Zweikampf mit der Geliebten*. This last contains the lovely Aria, which he afterwards transferred to *Faust*. There are hidden treasures of this kind, belonging to every age. The operas are shelved, and the world loses sight of them. *A propos* of operas that have been shelved (not hidden treasures, you know!), I wish I could sell my *Mathilde*. How very prosaic! But the publishers are so ready to print just now—if only the musical part of it were available! The worst of it is, ideas come when you are young, and success comes when you are old; you always want what you haven't got. Apart from printing and pay though, it seems a pity that all that music should be wasted. When one has been so happy over the writing of it, spite of all its deficiencies, one grieves over it, as one would over the death of a beloved child. It must have saddened dear Spohr, to see so many of his most perfect works, his operas, I mean, fading away so fast out of the history of music. All that appeared defective to those people who would not encourage his works, and allowed them to fade away, was not defective to *him;* in his ground, the music had healthy root, with room to blossom in, and yet it died.

After all, there is something great in the knowledge, that however beautiful the details may be, they cannot save a work, which has no life in all-pervading beauty. No charm of manner can possibly make up for want of style. It is want of style, to paint a fresco with the brushes you would use for a miniature; you must calculate the effect of distance, alike when you conceive, and when you execute your picture. Of course, I don't mean that Spohr injured the general effect of his music, as music, by finishing too minutely; I was thinking of larger dimensions, of the subordination of parts. . . .

Yours,
M. HAUPTMANN.

175.

LEIPZIG, *March* 18*th*, 1866.

. . . I send you but a few lines, to remind you of my existence, though my vitality is not much to boast of. " The hard problem of our illness," says Goethe, " has its existence half in over-haste, half in delay." I have little to complain of on the score of the first, but I am prodigal of the second, for all that I have to do remains undone. We are too dependent on " Brother Ass," as an old writer calls the body. O, that we could meet now and then ! With best love,

Yours,
M. H.

176.

LEIPZIG, *March* 31*st*, 1866.

. . . Helmholtz's book certainly deserves all the homage that is paid to it, but people ought to distinguish between physiology and psychology. Helmholtz absolutely ignores the latter, and he is in error, if he supposes that he has touched even superficially upon the Theory of Music. There he is completely at sea. The understanding of Music is entirely independent of everything qualitative, and it is a matter of utter indifference to me, whether I take my fourth from the zither, or from the bass trombone ; all partial tones and harmonics have nothing to do with the matter. It must be something definite, something measurable, all subordinate significations have nothing to do with it—as little as organ mixtures have to do with Harmony ; they can only be used, when they are not definitely heard, that is to say, when they cannot be distinguished. A painter wants a colour-box, not a Theory of Colours. For the practice and understanding of Art, it matters not whether Newton's theory or Goethe's be the right one ; he has only got to do with colours that are ready-made. Did I ever send you a pamphlet

On The Senses? It treats of six instead of five senses, and contrives to simplify the entire subject, and reduce it to a simple matter of contrast. I will enclose the pamphlet, if I can find it. I do not think that any subject can be understood in multiplicity; what looks like multiplicity can never be understood, excepting as the changed or changing condition of a simple unit. Heaven forbid that we should trace back a flower, in the form and colour of its leaves and blossoms, to the elements of its formation! the sensuous charm would be gone at once—that does not exist in the understanding. But there is no need to do this. The senses will always remain wholly unaffected by theoretical considerations; they have quite a different sphere. There is no bridge from the senses to the understanding. We are not to infer from this, that Theory is dry and lifeless — that is the "gray" dead Theory. In Theory, too, " Life's golden Tree of Life " exists, and the fruits of it are not dried up crab-apples, but juicy enough of their kind, though of course they are no more to be eaten, than a real crab-apple is to be understood. Everything has two sides, unless it be one-sided; and if it be, it is only a half, unless it be the middle of two more sides. . . .

Yours,

M. H.

177.

LEIPZIG, *April 15th*, 1866.

. . . Herewith the pamphlet *On The Senses*—a new *aperçu*—you will have to work out the details for yourself. But no harm would be done, if feeling were to be withdrawn from the same category as Sight, Hearing, Smell, and Taste— *i.e.*, if these senses, which are endowed with a distinct organ of perception, were to be classified apart from those senses, which are open to impression in every part of the body, as, for instance, Touch and the Feeling of Warmth. Of course, every part of the body is not equally sensitive to these last, but it is only a difference of degree, for though the finger-tip is more sensitive than the elbow, the elbow feels also, unable as it is to taste, smell, see, and hear. Sight belongs only to the eye, Hearing only to the ear, &c. Only those senses which are capable of measuring, are artistic senses—Sight and Hearing; the sense of Touch, specialised into Sight and Hearing—not the sense of Warmth, specialised into Smell and Taste, which absorb the object materially. That is not the way of Art. Art sees and hears, leaving the object intact, for she has only to do with its form, its quantity. Just think this over! there's something in it. . . . People flock from far and wide to see *L'Africaine;* they come by ordinary trains, they come by express-trains,—and yet I have not managed the short walk between the *Thomas-Schule* and the Theatre! Everybody ought to go once, if only to see the Upas tree, which they say is beautiful. That tree, like the plague in Halévy's Opera, *Ginevra,* seems to me to be the real motive or reason for the choice of the subject, for round it all, the other incidents crystallize and group themselves, just as a copper-wire may become the centre of chemical crystallization, which cannot be formed without it. There is something poisonous in all three cases. Wachtel, the tenor, is starring here, and has created a genuine *furore.* He has only appeared in *Le Postillon* and *La Dame Blanche,* both of which operas had to be repeated. They say his voice is marvellously beautiful. *L'Africaine* and *Le Postillon* are given only at double prices, yet the house is always quite full. . . .

Yours,

M. H.

178.*

Leipzig, *May 27th,* 1866.

. . . They gave a Motet of mine, *How lovely are Thy dwellings,* in the *Thomaskirche,* the other day. I wrote it originally for a Church Congress, and it was very well received.

---

* A short abstract of the original letter, which is in the main a reproduction of other parts of the book.

It opens with a pretty Duet between two sopranos, and the general construction is good. It was my first attempt to write anything at Alexanderbad; and after that, I never let the bathing season pass, without writing something, until last summer. How we used to enjoy meeting Spohr there! He was failing a good deal, that last summer of 1859—but more sympathetic than would have appeared to an outsider, as he sat silent at our table, out in the open air, leaning his chin upon his stick. He would put in a word sometimes, when no one noticed that he was taking any part in the conversation. He was always most good-natured about going wherever he was asked, when many another great man would have declined. However, if they serenaded him with nothing worth listening to, he did, now and then, lose his temper; and if they bawled at him like soldiers in a guard room, according to the motto, "He that hath a voice, let him sing!" it was highly probable that he would take no notice of them at all. One almost smiled, to see people fancying they could please him with such stuff as that. He could overlook a good deal, but not when it was utterly unmusical. He was much more indulgent to poets, provided there was nothing very objectionable in the metre or the rhyme. To me, Spohr's whole personality is a very pleasant remembrance. From the first years of our acquaintance, and even before that, he was my musical divinity; only by degrees, did other stars arise in my heaven. My reverence for him continued up to the very last. In his style and character as an artist, he is thoroughly genuine, never imposing on other people, never exalting himself above himself, always true to his own instincts. There are few like him. This is "the honest man," according to Hamlet, one out of ten thousand, who never "attitudinises," as Rameau's Nephew has it. Bach, Mozart, and Cherubini were such men; it is this that makes them what they are, and their greatness consists in their completeness. The more a man is, and the more he has, the less conceit he needs. Arrogance is always a *testimonium paupertatis*. Goethe says of Lessing, that he used to throw away his dignity, because he could take it up again at any moment, just as a good jockey can slacken his rein, and yet

make the horse feel that he is its master. The mere holiday
rider dare not do this, for he has to be on his guard every
moment. . . .

Yours,

M. HAUPTMANN.

179.

SULZA, *August* 18*th*, 1866.

DEAR HAUSER,—

. . . It is very odd that mountain climbing should make
you feel giddy. Did we but know the best remedy for our
complaints, in nine cases out of ten we should never go to
look for it, under a Latin name, at the apothecary's.
But in the first place we do not know, and in the second, if
we do know, we cannot get it. Fresh air, to be sure, costs
nothing, but when one cannot enjoy it at home, one must go
elsewhere, and that costs money, and time too. When a man
is tied by the leg, he cannot get away of himself, much less
does anyone else think of taking him off to a place where he
could get well. No! one has to remain quietly cooped up at
home, doing just what is worst for one, sitting indoors instead
of running about in the open air, exerting one's brain instead
of vegetating in animal fashion, planning how to fill up every
moment, so as to exclude every fragment of leisure. " Canst
thou forbid the silkworm to spin, although it is ever spinning
itself nearer to death?" How often have we wasted our
time spinning, when it was not the time to spin, when we
ought to have been butterflies, not caterpillars! If we had
only managed properly, we should have had time enough for
both, but to do nothing, when it is the time to do nothing,
demands an amount of energy that is not always forthcoming,
and we go on till we drop, under the impression that we are
making progress. It is one thing to know that you injure your
eyes, reading by twilight, and quite another thing to put down
your book till the lamp comes.

As to that passage in the *Harmonik*, about the resolution of
the Chord of the Seventh, you must wait until I get home. I
am in the position of Kunstrath Fraischdörfer in the preface

to *Siebenkäs*, when he confessed that he was almost stupid without his Herb Cap of Memory. There is such a passage in the book, but you have not quoted it quite correctly, and the view from the window is too pretty, to allow of my recollecting all those abstractions. Do you know what it was, that helped to make Goethe's writing so clear ? I am sure the reason of it is to be found, in the fact that he dictated everything ; he didn't write it, he *said* it, and it is impossible, in speaking, to make use of those laboured sentences, those algebraic symbols, which can only be taken in by the eye, not by the ear. Socrates set no store by written wisdom, only by life-like discussion, as it appeals to the ear in its growth and its development. But even the written wisdom of the Greeks is like speech. You can read aloud the intricate mathematical problems of Euclid, and the meaning is clear, without any of the symbols. This is what I call *plastic* style, and no German writer possesses it in the same way, and to the same degree, as Goethe, though Lessing comes very near him. The want of it is the great defect of my *Harmonik*. Less elaborate thinking, and a more ordinary method of expression, would have helped on the book. We should never try to say what cannot be said. Arrack and sugar alone make neither good punch, nor good grog ; there must be water as well, not to dilute it, but as an essential ingredient. We can think faster than we can speak, but it is only *spoken* thoughts that are intelligible to others, and the speaker should neither hurry, nor be impatient, but seek his own satisfaction in words, and know how to find it. . . .

Yours,

M. H.

180.

LEIPZIG, *August* 29*th*, 1866.

. . . Yesterday, I sent to Härtel's for your *Singschule*. It is very prettily got up, and I have read a good deal of it with pleasure. It tells me nothing that I did not know before, but I am glad to have the connecting-links supplied. I await

N 2

the popular verdict with some curiosity. The main point is, your uncompromising overthrow of idols (which is more than a negative good) and your merciless exposure of ancient objects of worship, reverenced by us only through the medium of hazy description. As soon as we draw nearer, and get the least into touch with them, the magic becomes less magical, and there are rents in the veil. It would give us no pleasure, to hear our best music sung by the pupils of Bernacchi; they must stick to Galuppi, Caruso, &c. I would rather not be too close to them, for I know little about them, and the general notion I have of their style makes me think, that we could hardly have been happy, in an age when such things were thought beautiful. The style was adapted to the prevailing taste of the time, and as such, it may, perhaps, be justified, but it must be limited to a past age, and the method of vocalisation incidental to it. Then the composer existed for the singer, whereas the singer should exist for the composer—for the composer of *vocal* music, of course. Here and there, we come across some splendid exceptions; Mozart made an enormous stride, when he sought to elevate the exception into the rule. . . .

Yours,

M. H.

181.

Leipzig, *November* 26th, 1866.

Dearest Hauser,—

. . . I must send you my essay on the Hexachord or Solmisation in the annual volume of the *Musikalische Zeitung*, for I cannot get it separately. I am like the rustic who won a lottery prize. He had pasted his ticket on the door of his cottage, and when the collector called for it, there was nothing for it but to unhinge the door, and transport it bodily, in a wheelbarrow, to the town. I only wish my volume could bring you a prize! . . . I have given up all thoughts of moving. An official residence like this has its advantages, though one gets into such a groove, that change seems impossible. The rooms, the stairs, the furniture become parts of oneself, though I suppose one could take them off like a pair of boots, if one were obliged to do so. I am writing in Susette's room—it was too cold in my own. In the church close by, they are hard at work, hammer and tongs, on Beethoven's Mass in D. All the world is there, I stay at home. I cannot force myself to think, that such a work as that is an expression of religious feeling. It is grand, powerful music, shifting with every change of the text. Such variety is never suggested by the words of the Mass, which do not require these divisions and classifications; they are not meant to be treated in that way, but rather in the style of the old Italian Masses, where the movements are subjected but rarely to a variety of expression. Too little here may easily become too much there, and I am certain it is wrong, to seize upon each individual phrase, and elaborate it minutely. In speaking thus of a great work, conceived in the heart, and born of the heart, a work which has inspired the veneration of the world, one must feel sure of understanding what it means: well, so far as it is good and beautiful, one does!

. . .

Yours,

M. H.

182.

Leipzig, *December 15th*, 1866.

Dearest Hauser,—

Like yourself, I am very so-so, after making every allowance. Two days after the Silver Wedding *fête*, I was so bad about the legs, that I could hardly crawl up to my bedroom, and I have been a cripple for more than a week. My people try and persuade me that I get better every day, but I am never at ease except upon the sofa; walking is out of the question. Susette must tell you all about the *fête*, the visitors, presents, *tableaux* of scenes in our lives, &c.— it's too long a story for me. I am touched by your appreciation of the mark I set under the Sonnet in the *Singschule*; no one ever approached you in those things. If you had but a small audience, they were fit though few, and it was just the right thing for them. It is only the proper man in the proper place that can elicit the proper expression, and then the singer is just as much the author of the song as the composer and the poet. Some sort of picture arises in the mind when one is writing, or has written it, but it is little more than a dream or a fancy, until the writer has heard it well done.

Later.

Susette has just read the beginning of this letter, and thinks it sounds as if my present lameness were the result of the Silver Wedding festivities—which is not the case. . . . Let me amend my ways, and tell you what a success the *fête* was—what kindness and affection were showered upon us from all quarters, from morn till eve! The *tableaux*, representing scenes from both our lives, were charming,— most cleverly arranged; there were Italian scenes as well, and others from my opera of *Mathilde*, with choruses and solos, set to words by Holstein, which were so good, that one can only regret that they were, from the nature of the thing, transitory. . . . I hear that a regular obituary notice of Rietz has appeared in one of the newspapers, together with a criticism of his compositions. Rietz, who is alive and kicking, will feel rather queer when he reads it. He wanted to come to our Silver Wedding, but was prevented from doing so, as his colleague, Krebs, was called away at the same time. We had no idea of the great preparations that were being made for the *fête*. Everyone vied with his neighbour in doing us honour. . . . The *Conservatoire* gave us a lovely timepiece, and we were completely set up with Leipzig china, and all sorts of other beautiful things. We might have been young housekeepers, beginning over again. . . .

Yours,

M. H.

183.

LEIPZIG, *June 9th,* 1867.

DEAREST HAUSER,—

I have so completely got out of the way of writing, that I can hardly form my letters ; one keeps dancing before the other—or an X, unbidden, shapes itself into an U, so that I cannot always say, what is cause and what is effect—whether I can't write because I don't, or whether I don't write because I can't. Besides, I have not heard from you for a long time ; I always thought I should get a letter, asking me why I did not write. I want that sort of stimulus ; one nail drives another. I am still a prisoner, my legs are no better, and perhaps they never will be. If one could only learn to resign oneself to facts which cannot be altered! but mortal man never ceases to hope. Now, it is the mild air of summer which is to do me good. Well, if it does not, whose fault is that ? One day telleth another.

I have enjoyed next to nothing in the way of music this winter, though there was plenty of good music to be had. The *Euterpe* was very active. They have done big works, with an orchestra largely reinforced, and new singers, as at the *Gewandhaus.* The Theatre too is almost always full, but I have not been at all. Who can say, whether I shall live to see the new one ? They are working away at it busily. Reinecke's opera *Manfred* will soon be given in Wiesbaden ; he expects a great deal from his subject, though the chief character is a different one from Byron's. It is impossible to help feeling slightly anxious about a new German opera, particularly when you happen to know the composer. It is different with a stranger ; then I don't grieve so much over the pages and pages he has had to write, so often to no purpose. Composers always remind me of the Princes in *Turandot,* where one after the other has his head cut off, and stuck up over the gate, as a warning. . . .

To the great delight of the public, there has been a revival at Leipzig, as at many other places, of *Così fan tutte.* Blessed

are those composers who can play fast and loose with beauty!
Would that this faculty of light handling were better understood! People do not know how to get weight without
heaviness, how to show that they are at ease in the midst of
difficulties. But consider what that implies! Think of the
power required for transfiguring the labour of workmanship,
so as to make it light, ethereal, and fragrant, as a flower of Art
should be. No living artist could write *Figaro*, not even
Mozart himself, could we bring him back to life again. *Fidelio*
is another matter, had we another Beethoven; a great deal of
him is chrysalis, the wings don't move freely. In the old
Harmony there is no thorough-bass, it consists of the juxtaposition of melodies in polyphony; it has no independent
existence, like the bit of marble with which sculptors
occasionally support their statues. Historians always
maintain that Biadana invented thorough-bass, which is just
such a support; it began, as it inevitably must, in a simple
organ accompaniment. Who in the Sixtine Choir, think you,
would have looked after thorough-bass? The gentlemen with
bouche fermée, perhaps? The others have other things to do;
they are masters of the situation, they cannot do servants'
work. Whatever there is to be said against thorough-bass, it
has this in its favour, that it is an accompaniment and
support to harmony, giving lightness and grace to melody.
Polyphonic writing was inevitable in earlier ages, for whilst
the *prima donna* declaimed her solo in front of the stage, her
vocal colleagues were ranged behind the scenes, and melody,
with accompaniment (Cantata style), was a new invention. I
daresay Emanuel Bach, now and then, found his papa's thick
polyphony a trifle too stodgy, so by way of recreation, he liked
to dabble in "little Italian ditties." . . . I have been at
work lately on a system of Harmony *in nuce;* as it is all
contained in a few pages, Bagge wants to insert it in the
Musikalische Zeitung. That journal, though it drags along in
the old groove, continues to justify its position. Whether people
understand it or not, it is the truth, and they will come to
see it. . . .

Yours,

M. HAUPTMANN.

184.

ALEXANDERBAD, *July* 27*th*, 1867.

. . . A Cantor in the neighbourhood brings me some of his compositions to look over, just to keep my hand in. How difficult it is for these poor people in the country! They never hear a note of music, and never get a chance of seeing anything; what a godsend it would be to them, if we could spare them some little thing out of our abundance! On the other hand, if I didn't know them already, I might make acquaintance with some of my own earlier compositions at Redwitz, two miles from here, where they are giving a Charity Concert, with *Ueber allen Gipfeln ist Ruh* and *Ehre sei Gott* in the programme. I never looked so far ahead, when I wrote those pieces. How things have changed, and yet the songs remain the same! Schiller, in his *Klage des Schönen*, says :

"Only what fades did I, the Father of Gods, make fair."

The survival of a four-part Song is only apparent after all, a slower kind of passing away, like the movement of the hour hand of a clock, as compared with that of the other two. And yet, we all arrive at the same time in Eternity,—with a good deal too, that we now think *eternal*. . . .

Librettists are in a bad way since Wagner appeared ; new conditions are indispensable. Librettos that were successful in former days still hold their own ; the new ones are doubtfully welcome, unless they have been purged in Wagnerian fires. We cry aloud for another Gluck, with his genius and his simplicity —don't mistake me, the latter quality standing alone is no good, and I don't mean childishness ; but we have more than enough of bombast. How is it possible, that operas which cannot be sung should be good operas? A short time since, all Naumann's compositions, which he had bequeathed to his son, perished in the fire at Irmler's pianoforte warehouse. For practical purposes, they were dead and buried ages ago, but they were a part of my life's history, and I am sorry they are lost. Haydn said that he learnt music from six Sonatas of Emanuel Bach's ; I can say the same thing of Naumann's Mass in A flat major. . . . Yours,

M. HAUPTMANN.

185.

LEIPZIG, *August 18th—22nd*, 1867.

. . . We had rare fine weather at Alexanderbad, but I
was too unwell to enjoy it; and yet if a man has red cheeks,
people think he is shamming. The society there was less
interesting than it had been in former years, but I can no
longer expect that people should entertain me, any more than I
entertain *them*, and I am a very bad hand at that now. Indeed,
I have done nothing for ever so long but complain that there
was nothing I could do. I had a letter from Benedict, who is
travelling in Spain. All his children are married and settled;
in spite of his visits to them, he complains of loneliness.
He has always been very active; and now he is beginning to
wonder, whether he always acted wisely. But we cannot
control ourselves in such matters. I think on the whole that
self-reproaches, except perhaps on the score of inactivity, are
out of place. Every animal is not a man, but to a certain
extent every man is an animal; I mean that man's instinct
for action tends towards a direction in which it can be
humanized. Benedict has sent a Sonata for Pianoforte and
Violin, dedicated to me; a work any composer might be proud
of; good music, cheerful and cheering, graceful and full of
character. I really know very little of his work, but this Sonata
is good evidence of his ability and of his artistic intentions.
Sound work of whatever kind is praiseworthy, as far as it
goes; of course there are many different kinds, and it must
be classified, but for all that, it stands or falls by its individual
quality. All roads lead to Rome, round-about ways as well,
but the straight ways are more direct and safer. Weber,
Benedict's master, went a way that was paved by the Abbé
Vogler, a grievous *circumbendibus*. Palestrina's is the
straighter course, and this was Mozart's and Sebastian Bach's
before him, not to mention Fux and many other good people.
Tannhäuser is sent back again by the Pope, and is for ever
wandering towards the Venusberg, and so it is with Wagner's
music. They think that the fifth or the chord of the $\frac{6}{4}$ can

form a basis and signify repose; but here is the contradiction, for one is sitting between two stools. Meyerbeer fared much better than his fellow-student, Weber, in this respect, yet when the latter writes naturally and agreeably, no one likes him better than I do, and he has certainly done more for German music than Meyerbeer. The latter, however, has worked his way through the Italian school, and has improved the technical part of his music in consequence. . . .

Loss upon loss! That splendid Church in Venice, *S. Giovanni e Paolo*, which I was so fond of, is burnt to ashes! Goethe says somewhere, that however willing we may be to turn to ashes ourselves, we should like to feel that such immortal works of Art were fireproof. Why should a Sixtine Madonna perish, when it possesses life eternal in itself, and could preserve it for future races, who perhaps may never hear of the picture, in the event of a fire,—which rude creature has a great appreciation of oil colours, though none of old masters? . . .

Yours,
M. HAUPTMANN.

186.

LEIPZIG, September 28th, 1867.

DEAREST HAUSER,—

Letters, telegrams, and congratulations from far and near, visits by the hundred! "Only Pamina is wanting still!" All this in honour of a Jubilee, and the fact of my having wielded a Conductor's stick, in one place, for twenty-five years! I suppose you have read something about it; anyhow, the newspapers have done their best to make it public. One letter from you would have been more welcome than a cart-load of others. But it was really a grand affair; from the afternoon of the 11th to the morning of the 13th, nothing but chorus and orchestra, orchestra and chorus, till the roof rang again. The following day I held a *levée*, and in the afternoon we had music in the church, a Cantata by S. Bach, *Herr, deine Augen*, to begin with, followed by my *Salve Regina*, an old Psalm recently printed, and the Mass in G minor. Everything was admirably done. . . . Rietz came from Dresden, with a deputation from the Orchestra and the *Tonkünstlerverein*. A great deal has been said, about the self-complacency I must feel, in accomplishing twenty-five years of office, and they compliment me on time well-spent, &c. I must confess, that I experience nothing of the kind. What have I done after all? True, I aimed at a good deal, but how fragmentary it has all been! And what work I have done is so poor and imperfect, that I cannot think it real. My treatises on Harmony and Theory are so unintelligibly expressed, as often to be useless to my readers; the best of them is always between the lines. Someone who really understands it ought to transcribe the meaning into popular language. Neither Socrates nor Christ wrote down His lessons, word for word; that was done by Plato, Aristotle, and the Evangelists. Truth must be reflected by someone who has first understood it, if it is to bring forth fruit. Pray do not think me presumptuous; I am only writing down what happens to come into my head at the moment, and now that I can no longer keep my thoughts on the right track, everything appears difficult, even what is easy. . . . Many persons live upon disease, not doctors only, but advocates and teachers. It is only a very few who live by producing things themselves; getting rid of what is bad is a much more profitable occupation. This reminds me of what Frau Spohr once said of an Englishman, who came to me for lessons in composition: "Did he cross the Channel, to learn from you that he must not write fifths?" Farewell, dearest Hauser! . . .

Yours,

M. HAUPTMANN.

LETTERS TO SPOHR AND OTHERS.

1*.

DRESDEN, *February 6th*, 1822.

DEAR KAPELLMEISTER,—

. . . One of my most ardent wishes would be realized, could I reckon on living near you, with a prospect of trying my powers under your guidance and protection. Such a consideration inclines me to look very favourably on the appointment which, according to your letter to Frau Spohr, is now vacant. I think too that the 400 *thalers*, supplemented by about 150 which I have made here, will enable me to live quietly and inexpensively, unless the cost of living in Cassel is enormously dear. Anyhow, for the last two years, I have neither had nor wanted more. On my return to Dresden, I was again offered a place in the orchestra, but I refused it, knowing by experience the deadening effect of the routine here, especially now that the work is incessant, and, on the whole, very uninteresting. Work with you, in a Theatre just beginning its flourishing career under your auspices, would be a different matter. I am quite independent, and on hearing definitely from you, if and when you expect me, I can start at a moment's notice.

We have had three performances of *Der Freischütz*, and but for Meier's illness, they would have been continued; the Theatre was always full to overflowing, and there was great applause, on the first night especially. Weber was called for. The Opera will command a crowded house, for many evenings to come, for there is much to see in it; it is beautiful in parts, and in some parts it is very beautiful. A real critic will soon find the music fragmentary, and wanting in form, but the general

---

* The following letters are addressed to Spohr.

public as yet is blind to these defects.   You remember
what the Manager in *Faust* says about this :

> " Give us a piece, and give it us in pieces."

Rossini's *Armida* followed close upon *Der Freischütz* at
Vienna, and having created an immense *furore*, it goes forth
into the world with the stamp of a genuinely classical Opera.
Under such circumstances, I set very small store by the
applause of the great public.   Hoping for your kind answer,

Ever affectionately yours,

H.

2.

LEIPZIG, *October 2nd*, 1842.

DEAR AND HONOURED KAPELLMEISTER,—

. . . The ceremonies of my reception by the authorities
were over nearly a fortnight ago, and since then I have been
at work.   My regular duties as Cantor consist of instruction
in choral singing from 11-12 and from 5-6, and besides that,
I conduct the Sunday music, which begins at 8 a.m.   I have
just made my *début*.   By desire of several friends, I rehearsed
my G minor Mass with orchestra, and in order to make a start,
I asked Pohlenz, who was temporarily acting in my place, to
conduct the band once more.   This Sunday is the opening
day of the Leipzig Fair, and the *Kyrie* and *Gloria* are usually
performed.   After the first orchestral rehearsal of my Mass,
the members of the band expressed a wish to hear it in its
entirety, in honour of my accession to office.   I asked the
Superintendent's leave, which was cheerfully granted, so at
the opening part of the service we had three numbers, and the
remainder of the Mass after the Epistle.   The cheerful zeal
of orchestra and chorus, and their interest in the music, so
lighten my labours as Conductor, that with all my want of
skill and experience, the task is easy, for it presents no
difficulties to a well-balanced and fairly efficient choir.   To-
day's performance gave complete satisfaction.

October 7th.

Mendelssohn, on his homeward journey from Switzerland,
passed through Leipzig last Friday.   He wanted to reach

Berlin on the 1st October, so he would not stop here ; but
yielding to eager solicitations, he agreed to conduct the first
Gewandhaus Concert on the 2nd, and returned here for
that purpose. The orchestral performance of Symphonies
under his *bâton* is quite first-rate ; such crispness and elasticity are rare. Mendelssohn, gratified as he is, will take none
of the credit ; he insists upon it, that with the many fine
players under his command at Berlin, and any amount of
zeal and hard work on his part, he cannot get the same result
there. The Leipzig people still hope for his return, but no
one can feel certain, for he himself is quite undecided. I
heard Schumann's three first Quartets at David's, and liked
them exceedingly ; they have greatly enhanced my admiration
for him. His earlier pianoforte works, conspicuous for mere
bizarrerie, seemed to me so patchy and aphoristic, that I
certainly underrated his gifts. Not that the Quartets are wanting in peculiarities both of form and of subject, but they are
intellectual works, both in conception and execution, and
there are many beautiful things in them. At the Theatre, they
have been giving Halévy's *Königin von Cypern.* The French text
is far better than the German ; it is incomprehensible to me,
how the translator could have made such a mess of it. In
the original, the King is an active person, who by his noble
conduct, enlists all our sympathies, whereas the German
librettist, with inconceivable stupidity, has transformed him
into a passive character, and his deeds become mere narrative. Narrative is ill adapted even for the stage, and it is
utterly valueless in Opera, where words are so easily lost.
As Caspar says, "What the eye sees, the heart believes."
But it is not only the text ; I like Halévy's music on the stage
better than ——'s. The opera is not very noisy, there is hardly
a note from the trombones throughout the whole of the first
Act ; in fact, it errs in the opposite direction, as might have
been expected of Halévy ; it is too delicate, the wit is too fine-
drawn, and his artificial tricks make it rather dry. Still, the
music is flowing, and very effective on the stage, for which, at
all events, it is better adapted than ——'s, redolent as that is of
the desk and the midnight oil, like so many other second and
third class German works. Heine says somewhere, that

never having been able to get reconciled to the complicated system of Linnæus in his youth, he had made one for himself ; he divided plants into two classes, eatable and uneatable. Similarly, and apart from other good or bad qualities, one might classify operas : those that are performed, and those that are not. I expect that Halévy's will rank among the first, ——'s among the second. After all, one is inclined to think anything that pleases such a large public as that which frequents the Opera, must have some positive good quality to depend upon, and the best operas that we have are the most popular, which proves that inferiority is not an essential nor permanent attraction, as regards the multitude. But if many works are popular, to which the *connoisseur* takes reasonable objection, technically and æsthetically, we may be certain that they have some intrinsic merit, for a thing cannot please, merely because it is bad. . . .

On Sunday last we went to the Härtels, and heard Henselt play. He came by train from Dresden, sat down to the piano at once, and never stopped for three hours ; he had been at it an hour and a half when we came in. I never heard more perfect playing, and doubt if it could exist in that particular *genre;* what with its unerring certainty, strength, and tenderness, its fine artistic self-control and quietness, it satisfies the most exacting hearer. To show his marvellous grasp of difficulties, he played two of Weber's Overtures which I put before him, and then some pretty new *Etudes,* mostly his own, I expect, though none of them were familiar to me. The Härtel piano held out bravely the whole evening ; it's a good sort of instrument, though I prefer the free, open tone of a Streicher.

3.

LEIPZIG, *December 1st,* 1842.

. . . . We had a wonderfully good performance of your *Weihe der Töne* in the *Gewandhaus,* the other day. It is a favourite Symphony with our audiences here, and you yourself would have been delighted. The effect of such music in a Concert-room, well built, well furnished, and well lighted, is quite different to that which is produced in such a place as the Theatre at Cassel, poorly decorated, and very bad for hearing. The best performances, under conditions such as those, are like pictures unvarnished and unframed. Here, our wind-instrument players, though some are first-rate fellows, cut a poor figure as soloists, but the *ensemble* is very satisfactory, and the rhythmical *nuances* are as animated as those of good Quartet players. Some time ago, an amateur bequeathed 20,000 *thalers* for the building of a School of Music at Leipzig, and the King of Saxony, approving of the scheme, has confirmed the bequest. We are just now busy with the organization. It is to be on a less extensive scale than the *Conservatoire*, and to bear a different name. I am to be made Professor of Composition. Besides that, I have other duties before me in the coming year. I have failed to convince Härtel, that I am unfitted for the editorship of the *Musikalische Zeitung*, a post which he long ago wished me to occupy. If I say I don't care about it, they tell me what a good deed it will be, to champion such a cause, promising me, at the same time, any amount of assistance in my duties ; so there is no help for it, and I have had to give my consent, though I fail to see what use it will be. Fink's own writings filled two-thirds of the paper. I am not up to that, so the journal must depend, as it used to do, on the old contributors and correspondents; where am I to get a fresh lot ? Theodor Döhler, the pianoforte *virtuoso*, paid me a visit last week ; he is quite in the first rank. I like his shorter compositions best ; they are *virtuoso* music of the better kind now in vogue. His longer works are imperfectly developed ; there is no middle, no second part. One leaves the head and tail of a red herring on one's plate at dinner—it is the beginning and end, but it is not the fish after all. Nothing should be self-centred, except the bud ; it must expand to find its own nature, and to become the fruit. Mendelssohn played his D minor Concerto the other day ; that is a different thing alto-gether—his aims are far beyond those of the mere *virtuoso*. Even when he is most brilliant, the essence of the music is still there, the idea that he has at heart. It is the same with

II   O

your Violin Concertos, which, for these reasons, are far ahead
of all compositions of a similar class. It is true, that these
modern *virtuosi* play music, which one must be a pianist
to understand, even though one actually *sees* it played ; but
the same effects are repeated so constantly, that they get
wearisome. We had several interesting items at Schröder-
Devrient's Concert—amongst them, Mendelssohn's Overture
to *Ruy Blas*, and Scenes from *Rienzi*, conducted by Richard
Wagner himself. His music stretches and strains the intellect, without giving it any solid satisfaction ; at least, it is
so with me. To be sure, the effect of an entire opera cannot
be estimated by the performance of a few detached numbers,
but they are enough to show the style, and I dislike it. That
style is an unmusical style, which emphasizes every detail,
disuniting joy and sorrow, and seeking to express each by
different means. To put words to music in that way, is to
imitate a watchmaker, when, as he says, he "puts a watch
into oil," meaning thereby, that he tips each little spring
with it. But words should be put to music, as fishes are put
into water—out of the dry, disjunctive element of the understanding, into the fluid, accommodating element of emotion.
This is what the Italians do, and those artistic allies of theirs,
Mozart and Spohr, who will not take it unkindly of me, to
reckon them on that list. It is not only Donizetti and
Bellini that we must think of, when we say " the Italians " ;
it is Raphael, Leonardo, Titian—flowers of the most glorious
Spring time Art ever enjoyed.

4.

LEIPZIG, *February 6th*, **1843.**

DEAR AND HONOURED KAPELLMEISTER,—
    Berlioz's Concert came off yesterday. Listening
to such music as this, for a whole evening, rather upsets the
nerves, though his fantastic oddities, here and there, are
very *piquant* and interesting. Such originality is quite *sui
generis*, and it should be balanced by some sharp contrast ;
last night, a fragment by any other composer, even a bad

one, would have been refreshing. While criticising Berlioz, you must always credit him with the power of writing beautiful music, whenever he chooses, or whenever he has no restraint to hinder him, in the shape of a demon, who forbids the proper expansion of his thoughts in quiet beauty. We heard the Overture to *King Lear*, *Les Francs Juges*, and that fantastic Symphony, *Episode in the Life of an Artist;* then we had two Romances, sung in the commonplace French style, by a very beautiful girl, who helps him in his Concerts. David wound up with a Violin Solo. The orchestra was strengthened; it consisted of 24 violins, 5 basses, 7 cellos, and 6 violas, 4 drums and 4 additional drummers, as occasionally he doubles the parts; ophicleides, 4 horns, &c., of course, besides harp and piano. When one hears people discussing Berlioz, one is irritated into perpetual contradiction; such is my feeling at least. Some people exalt him to the skies, others think him a regular *charlatan*, and declare that anyone, with the same amount of impudence, could do as much. Both factions are wrong, in my judgment. While condemning the falsity of his aims, I think that anyone pretending to be a critic, cannot deny him a very fair amount of ability. He plays his huge instrument with great skill, and he is a perfect master of the effects he intends to produce, harsh and grotesque as they often undoubtedly are. I think him most at his ease, and much more charming, when the devil is loose; when he means to be charming, he fails. One would rather see Seydelman and Devrient as ruffians than as lovers. Compared to the Witches' Sabbath in yesterday's Symphony, Weber's Wolf's Glen is a cradle song; it wouldn't be a bad thing, to transfer that piece bodily to *Der Freischütz*. We heard Mendelssohn's *Erste Walpurgisnacht*—the words are Goethe's, you know,—at a Subscription Concert, a few days since. It is an earlier work, which he has re-arranged, altering, I believe, only the instrumentation; everything is original, everything beautiful. We have the Blocksberg too, and all the appurtenances,—screaming dissonances, and plenty of them,—but then there is method in the madness, besides an additional element, which is completely lacking in Berlioz. Berlioz sticks to the dissonance, Mendelssohn resolves it.

I think you will be greatly pleased with Mendelssohn's new Symphony. I wish I had been in better cue that evening, but we had had an overdose of music, and I can only bear a certain amount. Nevertheless, it appeared to me to be very fine. I always think Mendelssohn is at his grandest in choral music Beethoven's Ninth Symphony is to be performed at our next Concert. The chorus, made up of amateurs and pupils of the *Thomasschule*, is always strengthened on such occasions; but it is somewhat prejudicial to the orchestral effect, that the singing should stand in front of the orchestra, on the same platform. Your new Overture has been twice rehearsed; it went so well the second time, that it might have been given straight off in public. At the very first rehearsal, Mendelssohn had only to interrupt occasionally. We were, one and all, delighted with the music. It was a relief to get a new work, which tells its own story and nobody else's. Surely, such art as that should not be allowed to get quite out of fashion! Meantime, however, if orchestral music is to have a characteristic tendency, it must be so, whether we like it or not. Apart from the relative perfection of execution, it seems to me like *genre* painting, contrasted with historical. The former, however good in its way, stands naturally on a lower level, and can never rise to an equal elevation.

Our new School of Music is to be opened next April— not on the 1st; Mendelssohn thought that ominous! A good many candidates have already announced themselves. Of course, there are no end of conferences and preliminary arrangements, but it is much cry, little wool,—and a beginning must be made somehow.

5.

LEIPZIG, *February* 28*th*, 1843.

DEAR KAPELLMEISTER,—

I am fresh from a Concert, given by Parish Alvars, perhaps the greatest harp virtuoso living; but we left after Gade's Overture to *Ossian*, with which the Second Part opened. He cannot get beyond his instrument, which has too many inherent deficiencies to admit of very varied effects. The better a man shakes on the harp, the plainer it is, that he ought not to shake at all. Arpeggio chords, soft and *diminuendo*, are perhaps a distinctive feature of the harp, as opposed to the pianoforte. Compositions for the former, as compared with those for the latter, should be of a simpler kind—more like a palm than an oak-tree. But for those chords and that simplicity, the harp is at a disadvantage. Its very poverty consists in its rich and complicated mechanism, which, after all, only makes playing possible; as for playing finely, that is out of the question, and I do not wonder that so few make up their minds to learn the harp. Of course we must take into consideration, that it is the only one of all our modern instruments, which has a beautiful shape, and sets off the player, the only one that has nothing ugly nor mean about it. Our pinched style of dressing is out of keeping with it; an ideal costume would be more suitable. Cut off the pedals, and just as it is, you have a far more appropriate instrument for a Sarastro than the violin or the hautboy. Gade's Symphony is to be given at our next Concert. The Overture is very pretty— rather patchy though, and far from being a masterpiece, because it never reaches any climax. It is difficult to analyse the essential quality, which makes itself felt unconsciously in all first-rate work, but here the *want* of it is palpable enough. Take a copy of Bach's Fugues and Motets! On paper, they seem to move, from beginning to end, in a perpetual labyrinth of parts; but when you hear his music, and compare it with that of any other composer, the one is a glorious tree—the other, bush and briar, that never rises above the earth, that has breadth only and no height. A five-part Psalm by A. Romberg (a stock piece with the *Cäcilienverein*) was sung the other day, in the *Thomaskirche*, as a Motet. Pretty enough, from first to last, but by the side of those massive Motets of Bach, how miserably thin and ineffective! Next to nothing, in fact; and as to the Second Part, the Fugue, my remarks on the harp shake would be equally true here. A thing of shreds and patches, with no go about it, as dull to listen to, as it must have been to write. Now for the reverse of this! Last Sunday, I made them sing a brilliantly effective six-part

Motet by Giovanni Gabrieli. The *Thomaner* were in ecstasies.

Berlioz paid us a second visit, the other day, coming from Dresden. He conducted the Offertorium of a *Requiem*, a sort of instrumental Fugue in D minor, slow time, in which the Chorus has nothing to do but to sing a and b in unison, thus :—

This is repeated a hundred times, over and over again, after pauses which are longer or shorter, for no definite reason, but just as the harmony allows of it ; at last we come to an harmonic Cadence in the major key, and the audience, after its long agony, is so relieved, that it really thinks it has been listening to a fine thing. But the Offertorium is very laboured, and intrinsically unmusical ; the effect is never truly religious, it is rather that of a procession of monks, passing across the stage. Sacred music in the theatre is of course an impossibility, for bare truth on the boards is no better than the live owl in *Der Freischütz*, or the Electoral Prince's tattoo in the *Wasserträger*. There is no danger of it in France anyhow, for they have never had any sacred music at all, take the expression as broadly as you please. So much of the real stuff as is to be found in Cherubini, he brought with him from Italy. Sacred music is the monopoly of the old Flemish, the Italian, and the German Schools.

6.

LEIPZIG, *November 3rd*, 1843.

DEAR AND HONOURED KAPELLMEISTER,—

. . . I was very much pleased with the Schubert Symphony (in C major), not as a finished work of Art, but because it is full of poetry. It is very long, and each part is spun out to a wearisome extent ; the close of the first movement is like a Finale, which I think very inappropriate, when there is still something to come. There is too much brass, from first to

last, and I daresay I could raise many other objections; but
when all is said and done, the work is far more interesting
than many others, the faults of which are less patent at first
hearing, though their orthodox mediocrity brings one to
despair in the long-run. Herr Hofrath Rochlitz has lately
forwarded to me the text of an Oratorio, *Saul and David*, with
a letter from you, in which you speak far too highly of my
abilities; but I have got out of the way of writing big things,
and I have no heart for attacking a work of such dimensions
now; I must get into harness by trying my hand at shorter
pieces first. Apart from this, I think your objection to the
Oratorio in question as correct as it is instructive. Speaking
generally, I have no liking for Choruses written only for men's
voices—it is not only doing violence to the nature of music, to
make men sing in four parts, it is a monotonous torturing of the
audience. Four-part music is for mixed voices. The ugliest
feature of the case is, that men should care to amuse themselves alone at their *Liedertafel*, with such a negation of
music. My chief complaint against the Oratorio is, that it is
laid out far too theatrically, and that, without scenery, it
would be absolutely unintelligible. As we see nothing in an
Oratorio, no scenery should be imagined for it; but that does
not imply, that the work should not be thought out in a
dramatic vein. Metastasio treats his characters in this
fashion, and yet we are not reminded of any fixed locality. I
like best such epic-lyrical works as *The Messiah*, *The Last
Judgment*, and *St. Paul*. I consider them best suited to the
needs of a composer, in so far as they minimise the temptation
to become theatrical. No doubt, severer claims are made on
the style of a modern writer than on that of his predecessors,
for in their case, to write an Air for an Oratorio or for an
Opera, was pretty much one and the same thing.

Hofrath Rochlitz is our near neighbour, and we have been
on very friendly terms, from the first. Next Saturday, we
sing as our Motet, a Latin Hymn for double Chorus by Gallus
(the German Hähnel), written in 1515, and my *Salve Regina*.
The four Prefects conduct the Motets, turn and turn about,
and I do not like to make any change, because it is an old
custom, but it provokes them to emulation, each one trying to

out-do his comrade, in the choice and execution of the music. Barring one Motet by Reichardt, I have not heard a bad thing yet, although there is not much music of this kind which is thoroughly enjoyable. I hope we shall soon venture on your Psalms; I was afraid to begin with them. The Chorus is firm as a rock in diatonics, with figures and *colorature ad libitum*, but in chromatic music, they are no better than their fellows. To sing chromatic passages in tune, presupposes a real education in music; something more than hitting the note is required; the singer must feel for himself the harmonic progressions. This, I learn, to my mortification, every time that I hear this passage in my *Salve Regina* :—

Mechanically, there seems to be nothing amiss, but when it comes to the performance, I am always in Purgatory. The sharpness does not lie in the vocal intonation, which is quite intelligible in these bars, and there are many other reasons to account for it. I had rather it should sound well than know the reason, why it does not sound well. But there is no justification for a composer, who makes a pianoforte accompaniment indispensable for the performance of choral music; and the old masters were far from wrong, in adhering to a very peremptory code of laws, to regulate such compositions as this. I am more ashamed of such a passage, than I should be of palpable octaves and fifths, which anyhow are no hindrance to pure intonation. I give the boys a good trouncing, but in my heart of hearts, I know that it is I who ought to be trounced. I heard Schumann's Symphony at our fifth Concert, and I am glad to know that you are going to be introduced to it. It never bores one for an instant. Freshness and life in every note; even though it be a little odd at times, it is always music—a Bettina, whom we would not choose for the mistress of a household, but who is as poetical as a fairy, and very suggestive and entertaining. . . . I saw *Czar und Zimmerman* the other day, one of our prettiest light operas; never commonplace, and a good specimen of that style. It is weakest in the sentimental passages, and those in which the composer aims at pathos; but the work is that of a dexterous artist, it sounds well, acts well, and impresses everyone most favourably. . . .

7.

Leipzig, February 16th, 1844.

People may talk and write volumes about music, without giving us any idea of it; real music defies description, and we must know the writer, before we can attach any importance to his praise or dispraise. . . .

Form varies considerably from time to time. Before the days of Beethoven, very indifferent geniuses were much more certain of their construction than far greater men have been since—just as, a hundred years earlier, a fellow who combined the trades of schoolmaster and organist, could write better Fugues than many a living conductor. They were the characteristic expression of the age, and the age deserves the credit rather than the individual. Formal skill is traceable, even in the Rococo Period of Architecture and of other arts, the cultivation of which was all the easier, as being solely the outcome of conventional tradition, rather than the spontaneous effort of poetical thought. As Goethe says: "It is easy to talk, when one has nothing to say." But when fresh emotions are experienced, and some outlet has to be found for them, poetry itself prevailing, and not the gift of cultivation, it is easy to see that the form of expression, artistically considered, can scarcely be so definite, so delicately finished, as that which appertains to a well-worn subject, and is already, to some extent, presupposed in the choice of it. This unfettered licence is, after all, only the want of artistic medium, and does not imply real freedom, though commonplace imitators take it for progress, because it suits them to consider themselves independent of laws, and to follow their inspirations "according to the will of God." As for the inconsequent crudities resulting from this, they are

about as much "according to the will of God," as it would be,
if apples and nuts were to grow on the same tree. The
practical artist, in every branch of Art, is he who is conscious
that his highest and best moments are those when he can
utter his thoughts in the simplest language, and connect
them together so as to form a whole, not when he is a prey to
abnormal fancies, depending merely on chance, and bearing
the same relation to ideas as accidents do to rational
necessity.

8.

1846.

. . . Gade's dramatic Cantata, *Comala*, was performed
here the other day. Ossian's words are admirably suited to
the genius of the composer. I doubt whether he is good for
anything much beyond sea-breezes ; as far as I am aware,
he never strikes any other chord, he can't keep away from
the seagulls. All his music is "An Echo from Ossian "—
not merely the Overture so-called. Snow-scenes, if well-
painted, and sea-pieces too, are ornaments to a picture
gallery ; why should not music, stamped with a Northern
nationality, hold its own among the other arts ? Everyone
has a good word for such graceful and sympathetic writing as
Gade's. But it is remarkable, that many a modern composer,
when writing vocal music, allows himself to be controlled by
the development of the subject in the text, although, if he
were writing for the orchestra, he would feel the need of
perfecting his work as an intelligible whole, apart from everything else, and would understand how to do so. To think
that this is not equally necessary in vocal music, is to mis-
understand the thing. The musical part of a poem is not
that which finds expression, when the words are expressed
successively, as in reading or declamation ; this only controls
the minor *nuances* of the music ; it is the complex emotional
result of the whole and its parts. . . . The poem has its
own formation, the music will have it too, only, in either case,

that formation must be organic. An eye, a hand, is something independently of the body, but to the body it is something, the actuality, the position of which can only be determined by reference to the whole. Musical phraseology, which is only connected with the whole by means of the first word and the last, has its root in the negation of music.

9.

LEIPZIG, *April 21st*, 1846.

. . . Jenny Lind has been here again lately, on her way to Vienna, where she must have arrived by this time. She was a little out of sorts, and not inclined to sing, but they persuaded her to give a Concert nevertheless. On the day following the public announcement, nearly every place was taken ; the receipts came to over 1,000 *thalers*. Nothing but pianoforte accompaniment; between the songs, Mendelssohn and David played. Except Viardot-Garcia, I never heard anyone sing with such execution and finish ; it is not sharply marked intellectual emotion, as with the French artist, but that deep, intense feeling peculiar to the North, which impresses me most in her. The poetry and brilliancy of Viardot give me the same sort of pleasure that I derive from the best pictures—say, those of Horace Vernet—in the Historical Gallery at Versailles. Her singing is artistic in the most definite sense of the word. Lind, though an equally faultless executant, works on her audience rather by means of sentiment, in the good sense of the word. On the same day that you gave Mozart's Requiem in Cassel, we had a performance of Cherubini's here. Written solely for chorus, and the grander for that reason, it is broadly and finely conceived, and you can see at a glance the main divisions of the work, as is always the case with Cherubini. One is never tempted to compare it with Mozart's, the opening of which is certainly quite a different thing, and, of course, you must never think of the details of Mozart, if you are to find satisfaction in any other setting of the same words. The opening of Cherubini's Requiem seems to me to be the weakest part of it, but it leads up to the majestic *Dies iræ* and *Domine Jesu*, which are gloriously effective. "A great work!" we say, when it is all over. Two or three styles are distinguishable in Mozart. It is so much a part of ourselves, that we would not have a single note changed; but it is hardly credible that the Requiem could have been put together, as it now is, all at one time. I suppose you have had a performance of David's *Desert*. He has been roughly handled by the Viennese critics. The public liked his music far better than that of Berlioz, who was there at the same time; but the papers praise Berlioz to the skies, over Beethoven's head, keeping David quite in the background. "Berlioz," they say, "has genius without talent—David, talent without genius." There would be a grain of truth in this, if genius without talent could pass muster—if the former depended more on invention, and the latter more on construction. But genius ought to show itself in construction as well as in invention. In this instance, the comparison lies rather between two sorts of talent—the poetical and the artistic. David lacks depth, but he has a graceful transparent way of writing music, and it is refreshing, now-a-days, to hear anything spontaneous, which has not been crammed and screwed up to the right point. . . . Wieland says somewhere, that when writing poetry, he used every effort to make it appear that he wrote without effort. I would specially commend his example to German operatic composers, who too often forget that the work at which they have been toiling for six months, is not to occupy more than from two to three hours in performance. Still less do they remember the exigencies of the stage, which make simplicity the one thing needful. Operatic music is to an operatic performance, what poetry is to a musical composition; both must be, to some extent, elastic. Reissiger's new opera has not yet been given in Dresden, because Flotow, the author of *Stradella*, had used the same libretto, and the directors think that his version is more likely to be successful. Of course, this must be very mortifying to a *Hofkapellmeister*—but Reissiger's operas have hitherto been of the ephemeral order, that are shelved for ever after the first performance. *Stradella* is given because it is practicable, and that is a matter of primary importance with the management. I think that *Stradella* and *Les Quatre Fils d'Aymon* are very like Auber in character, though inferior to his best operas. R. Wagner's Overture to *Tannhäuser* was given at a Concert here lately. Utterly hateful, inconceivably clumsy, long and tiresome! How could so clever a man have written it? Much as I should like to hear one of his operas, I cannot expect, from what I know already, that I should get any pleasure out of it. Wagner is no longer a young, inexperienced man, and the artistic vocation of anyone capable of writing and publishing an Overture like this, seems to me very doubtful. I thoroughly distrust a composer, who is the author of his own libretto. The idea seems to be all wrong, and I never yet found the result upset my convictions. It's a clumsy comparison; but it seems to me it is as if a man were to marry himself.

10.

LEIPZIG, *February 7th, 1847.*

DEAR KAPELLMEISTER,—

. . . Hiller has lent us Meyerbeer's Overture to *Struensee*, which you asked for. It is our first experiment with a large instrumental work of his; that fact alone makes it interesting to a musical audience. Besides, it is his vanity to be interesting at any cost. This is just like the rest of his compositions; you never lose sight of the composer for an instant.

I never heard Schneider's *Weltgericht* given in its entirety until last year, when Schneider conducted it in person, on the occasion of its twenty-fifth jubilee. I doubt if it will see another twenty-five years out; it is too hopelessly commonplace, and all those sham triumphs of Satan and Hell are only poetical untruths, no good at all, as meaningless as the flaxen-wigged imps in *Don Juan*, mere German Blocksberg furniture, of which Mozart and the Italian poets never dreamed. I am at a loss for *Passion Music*, as every year comes round; being a part of our Church Service, it must of necessity be taken from the Gospel narrative. In former days, Haydn's *Seven Words* and Graun's *Tod Jesu* used to be given, every alternate year. I cannot make up my mind to the latter, and do not wish to repeat the former, as it was given two years ago, so this year our choice has fallen on Astorga's *Stabat Mater.* The music is a little out of date, and here and there thin in quality, but the style is pure and the sentiment noble—pure gold by the side of Graun's tin-foil. I think that Schumann's Cantata, *Paradise and the Peri,* would be quite suitable for a larger performance, but the immediate printing of the work might be postponed to its advantage. The economy of the whole would have been made more effective by re-arrangement, though even as it stands, it is very delightful, when well performed. Schumann has thrown his whole heart into the work—too much of his heart, in fact ! . . .

11.

Leipzig, *June* 15*th,* 1848.

. . . I can well believe, that my political faith and confession of faith are hopelessly different from your own. I was partly in joke too, but that is not always so easy to see in writing. Nor have I anything to say against liberty, only I think the despotism of liberty is as uncomfortable as any other, and the stupidity that puffs itself is quite intolerable. This has nothing to do with the good cause itself—only with its adjuncts. . . .

The Commission of the Friedensclasse *pour le mérite* is awaking, none too soon, to a sense of its duties. I see by the newspapers, that you received your Order before the despatch of my last letter, which should have been congratulatory. Now, however, I wish you joy with all my heart. As the number of Orders is limited, I expect you will have Mendelssohn's; that is the only vacancy I have heard of lately. Who would have thought that he would enjoy his honours so short a time !

Rietz tells me, that the finished score of a Finale for his Opera of *Loreley* has been found, and that it is amongst the finest things he ever did. This, however, is the only completed number; a few sketches remain; that is all. Rietz has nothing to say in favour of the book, and I myself doubt, whether a slightly sentimental and essentially lyrical poet like Geibel, was the right man for a good dramatic libretto. It will be an everlasting source of regret to German Operagoers—like everything else that the Frankfurt Parliament has not had a hand in. When they are clear at last, as to the new strophe of Arndt's *Was ist des Deutschen Vaterland,* while they are all agog about Poetry and Music, I daresay they will see to it. Blum might speak well and to the point ; he has real knowledge of the subject, for he was our treasurer at the Leipzig Theatre, and no end of librettos passed through his hands. Please observe that I am only making bad jokes ; nothing serious is intended. But seriously, the row in Frankfurt about that strophe of Arndt's seemed to me very— German.

12.

. . . I am very glad to learn, that you are providing your Biography with musical *entr'actes,* particularly as the new Quartet forms the first. It is all in proper order—food and drink, sermon and singing. We have had some very interesting performances of Mendelssohn's posthumous works, in the *Gewandhaus.* First, the music to Racine's *Athalie,* which was repeated ; then, the *Lauda Zion,* written in 1846 for a Church Festival at Liège. Both are admirable works, dignified and full of style, each just what it should be. I think that his later compositions are marked by greater evenness and simplicity ; he is less self-assertive, and looks to the character of the music rather than to his own personality. Pray let me recommend you this *Lauda Zion,* as well suited for the *Cäcilienverein,* if you do not know it already. But it must not be forgotten, that the work was meant exclusively for the Church, and if, as a Concert-piece, it lacks some qualities which are generally too evident in the common run of Church music, that is rather to its credit than otherwise.

Ernst, the violinist, was here lately; though his Concert was poorly attended, he played superbly, far better than at the Subscription Concert, which was crowded. On the former occasion, I thought him the very first of modern players, but I have often remarked, that you cannot depend on him; at one time he plays incomparably—at another, in very inferior style. . . .

13.

LEIPZIG, *October* 28*th*, 1850.

That excellent violinist and good fellow, Joachim, has left us; they have engaged him as *Concertmeister* at Weimar, and though the salary is not exceptionally brilliant, he is better off to this extent, that he has less orchestral duty than formerly, besides getting five months' leave every year. Here he held the post of second *Concertmeister*, and greatly lightened David's duties at the theatre; now, David will have to lead in every opera, and lately four or five operas have been given every week. Liszt has also decoyed away our best double-bass. I hear that he is very keen about the progress of music in Weimar, and that he is highly successful. . . .

November 9*th*, 1850.

It would be a very difficult matter to find a competent substitute for Joachim. I now consider him, in every respect, one of the first violinists, and as an out and out musician, there are few that can come near him.

14.

LEIPZIG, *February* 9*th*, 1853.

. . . We had a great Scena from *Lohengrin* at our Concert, the other day. I am glad these experiments are being made; instead of hearing angry criticism and indiscriminate praise, we can now hear the music, and judge for ourselves. Brendel alone is woe-begone over the death and burial of all the music that used to delight us, but let that be! The extreme Left of the Frankfurt Parliament swept away the nobility, and many another old-established institution; the nobility, however, is still to the front, and the Left has been swept away off the face of the earth, by its own unreasonableness. We want no *Neue Zeitung*, to tell us that form is not the one thing needful for Art, but it seems to ignore the fact that spirit alone will not do either. The Creator gives a form to each of his creatures—to reasoning man, the noblest of all. Who ever dreamed of any other economy? Painters and sculptors have exhausted their powers over a model which they dare not alter; if they do, we call it bad drawing—and those who can draw, never attempt it. Of course, hooped petticoats and perruques are not part of the human form, and it is often difficult to discern Nature in such disguises, but mere drapery, which may conceal a chair or a table, just as well as a human being, is still less artistic. Before he composed his Ninth Symphony, Beethoven had written a First and a Second, let alone the Sestet, *Adelaide*, the early Quartets, Sonatas, and I know not what besides, as an introduction. He had his period of happy, innocent childhood, his feelings of reverence for the works of his forefathers, and for all that humanity had found good. That is quite different from Philistinism: such a training is no sort of hindrance to original genius. Who is a more fervent worshipper of Mozart and Haydn than Cherubini? yet he became Cherubini, and you became Spohr; with all your individuality, you never lost touch with the men before you. That fact constitutes the legitimate title-deed of your existence. A man who begins on his own hook, ends on his own hook. Gluck says, that whilst engaged in writing an opera, his one object is to forget that he is a musician, and yet, whenever he is most successful, he isolates himself artistically. In his Preface to *Alcestis*, he expresses his surprise that people do not adopt his operas as models, and that music still goes on in the old groove. That is amateurish in him; where he is less self-conscious, he exercises a certain influence over other composers, though we cannot say that he founded a School. Wagner's aims, to some extent, resemble those of Gluck, and he is just as arrogant too. What can be more bumptious than that Preface to his friends, at the beginning of his three librettos—a work familiar to you, I daresay? That old pedant, the Abbé Vogler, was just as cock-sure of his own infallibility. I think a little modesty would be more becoming on the part of those who, indifferent as they profess to be about composing independent, or as they term it, *absolute* music, have yet to prove that they can do so. Did Raphael, when at work, try to forget that he was a painter? As if we could forget what we were! We can only forget what we have been taught superficially; rational cultivation cannot be forgotten, it is a part of ourselves.

We have had three performances of *Tannhäuser.* I grant you they applauded loudly, but it was not the clapping of an audience that had quite made up its mind. Time alone will show the reality or the sham. Many years ago, I heard the opera given very finely in Dresden, and I was present at the first performance here; on neither occasion did I leave the theatre in that calm and happy frame of mind, which should be the result of a good work of art. The composer has toiled for months over this opera—we have to hear it all in three hours; he had days of repose in between—we have not a single moment; such a strain as that can only produce exhaustion, more especially as the whole work has none of the ordinary divisions that we are accustomed to in dramatic music. The Pilgrims' Chorus, which occurs again and again, might have served to indicate repose, but even here, melody and harmony are tortured, and the chorus made to sing out of tune. I suppose this is the apt expression of contrition on the part of the Pilgrims, but surely, from a poetical and artistic point of view, it was a very fitting opportunity for a peaceful episode. Even the song of the shepherd-boy, after the first passionate scene in the Venusberg, is only a melodious, or rather an unmelodious, curiosity; and how indecorous of that youngster, after dropping on his knees, when warned of the Pilgrims' procession, to fill up the pauses of the chorus with his tootling! The incessant use of the 4/4 Tempo in the declamatory passages of the Tournament of

Song bores me to death, and in the third Act, Tannhäuser's everlasting story, about the consequences of his journey to Rome, is not a happy thought, dramatically. *Musically*, I liked a good deal of the fragment of *Lohengrin* better than all *Tannhäuser* put together ; there are some splendidly effective choruses in it,—but they say that *Lohengrin*, as a whole, is also very tiresome. However, Wagner seems to mean business, we see the whole man in his music, and this we must respect, of course. The poetical element is certainly very remarkable, but there is no artistic element to lighten the wearisome burden of passion. We simply groan under a weight of bare realism and amorphous sound. There is something wrong somewhere, when a man comes away from a drama or an opera, feeling as if he had been beaten.

15.

LEIPZIG, *March 3rd*, 1853.

DEAR KAPELLMEISTER,—

I am venturing to send you a book on the Theory of Music, hoping that you will be so kind as to accept it, and let it take its place on your bookshelves. I shall not expect you to read it. It is by nature abstract, and happily for the world, your business is with the concrete, with the production of life—not with the investigation of those natural laws, by which it is inspired and governed. There are no hints for practical composition in my book ; it deals exclusively with the natural laws of formation. Indeed, it is to a Manual of Composition what Chemistry is to the art of cooking. Not that I mean to disparage the Cookery Book, far be it from me to do so ! When we sit down to table, we want something that tastes nice, and to that end a good receipt is worth much more than the accurate knowledge of every component part of each one of the chemical ingredients. The cook's own good taste will always be the best guarantee of success. Perhaps you may find time to glance at a page here and there, and Wolf might like to look at it. We often used to meet each other half-way, in the old days, when he was busy with the laws of Architecture, and I with those of Music.

16.

LEIPZIG, *March 3rd*, 1854.

DEAR KAPELLMEISTER,—

. . . I return you the Septet, with hearty thanks from all of us. It was given with the most signal success on Thursday, at our last Quartet party. Everyone was delighted with the performance. Moscheles was at the piano, and I do not think his rendering could be improved upon. The wind instruments were as good as could be, alike in *pianos* and *fortes*, and the violin and the cello left nothing to be desired. Pianists who think they can equal Moscheles, or beat him hollow, are in number as the sand of the sea. They look upon him as a superannuated old gentleman, very far behind the age, whom they are bound to respect, because in less *exigeant* days he once was famous, but that is all. They have no eyes to see what a true artist he is, what a real master of his craft! No raw material for him; he works it all up into gold. It is often said that you cannot see the wood for the trees, but our young pianists cannot see the trees for the wood. Yet every tree, every little leaf upon every tree, has its own organisation as part of the forest, as the condition of its existence. The player, like the composer, is bound to see that the parts are dead without the whole, and the whole without the parts. With the ordinary *virtuoso*, a shake is a shake—a mordent, a mordent. How different these things may be, occurring in different compositions, that artist alone can show, whose technical proficiency is made a means for the expression of truth, not for the display of execution. Judgment alone will not effect this, but judgment is necessary, and " He has no judgment at all," says Jean Paul, " who imagines that genius can exist without it."

17.

LEIPZIG, *January* 18*th*, 1855.

. . . Rubinstein, the Russian pianist, is here now, and they have been doing a Symphony of his, called *Ocean*, a Fantasia for Piano and Orchestra, and a Trio. Very effective, all three of them, and he was cheered to the echo. The Ocean heaved exceedingly (that's his nature, and it does not trouble him), the Fantasia heaved less, but at the same time it was less interesting; the Trio had no false pretences about it,—it was brilliant, easy to understand, pleasing to listen to. The man had swum ashore, you know, and was a different creature, dress clothes and all. On the whole, the worst of these compositions is, that they lose in substance what they gain in definiteness. When the mist disperses, the neighbourhood is not so lovely as we thought it was. Still, Rubinstein has very striking gifts, and he is a tremendous fellow at the piano; it would be no easy task to play his compositions after him.

I hope your Arrangement of Fiorillo's Studies will soon appear in print. I can quite imagine that you have had trouble enough with them. One need not be particular as to melody, but if a proper harmony is to be put to it, want of construction becomes apparent directly, and it takes the hand of a master to patch the garment together, without showing the seam.

18.

LEIPZIG, *March* 27*th*, 1855.

. . . Gade's *Erlkönigstochter* was produced at the Pension Concert yesterday. It is a dramatic ballad, *à la* Schumann, very graceful and flowery in its way, only I think its way is the wrong way. There is too much caprice about the thing; who's to know where it's epic, and ought to be sung by the Chorus, and where it's dramatic, and ought to be sung by the soloists? Such poems as these were never intended for music, and the best of them cannot be adapted to it.

An Opera of Moritz Hauser's is being rehearsed here, under his direction; it is to be given on the 26th. He has become an excellent musician, and is a clever fellow in every way—a really able artist, I think—very outspoken in his opinions, and not at all fond of the Music of the Future. An Operatic composer has a hard time of it just now, for he sits between two stools; half his audience won't have anything old, and the other half won't have anything new. It is like the two wives in the Eastern story; one couldn't bear her husband to have black hair, and the other detested white, and so they pulled his wig to pieces between them.

No; I cannot enjoy ——'s compositions. He is one of those young writers, who have had no happy, ideal infancy in Art, who begin straight away with *Paradise Lost*. They have no lovely recollections of the state of innocence, as Beethoven had, even in his latest and most despairing works—no echoes of "the loved one far away," and all that vanished blessedness. In exchange, we get nothing but dry vexation, *blasé* disgust with reality, and arrogant egotism that has, and can have, no sort of belief in itself, and yet would fain persuade itself and others, that it is somewhat. Where there is no tension, they think everything is slack and insignificant; as to Beauty, it is not so much as mentioned in their synagogues! *Sound*, that most beautiful of all media, which every other art might envy Music, is crushed and tortured at their hands, until it is reduced to mere screaming and whining, and so they give forth a sound which is no sound, and music which is not music, and compared with what we are expected to listen to now-a-days, all that appeared rough and harsh in the writings of earlier composers, seems as gentle as Heaven itself. . . .

19.

LEIPZIG, *April 5th,* 1855.

DEAR KAPELLMEISTER,—

. . . Your *Weihe der Töne* was performed at our last Concert. My delight in that fine work is an old story; it was enhanced the other day, when I saw the great effect produced by it upon a very crowded audience. After all the torturing I have endured at the hands of so many modern composers, your music is in very truth a *Consecration of Sound*— a fair mind in a fair body—rest after great restlessness ; we could not have wound up our Concerts better. The difference between real and unreal Art impresses this lesson on me— that as true freedom depends solely on the observance of law, so lawlessness is nothing but slavery and sorrow. A work of art, concentrated and perfect in itself, expresses the inexpressible much more clearly than one which caprice has put together anyhow, notwithstanding the multifarious aims of the latter. A composer who goes the whole length of his tether, who is always on the outside edge of what is admissible and comprehensible, exaggerating himself and striving to outbid his own nature, because he finds the whole world too narrow for him, such a man conveys to us nothing but a sensation of cramp, which, if his aims were in accordance with reason, would be impossible. The smallest whole is infinite, the largest heterogeneous mass is and remains painfully wanting in all that should content us. It is the work of a defective artist, wanting in accuracy and rational purpose ; the Spirit of Art says to him, as Antonio said to Tasso : " It is not my part to grant, what it was not your part to ask."

20.

Leipzig, *November 23rd*, 1857.

The news of your retirement affects us very much in the same way as it does you. At first we felt very regretful, then the reaction came, and now, when we recollect that you are free from all sorts of cares and worries, we can cordially join in the congratulations that you are receiving from your own family. You still remain the pillar of good music ; the Conductor's desk has nothing to do with that. . . .

I rather doubt your caring much about Rubinstein's *Ocean*, except for its unmistakable cleverness. . . . He writes with terrible facility ; though hardly of age yet, he has published over fifty works already, and has I know not how many more in his desk. His playing is of the rarest order—the execution as marvellous as it is beautiful. Add to this, that he is a man of tact, and easily accessible—*mens sana in corpore sano.*

Frau Lind Goldschmidt has been here lately—still the incomparably beautiful singer, still applauded to the echo. I daresay you will read in several newspapers legends of "fallen greatness," "a perfect wreck," &c. Believe me, she is as delightful as ever she was! We heard her this summer in Dresden, and thought her voice finer than before. As for her execution, Viardot's alone can be compared to it. Viardot dashes at her music still more recklessly than she does.

21.

LEIPZIG, *November 3rd,* 1858.

DEAR KAPELLMEISTER,—

An old Motet of mine, *How lovely are Thy Dwellings,* which I wrote at Alexanderbad, was repeated at our last week's Concert. Its popularity reminds me of Goethe's saying, " Miracle-working pictures are seldom good paintings." Not one-hundredth part of the praise lavished on this Motet has been bestowed on infinitely better things of mine. It starts with two soprano solos in thirds, and this puts people in a good temper to begin with. Yesterday, the *Euterpe,* the second Concert Society of Leipzig, gave a performance of *Elijah.* I was not present. To-morrow, on the anniversary of Mendelssohn's death, we perform Beethoven's *Eroica* and *Athalie;* E. Devrient is to do the declamatory part. I have heard this last work several times, and with real pleasure. It is far more suitable to the poem than modern music is to old Greek plays, such as *Antigone* and *Œdipus,* where the writer necessarily falls short of himself or else of the poet. I doubt if Mendelssohn would ever have assented to these arrangements, had they not been required *par ordre de Mufti.* The music to *A Midsummer Night's Dream,* barring the

Overture, was another royal command ; but in that instance, Mendelssohn addressed himself to the task with such sympathy, that we can only congratulate ourselves on the King's injunction. . . .

Will this interest you? The Physharmonica, with all its improvements, was found impracticable for rapid passages, the metal tongue not being made to vibrate so instantaneously as is requisite for short notes or roulades. So Kaufmann, of Dresden, has invented an instrument which he calls a Harmonium, and it is an excellent substitute in every way. On the pressure of the keys, one single little hammer strikes a clapper inaudibly, so as to let the current of air produce a note instantaneously. Dr. Pfeiffer has adopted this instrument for the use of his Choir in Alexanderbad ; it is very easily played, and is better suited for choral music than a small organ. . . .

22.

LEIPZIG, *April 4th*, 1859.

DEAR KAPELLMEISTER,—

Many happy returns of the day to you! That is the wish of all our hearts.

It has been my privilege to spend many happy days in your neighbourhood—a year in Gotha, six months in Vienna, twenty years in Cassel—but I daresay you yourself scarcely remember the music which made me love you even before that time—to wit, your first volume of songs, and an orchestral Overture in C minor. Franz and I got this last performed at a *Café*. I remember it as if it had happened yesterday. It was beautiful summer weather—I was only seventeen—no criticism stood in my way—and the inevitable desire to know how things are done, which must come later on, troubled me not. The music went straight to my heart, so that for days I walked about in a dream, thinking of nothing else. As for my architectural studies, they went to the dogs altogether ; in fact, it was this Overture that made me a musician instead of a builder. After that, Hermstedt came to Dresden ; he used to play your glorious clarinet music beautifully in those days.

He was a friend of ours, and a constant visitor at our house, and he it was who insisted that I should be sent to you at Gotha. I had some knowledge of thorough-bass, and had been studying composition for some time under Morlacchi, who was always dreadfully discontented and irritable, as was quite natural, seeing that he did not himself understand what he was trying to teach. I still possess some of the attempts which I made under his guidance; the harmony is incorrect, and the style is neither German nor Italian. The first efforts that I made with you are quite different; the harmony is according to rule, and they have some sort of form. That is all your doing; I had nothing to say to it. A certain instinct of correct writing I did possess, however, and the principle of it once grasped, even Morlacchi could have done me no real harm. Many smaller pieces, songs and so on, that I wrote whilst still at Gotha, just for my own pleasure, are correct in point of harmony, and more spontaneous. What Morlacchi, with all his ill-temper, could not accomplish, you showed me, with a few kind words and by your own example, at my first lesson. I suppose I began the violin too late, for I had had no regular instruction before I went to Gotha. I practised industriously for a good long time, and played best when I was at Pultava, with no one to hear me, except one of the Prince's officials. He was a very decent performer, and I had such a craving for sympathy, that I proposed duets with him. However, no duets were forthcoming, so I tried to write out two of yours, and as that was not very successful, although I knew them perfectly, I ended by writing two myself. That I was able to play them well, is a sign that I had made some progress, for they are dreadfully difficult; but it takes too much time and study in after life, to keep up even such technical proficiency as that which a man acquires when his first years are past, and so my violin was laid on the shelf, and I can only regret, that I did not give the tenth part of the time I wasted over it to the piano. But I never had perseverance enough for that. When I was still at Gotha, I used to have pianoforte lessons from a bad violinist called Pitscher, or some such name; but when he wanted me to learn Mozart's Sonatas to his accompaniment, I know it always ended in my taking the violin and letting him play the piano. So perhaps it's no wonder, that I did not make much way with the instrument !

I ought to have told you about the *Gewandhaus* Concerts, for we had a good deal that was both new and interesting, and here have I been maundering on about old times ! I hope to make amends in my next. I wanted especially to tell you about Schumann's music to *Manfred*, which was given twice, to the great satisfaction of everybody. On Good Friday, we do the *St. Matthew Passion* again. Farewell. Our kindest greetings to you and yours !

Yours, with unalterable affection,
M. HAUPTMANN.

23.*

LEIPZIG, *March 15th*, 1857.

DEAR HERR BAGGE,—

I am very grateful to you for your article about the Motets and Hymns. It is, I fear, only too complimentary, and people who are not inclined to view them with such partiality will be disappointed. However, it is worth a great deal to me, to know that you like them, and that your *Verein* enjoys singing them. I have also set three of Oser's poems to orchestral accompaniment, for use in Church, but they have never yet been performed. Quite unintentionally on my part, they turned out rather differently, and I really do not know how they would sound in a Church, nor whether they are suitable to it. It is always the character of the poem that gives the tone and style of the music—at least, I find it so. Italian words suggest Italian music ; Latin words, Latin music, and so on. The Lap language I have never yet attempted. Oser's songs are very subjective and emotional, and this feeling has tinctured the work; but they lack the exaltation of the Psalms and the older Hymns of the Church, and that is one reason, amongst others, why the style of the music is not very elevated. . . .

---

* Letters 23 and 24 are addressed to Selmar Bagge, violoncellist, composer, and Head of the School of Music at Bâsle. He was the Editor of the *Deutsche Musikzeitung* and the *Leipziger allgemeine Musik.*

Where there is no repose, Art itself is wanting. " It is the
feeling for weights and measures, that makes men of us," says
Goethe, à propos of a villa belonging to the mad Prince
Pallagonia of Palermo, the architecture of which is purely
capricious, and in direct contradiction to every natural law.
In his eyes, whatever was straight was crooked, and vice versâ.
But there is only one straight line, and that is the same
everywhere to *human understanding*. Even the crooked line,
vague and unintelligible in itself, is only to be understood by
reference to it. The Greek tragedians stood in need of a
Chorus, to represent rational reflectiveness as opposed to
passion—ἦθος as opposed to πάθος—but great and lofty as their
poems are, there is something yet higher and truer to Art in
the idea of a medium which no longer requires such a contrast
as that between the Chorus and the *dramatis personæ*, to
make the " weights and measures " felt in the very essence of
passion. If Music, in her most passionate mood, keeps even
time, there is no necessity to beat time audibly, for even
inaudibly and invisibly, it is the regulator of that which has no
rules—the ἦθος of the πάθος—which is necessary to make passion
dignified and enjoyable, because it is not torture and agony in
themselves, but the conquest of torture and agony, which is
really beneficial to us. But very few people understand what
is meant by Form, most of them confuse it with Modelling.
Modelling is the rule, Form is " the law in obedience to which
the rose blossoms "; the former is only right in individual
cases, the latter is right in every case, for it is Truth itself, by
virtue of which every individual case has its reality, and that
can never be Philistine. The very worst Philistines are those
who do not understand its nature, who try to deny that there
is any necessity for it. There is another thing to be said for
Form, though this also is liable to be misunderstood. It is
the morality of the sensuous subject. Morality does not
exclude sensuousness, it includes it, compelling it to adopt a
human instead of a bestial mode of expression. No one
attempts to say that immoral expression is beautiful artistically, and yet, how much of it there is in the impassioned
agony of modern music, and how painfully the effect makes
itself felt ! If the composer himself could not carry his

burden without staggering, it is impossible tha his audience should do so. He is not an artist, he has no notion of *the meaning of Art*, although he may possess the gift of *poetry*. Poetically, a man is passive—artistically, he is active. Poetry is not a merit, but a gift.

24.

LEIPZIG, *February* 11*th*, 1860.

. . . Your Choral Unions seem to be getting on capitally. They fill up a decided gap among the Musical Societies of Vienna. It is not to be wondered at, that some hundred amateur singers should come together in such a large town ; the only wonder is, that they did not do so before. In Protestant countries, where the congregation sings in church, however artistically, people who are not musicians acquire a certain proficiency, which they have no means of acquiring in a Catholic country, where they only hear the music from the other end of the Cathedral, and take no part in it themselves. There will never be any amateur Choral Societies in Italy. To speak the truth, the Italians are not thoroughly musical. The people sing abominably. They have some sense of melody, but none whatever of polyphony ; you never hear them singing in parts. The Southerner is too happy out in the sun, amongst the flowers, to care about sounding the depths of harmony. He keeps to the surface of melody, and only asks for a firm foundation of bass, on which to stand. He troubles himself mighty little as to what comes between the bass and the soprano, that is thorough-bass, harmonic padding. Of course, the *Tu es Petrus* of Scarlatti, and a thousand other great examples, full of the purest and most exquisite polyphony, may be cited against me, and I am quite ready to confess, that they are dearer to me than my own abstract opinion.

25.*

LEIPZIG, *March 18th,* 1851.

DEAR FERDINAND,—

. . . I am glad to hear that you are working at composition. Do try to be plain, and keep to the old rules as far as possible! What is good is not necessarily peculiar nor out of the way; the right way never has changed. I think that the affectation of differing from others is as bad artistically, as it is morally. If you know, directly you hear a piece of music, that it is by So and So, I call that inherent weakness rather than strength. But if you know, directly you hear it, that it *sounds* as if it were witten by So and So, the case is hopeless. Your own weakness may be pardonable, but it is unpardonable to imitate the weakness of another, and then set up for being original. The kindest criticism we can pass upon such work as that is, that it is altogether superfluous. No master is entirely free from mannerism, but that mannerism is never thoroughly evident, until imitators have made it so, for they can imitate that and nothing else. Each, according to his measure, has his share in what is good and in what is open to all, but let him beware of trying to appropriate more than belongs to him! Imitate the great men in this alone; *be yourself.* There is no plagiarism in that; it is common property, like air and light.

26.

LEIPZIG, *January 13th,* 1855.

DEAR FERDINAND, DEAR BRENNUNG, DEAR PROFESSOR,—

When I think of the bright, clever, hardworking boy who came to us straight from Brotterode, I feel a little difficulty in addressing the well-to-do Professor at the Cologne *Conservatoire.* Do you remember, how you played a Fantasia

---

* Letters 25 and 26 are addressed to Ferdinand Brennung, a pupil of Mendelssohn and Hauptmann, and subsequently one of the first organists of Germany.

of Thalberg's, with lots of pedal and wrong notes, and began
all over again, like a child who has ridden bare-back by
himself, and then has to go through the riding-school ? Well,
we have both grown older since then—older by the same
number of days, though not in the same proportion, for you
clearly have the best of it there ! In spite of that, I mean to
stick to the old *Du* and the *Ferdinand* I used to know. The
children get through one birthday after another, and will soon
be children no longer. You would hardly know Louis, who is
ten years old now, and you certainly could not recognise the
little fellow, who is going on for six, and is a regular duck.
Helene too has grown very much. . . .

27.*

LEIPZIG, *May 17th*, 1854.
DEAR HERR HILLE,—

I expect you have been waiting some days for my
letter of advice that you should go to Italy, but I had
much to do that I could not put off, and to-day is
my first opportunity of writing. In the enclosure, I have
made a great point of your going to Rome instead of Milan,
for there I have a special object in my mind's eye,—the
Sixtine Choir, which, whatever may be said against it, will
always take rank as a sort of classic. Compared to it, the
Choir at Milan is as a Düsseldorf painting by the side of a
Raphael, which though weather-stained, spoilt by incense,
and restored, will always be to a fresh, newly varnished
picture, what pure gold is to gilt, or the artificial to the
natural. Musicians would stone me to death, if they knew
that I exalted the Choir of the Sixtine over that of Milan—a
few old singers over a lot of vigorous lads in a high state
of discipline, at the beck and call of their drill-serjeant.
But I still stick to my opinion, even though it seems that the
present state of things is not thoroughly satisfactory ; twenty
years ago, indeed, a good deal wanted altering—but that does

---

* The following letters are addressed to Eduard Hille, an intimate friend of
Hauptmann's.

not hurt the idea, the soul of the thing. Old age has nothing of the elasticity of youth. The aged Goethe is not the youthful Goethe, but he is Goethe still, sound in mind in spite of the infirmities of age, more powerful, and worth more to mankind than a hundred thousand of young Germany, crescendo-ing into *Weltschmerz* pianissimo. I trust that your hopes of visiting Italy will be realised, but don't stop short at Lombardy ; that is not Italy, you get her first at Bologna and Florence. Rome naturally follows, and you can make an excursion to Naples. I don't insist upon Sicily as a *sine quâ non*, because I never was there ; but you must visit Pæstum, if only to get a notion of what the ancient Doric workmen could do. Herculaneun and Pompeii, of course— although they have no direct influence on the study of Protestant Church Music ! Vitruvius says that an architect must number Music amongst his other accomplishments. I daresay, by-and-bye, they will require a musician to study Architecture. In fact, I might as well have let fall this suggestion, so as to attack the authorities on all sides, and make them see that they are bound, at all hazards, to send you to Italy.

28.

LEIPZIG, *May* 24*th*, 1855.

DEAR HERR HILLE,—

Apart from the fact that your letters are always a great pleasure to me, I am especially glad of the last one, because it compels me to answer the one before. There is a fatal sort of multiplication about the neglect of duty. One week goes by, and then another—as I have not written for a fortnight, I think I may just as well not write for another fortnight—as I didn't write this month, why, a month later will make no difference, and so on. It is just like metrical evolution—or the feeling one has about the divisions and periods of life. A child of a year old repeats the whole number of his days before he is two, but it takes two years to repeat them before he is four, and four years to repeat them

before he is eight. The single year becomes less and less as
he goes on. What an epoch in a child's life are the first
cherries of the season! What a joy are the first three strawberries! Now, when cherries come in again, I feel as if I had
eaten cherries yesterday. Very well! Buy the first cherries,
and peas, and strawberries for the children, and think what
they were to you when you were a child, not what they are
now you are old!

> "How cherries and berries taste,
> Children and sparrows know best,"

says Goethe. It is just the same with other and more
important things. "In youth there's no truth," says the pro-
verb; but youth does not need it. The young enjoy themselves unconditionally, not indirectly—on condition—by
comparison—after mature reflection—as we do. Of course
our enjoyment is more intellectual, less material, and we are
bound to arrive at that stage, if we are ever to become men;
but nevertheless, we should be careful to respect the spirit
which makes the common people enjoy a ballad, when they
neither know nor care, whether it is a good composition. For
him who likes it, it *is* a good one. I have strained the privileges
of a letter-writer to bursting, with all this chatter about correspondence, multiplication, cherries and berries, sparrows, age,
youth, and *Volkslieder*. It may be lawful in the epistolary style,
that the end should have nothing on earth to do with the beginning, and that one sentence should be connected with the other,
simply and solely because the last word happened to suggest
it; but I am afraid I have gone too far. If I were inclined to
be malicious, I might claim forgiveness on the score of your
enthusiasm for Wagner, who very often connects his musical
phrases, or bits of phrases, only by means of the last word,
and when acting strictly in accordance with his own principles, without the beneficent though involuntary interference
of Nature, accentuates every word individually. You hear the
words "Joy" and "Sorrow," for instance, and one is joyful
quite by itself, and the other is sorrowful quite by itself, but the
music is neither joyful, nor sorrowful, nor musical. I cannot
think such cherries as these will retain their flavour. . . .

II   Q

The imitators of Mozart were but few in number, compared with those of Berlioz, Liszt, and Wagner, whose name is Legion already, and who are increasing every day. Mozart's originality is not external; outwardly, there is no great difference between him and his contemporaries. An educated man, a distinguished man above all, cares little about distinctions of dress and deportment. His originality consists in this—that he has himself felt all that he says he feels, and does not reflect the feelings of somebody else. Goethe represents merely the experience of his own heart; there is no need for him to employ fancy, as other poets do,—even Schiller, who disfigured his earlier works with hollow, bombastic, or sentimental phrases, that have no root in the heart. But this personal experience is shaded with such delicate subjectivity, is so intimately connected with the whole poem, that it is quite impossible to detach it from the rest, to pick it out and imitate it. You must be nothing less than Mozart, nothing less than Goethe, if you want to write as Mozart or as Goethe wrote. True, Goethe has had his imitators, and their day is only just over; but they imitated only his mannerisms, and, for the most part, his later mannerisms. The very greatest men are not free from a certain taint of this kind. Mozart has it less than anyone else. But the latest examples of originality are all mannerism; their authors behave as no poor child of man ever behaved before, they are singular everywhere and in everything, they hold that truth is synonymous with novelty, they want to deliver us from our freedom, because their own mock-artistic nature makes them feel it to be a bond. They want to make us a generous present of their own fettered, slavish personality in exchange for it,—*i.e.*, a miserable unit, instead of the divinely human Spirit of the Universe, as it has expressed itself throughout all time, by the inspired lips of inspired mortals,—intelligibly to all men, not above the comprehension of the lowest, nor below that of the highest. They are all mannerism, and it is easy enough to imitate them; all peculiarity is mannerism, savouring of the nature of the Philistines. Flesh-tints are made up of an indistinguishable combination or blending of yellow, blue, and red, and anyone whom *le bon Dieu* had left unfinished, would have no small difficulty in colouring himself right—at least, it is the great problem of the greatest painters, and few even of those succeed. It is an easier matter with a parrot or a thistle-finch, whose various colours are prettily divided, but as Man, though he has two legs like a bird, is rather too big and owns no feathers, it might not be so easy to turn him into that kind of creature. However, he might produce a striking resemblance between himself and a baboon with a red and blue snout, if he handled the brushes properly.

I am so glad you are fond of our dear old Spohr. I don't call him old, because he is over 70 (for really he does not look it), but because he has always been just the same, and will be, as long as he lives. Not that I care much for his *Irdisches und Göttliches*. It is a weakling, born out of due time, and not to be compared with *Die Weihe der Töne*. . . Objectivity indeed is not his strong point. I love him best in his purely lyrical moments, when he lets himself go, and does not attempt to produce anything except his own soul. Of course a decided character will express itself everywhere, and therefore you ought not to hear too many works of his, one after the other ; a single work that lasts three hours—yes ; but three hours of Spohr *miscellanea*—no thank you ! (There are very few indeed who could stand that test.) His compositions have a very definite status in the musical world. Much of his harmony has become common property—like Cherubini's—and people use it, without so much as knowing it is Spohr's. Even Schumann in his later period, in *Paradise and The Peri*, for instance, acts Spohr now and then, to the mutual satisfaction of himself and his audience.

An Opera by young Hauser, the son of the Director of the Munich Conservatoire, was brought out here, a short time since. It contains many beautiful things, and the music is good music throughout—and yet it does not hold its own. There is too much repetition in the text, and cutting out is no good ; but I hope he will not let himself be discouraged. There was great applause the first night, and he was called three times before the curtain ; but the second time, when it was given for the so-called *benefit* of the composer, the Theatre was almost empty. My poor fellow-countrymen !

For six months or a whole year they are all fire and flame, as
busy as they can be, happy in the completion of their work.
Then begins the weary fight to get it performed, which may
last for years.   After that, it is given two or three times—
and there's an end of the fun for ever!   Nothing daunted,
they will set off writing new music to the first bad libretto
they can get hold of, the very next day.   I think it's the
Talmud, which says the happiest thing is, never to have been
born.   Who they are, that enjoy this happiness, I don't know.
But the kindest wish one could frame on behalf of most
German Operas, would be, that they should never see the
light; then the composer would keep his happiness in the
making of them, undisturbed, and live in hope for the rest
of his days.

29.*

LEIPZIG, *October* 20*th*, 1861.

MY HONOURED FRIEND !

Accept, first of all, my hearty thanks, for so
kindly remembering the twenty-fifth anniversary of my accession to office !   One ought really to be allowed to anticipate
such celebrations, during one's earlier years, for when age
sets in, they are a useless tax on the vital powers.   I never
would throw a stone at certain people, like Goethe and others,
who are accountable to the world for their self-preservation,
because, on such occasions, they preferred to absent themselves.   Commonplace people like us cannot take these
liberties ; we must grin and bear it.

I return you the Mass, which I have not been able to hear,
for I am not always up to my duty now, and am unable to
attend every rehearsal.   But I am anxious about returning
your MS. at once, for you may have no second copy; if ever
I am able to get about again, I shall take the liberty of asking
you for it once more.   The Mass will sound very well in
Church ; unlike most of our modern things, of which the
Sixtine Choir would say : *Non è roba da cantarsi,* it is written

---

* This letter is addressed to Ferdinand Hiller.

in the genuine style of vocal music, good for all time. But
the blame is invariably to be laid on the composer, if the
music does not go—and the keeping out of what has no
business there, often helps the effect more than anything
else. The most difficult are not the most effective
passages, even when painful practice has made them easy.
It is the innate difficulty of the music, which constitutes its
unnaturalness. A light hand is of supreme importance to the
artist, and it is honourable to their intelligence, that Germans
use the word " playing," when they talk of Art. Playfulness
is one thing, childishness is another ; the main object should
be, to make difficulties easy. I hope you will have the Mass
printed ; there are plenty of Choruses in existence, but not
much choral music so good as this. *Au revoir* then to the
Mass, for which I thank you most heartily. My people
join me in kindest regards.

Yours, very sincerely,

H.

30.*

LEIPZIG, *February* 23rd, 1853.

HONOURED SIR,—

I must beg you to excuse my long delay in
answering your kind and confidential letter. . . . Even
now, I cannot pretend to say that I know your opera through
and through, though I have attentively studied some of the most
important numbers, and taken a general survey of the construction. I wish I had had the libretto as well. . . . You
have a real talent for technique, and it is easy to you, to clothe
your thoughts in music, and to understand musical situations.
I have no fault to find with your harmony and melody ; you
understand metre, and the development of musical ideas. All
this may seem unimportant from a modern point of view, but
I am of a different opinion. . . . I have seen some of your

---

* F. v. Holstein, to whom these letters are addressed, was born at Brunswick,
February 26th, 1826. He had served as an officer in the Schleswig-Holstein
Campaign, before he entered the Leipzig Conservatoire. His musical reputation
is founded on two Operas, *Der Haideschacht* and *Der Erbe von Morley*

earlier songs, which gave promise of the vein of poetry that characterises your opera; your method of expression, however, was more *naïf* and direct in the songs. I observe that in form and phraseology you adopt the more modern style of German-French-Italian Opera, which, as far as we are concerned, generally fails to hold its own. However little unconditional sympathy I may have with the most modern aspirants of this class—I mean those who allow poetical to supersede artistic feeling—yet, to my thinking, the days of regeneration are at hand. Conventional phrases and turns of speech have lost all their charm and freshness—so much so, that many a German opera, well conceived and well written, passes away without leaving a trace behind it. . . . Of Marschner's numerous operas but two survive. Lindpaintner's are all dead; so are Reissiger's, and many, many others, though they were written by very good men. Only two out of Spohr's ten hold the stage. . . . I do not believe that Weber's *Freischütz* is so far above many other operas, dramatically or musically, as its far larger circle of admirers would lead us to suppose; but *Der Freischütz* was not the 100th Opera to the 99 before it, as so many others had been. Without aspiring to be anything new, the music was something new; it was quite fresh, and the form arose out of the nature of the subject, and was good, or at least tolerable, because it was not done to a pattern. Whatever form may be adapted for an opera, it should be a repetition of the idea started by Gluck. He, in his day, felt himself compelled to fall back on simplicity and originality, and by virtue of his genius he so far succeeded, that after the lapse of nearly a hundred years, his operas retain the essence of their former beauty, and are still listened to with delight. His music is ever new, because it never was modern, it was only true; truth is for ever new to us, the modern music of *every* age takes good care of that. I could wish that your opera too had less of the modern flavour about it, though I can say, with perfect sincerity, that I think there is real talent both in the conception and in the execution, and you have surprised and pleased me, by the ability with which you avail yourself of your technical resources. If your great love of music will not

allow you to find your vocation in any other employment, I
should be less inclined to dissuade you from it than I have
been, in many other cases, where honesty compelled me to
adopt this course. No doubt you have seriously considered
the sacrifice of your present position. It is not my place to
recommend you to consider it. But I heartily wish that your
new calling, should you decide to follow it, may prove a happy
one, not in that sense which the world counts happiness, but
in the sense of quiet self-satisfaction.

Yours, very sincerely,
M. HAUPTMANN.

31.

LEIPZIG, April 1st, 1853.

HONOURED SIR,—

. . . I am sorry you are coming to Leipzig at a time
when, with the exception of the Opera, there is nothing going
on. We exhaust our energies in the winter; but, of course,
you will have all the more leisure for study now. I shall think
myself happy, if I can be of any assistance to you, but I am not
fond of giving lessons, except in Harmony and Counterpoint,
and that is not Composition in the wider sense of the word.
. . . Repose is the great thing to cultivate. The want of it
has occasioned the failure of many a modern work, which was,
to all appearance, brilliantly successful, when heard for the
first time, but which afterwards faded away like a bouquet of
flowers, because it had no root. So far as I know your writings,
they show great natural appreciation of harmony and metre;
whether you know *why* it is that you write correctly, I have
yet to learn. If a perspective drawing be right, there is no
need to enquire, whether it was natural instinct, or theoretical
knowledge of perspective, that made it so. In certain cases,
however, the instinct of correctness may desert even the
cleverest writer, and then he must have recourse to the law,
and study rules. Perhaps, in this way, I might be useful to
you. As regards orchestral writing, and all practical matters,
you will find many a cleverer instructor. If you want to write

another opera, under safe guardianship, I should advise you to go to Spohr. You would not lose your individuality. He is not at all one-sided in his criticisms, and does not insist upon other people's music being all of it just like his own; for instance, he knows how to esteem what is good in Wagner—a man utterly opposed to him—though he does not overlook his failings. To work for a time under him would be most useful to any young musician, in the way of practical help. His theoretical knowledge is none of the profoundest, but he unites in himself many qualities which are only to be found singly elsewhere. Do just as you think best, only you must not expect to find here what you could get much better there. Of course, as I said before, I am ready to help you in any way that I can.

Yours, very sincerely indeed,

M. HAUPTMANN.

32.*

LEIPZIG, December 16th, 1855.

My dear and honoured Friend,—

I must congratulate you heartily on the first volume of your *Life of Mozart*, which is now almost complete. . . . No one could come up to you, in point of loving industry. It would be far easier to imitate the enthusiastic phrases of Oulibischeff, or the made-up anecdotes of Rochlitz. With you, one is always on firm ground, and your fidelity and industry make one take an interest, even in the discussion of things one knows very little about, of which there are plenty in this volume.

Everything in it is not meant for everybody; many a reader will skip. But that is no matter. The very fact that they can find in it the continuous development of culture up to the highest

---

* The following letters are addressed to Otto Jahn, author of *The Life of Mozart*, one of the most famous of German philologists, archæologists, and musical critics. He was dismissed from his Professorship of Archæology at Leipzig, on account of the part he had taken in the disturbances of 1848 and 1849, was subsequently made Professor at Bonn, and died at Göttingen in 1869. See *Paul's Lexicon.*

point, a point never reached before nor since, by reality nor the imagination, will make it an inestimable treasure to many. . . . Our modern artists, without exception, are amateurish in their ways of doing things. Who, now-a-days, could write such a work as Mozart's little Mass in C, for two hautboys, trumpets, and drums? Mendelssohn could not, Spohr could not, and this, not because it is by Mozart—for I am not alluding to its poetic quality—but simply because it is by a good workman of that time, and its construction is so natural, easy, and certain, that you could not alter a note of it, without spoiling the effect. It may be said in answer, that the cleverest of our composers have a certain *savoir faire*, which keeps them safe, and this is not to be despised; but if they have, it is rather an individual peculiarity, which no one else could betray, without being accused of plagiarism. Mozart, in his Mass in C, speaks not in his own voice, but in the vulgar tongue. The atmosphere in which we live, is scarcely favourable to a young composer, no one learns to write in a pure style; how, indeed, should he seek and find pure expression for thoughts which are in themselves unhealthy and impure? It is utterly untrue to Nature, to see a silly little boy struggling to reveal his infinite misery, when he ought to be able to express all that he can possibly feel at that age, by means of the chord of C and G major.

33.

Leipzig, *December 30th,* 1855.

My dear and honoured Friend,—

. . . I believe I have said before, that it is easier to think Beethoven a great genius, than Mozart. A letter I have just received from —— confirms me in this opinion, though he is speaking of Mozart as compared, not with Beethoven, but with Haydn. He has been hearing a Trio of Haydn's, and he declares that in its perfect *naïveté*, it surpasses everything that ever was written—even Mozart, having regard to his style alone. Haydn is freer and more various in his choice of forms than Mozart, who received his education in Italy, and was carefully looked after and trained in the way he should go, from his earliest years upwards. Haydn, I suppose, was more of a self-educated genius; he had models to copy, but no school-master to superintend and correct his exercises. The lofty genius of both men enabled one to achieve freedom in the midst of pedantry, and the other to create form, where no limits had been imposed. Both were equally great, but one could never have done the work of the other. Mozart could not have written *The Creation* and *The Seasons*, nor could Haydn have written *Don Juan* and *Figaro*. Compare the Arias of the two! The easy, vegetable style of Haydn is foreign to Mozart's nature. Stems, boughs, leaves, and blossoms are not his business. He goes in for the animal organisation, for creatures that have hands and feet—the unity of Greek architecture, not the manifold charms of Gothic—though, of course, he is no more lacking in charm than Haydn is lacking in unity. . . . If people think the step from *form to uniform* is a step forwards, it is a melancholy sign of the present condition of Art.

I am delighted to think, after the lesson you have given us in Mozart's perfect circle of perfect form, that you are about to enlighten us also concerning Beethoven. In his latest compositions, where he is quite himself, apart from anyone else, it cannot be denied, that he has scarcely succeeded in finding the right form for his overflow of poetry. We are not always excused that "process of fermentation," which it is your boast that Mozart never allows anyone to witness. But when, after a period of drought, genius, full of new wine, attempts to pour it into the old bottles, and they, though not yet broken, are all too narrow to hold it, the result is that the wine brims over and escapes. It is easy enough, to say that everything which is a fit subject for Art postulates its own form, as a condition of its existence ; but he is a mere *dilettante*, who thinks he has explained anything in that way, who finds it easy to believe that works of Art spring fully equipped from the head of the composer in all their perfection, just as he hears them in their finished state,—who lays it down that alteration implies defective genius, and that inspiration is always inevitably correct. The acme of perfection has been reached, when no trace of effort is perceptible, but it is impossible for anyone to reach this point without effort. Technique, and much more than technique, demands it; passion must be etherealised, lest it overwhelm us; sorrow must be handled in such a manner as to cause joy—not because we cannot sympathise with those who suffer, but because we contemplate a harmony by means of which all dissonance is, in the little universe of Art, resolved—as it is actually resolved in the great universe which we inhabit. The artist who torments, oppresses, and crushes us to bits, is not an artist at all, though he may fancy he has moved us more than any one of the classical masters. What do I care about his inconsolable agony? I would rather not look at it. I am like that honest Squire, who, seeing a lame beggar, dressed in rags, coming into the courtyard, called out to one of the servants: " John, just take a whip, and drive that fellow away! I don't like feeling so sorry for him."

M. H.

34.

LEIPZIG, *May 8th*, 1856.

. . . There is a great deal in your book about this precious future of ours, and much that affects the inner principles of its vitality or the reverse; but Gluck's flag still flies proudly, independent of all change. Your remarks upon the absurdity of comparing poetry and music with drawing and painting could not be improved upon. Thank Heaven, the good composers, from time immemorial, have had something better to do than to illuminate the contours of words! They are clumsy children, who have gone over the outlines with their brush, throwing such life into their text, that it is still a joy to us, even to this very day, though without the music, it would long since have gone the way of waste-paper. Shall we say that the Art of Music stands alone as an Art?* If I call to mind a fragment of *Don Juan* or *Figaro*, I remember not only the music, but the

---

* *Sonderkunst* was a term of Wagner's.

entire dramatic situation, the joys and sorrows allotted to
each person in the story—not according to the actual words,
which are often rather trivial than otherwise, but according to
the musical expression of them. The consequence is, that the
text of such a work can be translated without serious damage,
the opera remains the same ; but different music, set to the
same words, does make another opera, and here the parallel
with painting breaks down, for the same drawing, recoloured,
does not constitute another picture. By-the-bye, talking of
pictures, the fifth and concluding number of Richter's *Goethe
Album* appeared a few months since, though we were led to
expect a good many more. Take them for all in all, the illustrations, though charming, like everything else that Richter
does, are to my mind less satisfactory than his other works.
To be sure, Faust's Gretchen and Egmont's Clärchen are only
bourgeoises, but where shall we find an actress who satisfies us
in those parts ? I have never seen Gretchen yet; she is always
silly or affected, though many an actress succeeds with
characters equally natural. But there is always something
behind Goethe's naturalness, a symbolic ideal ; to represent
this on the stage is as difficult, nay, perhaps as impossible as
it is to reproduce it in a picture. Reading or thinking, I have
the poet and the poem before me ; if my vision extends farther,
the poem and whoever represents it. Goethe in person is no
nearer to me in a Theatre, if I may venture to say so ; all
that I have of him there is what he makes his characters say.
The more the character resembles that of the author himself,
the easier it is to reproduce. It is, of course, far easier to
represent Iphigenie than Gretchen, for in Gretchen he is
obliged to suppress much of his own individuality, which is
strongly marked in the original conception of that delightful
creature, Iphigenie.

It seems to me, that Richter fails to give any meaning
to the *naïf* figures of Goethe, fails to give any dignity to
those which belong to the first period of reflected poetry.
Hermann and Dorothea, characters essentially Goethean, are
very commonplace ; you might find them in any village.
No doubt, the artist is at a great disadvantage, for we
carry about with us definite ideals of Goethe's characters,

and as they are all different, no one is satisfied with any but his own. I allude more particularly to the really living *dramatis personæ*. I could put up with illustrations of the Second Part of *Faust* or *Die Classische Walpurgisnacht*, and they would not violently disturb my ideal—nay, I could stand Eugenie, with those personified abstractions of rank. The Second Part of *Faust* would be a good opportunity for Genelli, whose art is cold and abstract.

You are sure to have come across the advertisement of a scheme for the new Handel Society. Gervinus was the first to start it; he has followed it up with great earnestness, and is confident of success. He came here, before he went to Berlin to consult Dehn and Dr. Chrysander. Chrysander had been working for a complete edition of Handel; he was in London for a long time, getting materials. The work was to consist in all of sixty volumes, containing sacred, operatic, and chamber music. It was a much better plan than ours for the complete edition of Bach, for every year we have to consider what the next volume is to contain, and when we shall finish, Heaven only knows! Still, we are publishing a great deal of which the world knows nothing, and some of it is very fine. Did I tell you, that we have heard the whole of the B minor Mass? A Choral Society here set to work at it the other day,— with commendable perseverance too ; the result was a really good performance. Of course, a large band is impossible in a private house, but it was quite adequate. Unfortunately, I was too ill to attend a repetition of the work last week in the *Paulinerkirche*, but I hear it gave great satisfaction to a larger, though not a large, audience, who, I expect, heard the work in its entirety for the first time. Need I say, that when I heard it, I listened from beginning to end with the deepest interest? It lasts nearly three hours, and it contains the sublimest things, which no one but Bach could write ; neutralised, however, by long stretches of that dreary work-manship also peculiar to him, especially in the long-drawn, never-ending Solos. He certainly is very unequal, one dare not say in value (for even in the dullest passages every detail is full of artistic significance), but in poetic conception. We hear a great deal that we should not care to hear often, and again, much that defies criticism, the beauty of it lying not in the construction, but in the overwhelming effect upon the individual hearer, which anyone, even an ignoramus, must feel. The origin of this great Mass will ever remain a mystery. It could not have been designed for the Catholic service, for Sebastian Bach must have known perfectly well, that music which it takes three hours to perform, would be impossible in any church, and besides, there is no Offertorium nor Graduale. The inference is, that like Beethoven's Mass in D, which is also too long, it was written entirely to please himself; but how does this agree with the fact that it is a *pasticcio*, in which portions of the Cantatas are continually recurring? He sent the *Kyrie* and *Gloria* to Dresden, in order to get a title from the Electoral Prince; that was in 1733, and he was nominated Court Composer in 1736. Of course, not a note of the Mass has ever been given in Dresden; it was found too long for the service. The *Missa brevis* too, though very long, was found impracticable for the *Katholische Kirche*. The B minor Mass is equally impossible in the *Thomaskirche*, where the chief part of the musical service is performed after the Mass is over. Why then did he write it? The whole question is so hazy, that it makes the editor's task a very difficult one. Even as regards the notes, several alterations in the Dresden parts had to be made, when they were compared with the MSS. at Berlin. I have always thought that, before the Mass is published, one of us ought to go to Zürich, and try to see the Nägeli copy.

Yours most sincerely,

M. H.

35.

LEIPZIG, *September 15th*, 1856.

. . . One has an instinct in favour of Mozart, without in any way wishing to detract from the greatness of Gluck, who is as great as the highest artistic principles can make him—and this too, although much of Mozart's earlier work sounds more old-fashioned than the still earlier work of Gluck. Not being enough of an artist to move freely within the shackles of form, Gluck abandoned form altogether, the particular forms of his own age included. They did not fetter Mozart, he made them elastic ; they were no mere models, they were organically essential to Art, as he understood it. He was no revolutionary, he was not even a reformer ; he left a good deal just as he found it, only—though in externals his work may often belong to some perfectly definite period—it is a different thing, because his hand has touched it, and his spirit has leavened it.   People note the difference of form more than its total absence, but if they could only hear it thoroughly well rendered, even an *Idomeneo*, old-fashioned as the details might appear, would convince them of the beauty, spirit, and freedom which are compatible with the strictest regulations — the form enabling the music to bear its own weight, as it cannot do, when it is borne down with the materialism of chaotic emotion.   I have heard few of Gluck's operas, only *Armida, Iphigenia in Aulis,* and *Alcestis,* once each, and at long intervals of time.   They never completely satisfied me ; it seemed so often as if the composer intended to be true, but true to the words alone, in consequence of which he was false to the music.   Words break off suddenly ; you cannot break off music like that.   Music is always the vowel, of which words are the consonants, and here, as everywhere else, the accent ought to fall on the vowel, the principal, not the secondary sound.   However faithful to the words the music may be, we always listen to it for itself as well, and we ought to be able to do so.   .   .   .

M. H.

36.

Leipzig, *December 17th,* 1857.

Dear and Honoured Friend,—

.   .   .   Many people are afraid, that when you have finished your great work, you will have no inclination left to attack Beethoven.   But you really *must* write his Life, and I should

like you to give us Haydn's into the bargain, so that we might
have the beginning, the middle, and the end. It is not merely
because he happened to live after Haydn and before Beethoven,
that Mozart stands between them; his music makes the two
extremes possible—it is classically romantic. His Italian
education taught him to look to old established rules and
precedents (the latter merely conventional) for the construction
of his form, and therefore he is at times, and in the detail of
his work, more old-fashioned than Haydn. Haydn, Bach, and
Beethoven never were in Italy, nor at the Academy; they
grew up wild, like the trees of the forest, not in a nursery-
garden. They have no fashion at all, so that it is scarcely
possible for them to become old-fashioned. Handel is so, often
enough in his Arias.

Bach's *Gottes Zeit* was performed at the Euterpe Concert
yesterday. There is not a single conventional bar in it—
it is the very heart of the man. Of all the Cantatas
known to me, I can remember none which is so perfectly
expressive from a musical point of view, both as a whole and
in every detail; but if it were possible to blind ourselves to this
aspect of beauty, and to consider the whole thing, in
accordance with the laws of musical architecture, we should
find that it is a curious agglomeration of involved movements,
all higgledy-piggledy, promiscuously thrown together, just like
the chance phrases of the text, without any attempt at
grouping or central elevation. In most of Bach's Cantatas,
the central elevation occurs at the beginning, in the form of
a broad introductory chorus, a sort of steam-engine, dragging
after it a row of Recitative and Aria trucks, ending up with a
choral mail-coach. In *Gottes Zeit* even the first chorus does
not stand markedly by itself, it is always passing over into
something else. Compared with what has gone before, the
conclusion is very jubilant. An Academician, a member of the
Italian School, with a scheme of the whole and its parts in his
mind, could not possibly have admitted so much that was
accidental; but for all that, it is full of infinite beauty, and we
should be able to rejoice in both styles alike, in Raphael and
in Albrecht Dürer, as also in much that lies between the two
(not in Liszt's *Mazeppa*, for that lies outside). Nor did I much

enjoy Beethoven's great Quartet-Fugue, *tantôt libre*, *tantôt recherchée*. It was originally written as the concluding move-ment of the Quartet in B flat, Op. 136 (?), but Haslinger would not accept it, and made Beethoven compose another Finale—after which it was published separately. The combinations are forced and unnatural; it has a sort of " Do-what-I-want-or-else-I'll-eat-you-up " effect. Bits of it are quite horrible. I cannot help feeling amused, when people who know nothing about it pretend to be enchanted. To tell the truth, I think it disgusting,—though I should not say so, if they would only confess that they think the same. Here, as in so many other instances, it is a terrible thing for the great man's reputation, when fools pique themselves on understanding him.

M. HAUPTMANN.

37.

LEIPZIG, *June 6th*, 1860.

DEAR AND HONOURED FRIEND,—

Nearly five months have elapsed since I received your last letter, written when you had finished with Mozart. I am wrong, it is six months, for the letter is dated December 5th, 1859. That is pardonable enough in talking, but when it comes to writing, a man should look ahead before he starts, or take another sheet of paper, if he makes a mistake. Years and years ago, when I was learning English, there was a sentence in my phrase book, in case you wanted to talk about someone and could not recollect his name—" *How do you call him ?* " The phrase book was written by one Haardorf, a German, and my tutor, an Englishman born and bred, was sorely exercised in his mind at anybody presuming to talk of another without knowing his name. Was ever anything so preposterous ? He was a Mr. H. Subsequently, I had lessons from an Earl of Seymour, who also flew into a passion over this same ridiculous passage. How furious would these two Britons have been with my opening sentence ! After all, there is something in the way the whole nation insists upon collectedness and self-possession. One of my teachers was, I think, the youngest son of a Count, and the other quite a common sort of man. It is very unlike the German dressing-gown-and-slippers fashion of doing whatever is most comfortable at the moment. Each has its good points; I am only talking of the difference, which is also made prominent by the different education that turns out the precise German and the easy-going Englishman. The transition from extreme carelessness to extreme discretion may be seen in the same individual; Goethe's early letters ought to be read only in manuscript, his later ones only in print. . . . Your fourth volume is excellent from first to last, and the chapter about the *Requiem* could not be clearer nor more exhaustive. The *Sanctus* and *Benedictus* are charming movements, but I willingly believe they are not by Mozart; apart from the instrumentation, there are certain peculiarities which convince me of this. The same may be said of the Mass in B flat, which I am just now rehearsing for next Sunday; even if it had no clarinets, certain details would show that it is not by Mozart, and yet the tone of a great deal of it is absolutely Mozartian, and you cannot help wondering, how anyone else could have been so steeped in his spirit, especially as no other of his contemporaries ever tried to do anything like it. The fact that, only a little while ago, it was easy,—easier even than it is now,—to imitate Mendelssohn, Spohr, and Schumann, does not affect the question, for as they stamped themselves on every bar, their mannerisms were easy to catch. It is amusing to see our youngsters in the *Conservatoire* composing whole pieces, which are Mendelssohn from beginning to end, without so much as a suspicion that they are plagiarising. It is not a casual drop here and there, the whole bucket is drawn from Mendelssohn's well. They are like the caterpillars on the mignonette, just as green as the plant they feed on. Purity and health are the essence of Mozart, these must be qualities innate in the composer; you can catch an illness from anybody. . . .

I expect you have seen the two first numbers of Spohr's Biography; Oetke does the greater part of the editing. . . . It is funny that he should have made so many mistakes about his stay in Vienna; he must have written it out from memory, instead of keeping a journal. He will have it that I had an appointment there, which was not the case. I was in Vienna from April to August, 1813, and I met Spohr at Prague, when he was on his way to Gotha, to fetch his brother and the children. They were all going back to Frau Spohr at Vienna. Some time after his return thither, I wanted to go back to Dresden. He was averse to this, hoping that I should be appointed to the orchestra at the *Theater an der Wien*, where he was first violin (the *Kapellmeister* being a mere title). I had satisfied my examiners, and it seemed a likely thing enough, but when I heard that my election meant the dismissal of another really good player (Scholz by name), I declared that, grateful as I was to Spohr for his good will, I could not accept the appointment under such conditions. Though I never took my seat in the orchestra, the Theatre itself was, at that time, a great delight to me. I had followed Maria Weber from Prague to Vienna, and during his stay there, we lodged together at the *Fliegender Klöppel*, near the Kärnthner Thor. Weber had succeeded Wenzel Müller as State *Kapellmeister*, and he only stayed five weeks in Vienna, engaging instrumentalists for his orchestra. Spohr makes out that he was appointed straight away from Vienna, though at that time he knew as well as I, that it was not so. This is only one of his many slips of memory, and there may be more which have escaped me. But Malibran's romances in his Biography of Spohr, are much more diverting; for instance, his description of the rapturous reception of *Faust* in every theatre of Italy, and the account of Spohr's triumphal procession through that country. Why, Weber brought out *Faust* in Prague, and Spohr never heard a note of it till it was given in Frankfurt, four years later! They are going to publish some of his letters, which are written in the same plain, flowing style as the Biography. He always sticks to the matter in hand, the subject suggested by his correspondent; indeed he seldom wrote unless driven to it.

M. HAUPTMANN.

38.*

DEAR DIRECTOR,—

. . . The accompanying volume is full of my musical theories, in which you used to take an interest. I shall be greatly pleased if, on reading the book consecutively, you manage to make out the *rationale* of it ; an idea is far harder to express than mere thoughts. . . We have been so long accustomed to content ourselves with untheoretical theories, and to see the most beautiful things composed by persons who know next to nothing of rules, that it seems hardly necessary for the practical man to go any deeper. But Art has always been ahead of Science, and there is a time for everything. I should be sceptical about the productive power of a young composer, who laboured exclusively in the field of acoustics and the laws of metre. These are for others to find out. The poet ought not to study philosophy. At all events, he must, like Schiller, have a rich vein of poetry to fall back upon, if he is to do it without damage to his productive power.

39.†

LEIPZIG, *May 24th*, 1861.

. . . I do not think that the egotism of the latest style of emotional music can be favourable to sacred composition. However significant the *Graner Mass* may be, musically speaking, and whatever credit the composer may deserve in this respect, the very style of his writing makes him too self-important, as compared with the Almighty ; humility is conspicuous by its absence, and when it does occur, it is so very pretentious, that it exalts instead of abasing itself. In the room above my head, which is the Rehearsal Room of the

---

* This Letter is addressed to O. Kade, Director of the Grand Duke's Choir at Schwerin.

† This Letter is addressed to L. Köhler, composer, and founder of a School of Music at Königsberg.

Thomasschule, I can hear them practising a Prize Motet by Doles, Sebastian Bach's successor, for next Saturday. Bach, too, often displays the organist in his Motets, but the fundamental harmony underlying the display is always really sacred music, and awakens universal sympathy, no matter at what distance of time. The spirit of youth in Music is like a drop of dew in amber, no time can harden it. Mere imitation, on the other hand, easily becomes lifeless, however lively it may be to start with, and it betrays the age in which the imitator lived. The followers of Bach are more old-fashioned than their model. " First the Prince, at the head of his procession ; then, when the way is plain, the rest of the baggage ! " A sacred picture by Rubens may be a wonderful example of composition, drawing, and colouring, but it lacks the reality of feeling, which makes us overlook the inferior execution of all these things in a sacred picture by Albrecht Dürer. Not that I mean to compare Sebastian Bach with Albrecht Dürer—still less Doles, Homilius, Rolle, &c. (down to Schicht), with Rubens, who, at his worst, is always powerful ; but in Music as in Painting, it takes a man of an ecclesiastical turn of mind to work for the Church. There were particular prescriptions at one time, as to what might or might not be done in Church— *e.g.*, the chord of the added Sixth was not allowed, and so forth. If the religious feeling of the composer does not direct him to use the chord of the added Sixth, let him refrain by all means ! but the omission of it will not change secular into sacred music, any more than the occurrence of it, if suggested by a religious inspiration, will have the opposite effect. " It is not against my oath to drink wine, but if wine is against my oath, I will not taste it," says brother Martin in *Götz von Berlichingen*. In Church music, I would not, as a rule, give so much weight to the words of the text, as to allow them to influence the form, and thereby make it incoherent ; if the general colour of the music can be got to correspond with the words, its formal development need not be disturbed—for why should each new phrase constitute a new piece of music, and the whole sound like a conglomeration of fragments ? I should like vocal music to be intelligible, musically, on its own account. I wish every Song with

Words were, at the same time, a Song without them. I am well aware that my taste is exceedingly antiquated; now-a-days, people don't want music for music's sake, they want it for the sake of emphasizing words—but after all, this is not such a very high aim as to make me despise my own. " Woman is woman's highest title," says Logau, and as he esteemed womanliness above every other feminine distinction, so I cannot help thinking that music ought, in the first place, to be musical. It may be as characteristic as you like, notwithstanding. The human countenance expresses every emotion perfectly, without changing or transforming any of its component parts. Let the artist remember that he is mortal, and be content to work according to the laws of God and of Nature! He may alter, he cannot improve upon the method. . . .

M. HAUPTMANN.

40.

LEIPZIG, September 7th, 1862.

. . . As for what you say about hunting up specimens of old music, and particularly old spinet music, in our School Library here, I confess, with sorrow on my own account as well as on yours, that we are very poorly furnished in that respect. We have some interesting relics in odd nooks and corners, such as operas by Lulli and Rameau,—and Heaven only knows how they came there! but there is no regular series. Our collection was made hap-hazard, for in old times, as at present, the Cantor, I suppose, had to procure his own materials, and they became the property of his family, after his death. So we have nothing of Sebastian Bach but a defective series of forty-three sacred Cantatas, and these only in parts, not scored. All that he left remained in the family; Emanuel had the vocal, Friedemann the instrumental music. I myself procured everything else of his that we possess, except the six printed Motets, during the first years of my office here, in which I spared no expense, to get together a serviceable répertoire. The Cantatas of Bercht, Otto, and others, accumulated by my predecessor, whose library had been purchased, may be all very well in their way, but with a good orchestra at command, they are scarcely the thing. You cannot do better than consult Dörffel, if you want to know about ancient music; the musical department of the Town Library is his special province, and he will be delighted to tell you of any work that will be useful to you. Corelli's *Clavier Sonatas* are, so far as I know, nothing else but the violin pieces; I have not myself seen them, but I have heard that they were adapted for the clavier as well. With regard to the old Flemish compositions, I have never had a feeling that they are in the main harmonic. What distinguishes these from the more modern works, *i.e.*, Sebastian Bach, seems to me to be this—that in that old music, the chord of the Seventh—that decisive turning-point of Harmony—is entirely wanting,—that every dissonance is only suspension, which does not affect the inherent consonance of the whole, since it is external to it. Again, the Flemish works are in the main melodic combinations, and in the oldest of them, harmonic effects constitute their weak point, just as with us melodic effects in polyphony are usually weak; a feeling for chords is second nature to us, and, as it were, our starting point, while among the ancients, melodic combinations preceded harmony. Thus, as a general rule, four parts are enough for us; but the ancients would have as many melodies as possible sung simultaneously, and if there were few melodies, they thought an empty Fifth sufficient for the harmony; indeed, they considered it more satisfying without the Third, which appears to have had too much harmonic charm for them. I am glad you find Klengel's Canons suitable; they are very little known, I believe, and are a dead weight to the publisher. The critics, as a rule, do not esteem them highly. How foolish to talk of the *Temperirte Clavier* in the same breath with them! What can compare with Bach's Fugues? We want no reviewer to tell us that Klengel is not a Sebastian Bach; even if he were, the element of polyphony, which was Bach's breath of life, exists no longer, and it would be impossible for him to revive it. The cactus and the palm are quite different things in the open air and in the forcing-house, where the temperature must be artificially warmed, if they are to live. But that simile is hardly correct, for much of the music of the old school, though not of Sebastian Bach himself, is crystallisation. You do battle bravely and kindly for my *Harmonik und Metrik*. I care for it as Goethe cared for his *Farbenlehre*, and it has met with much the same sort of fate. A single appreciative word about this "Essay" gives me more pleasure than any amount of praise bestowed on my compositions. I should naturally have expected schoolmasters to take some notice of my book, but they are the very men who appear to be least concerned in the matter; on the contrary, it is the learners who take an interest in the work, and it is quoted in manuals of philosophy and æstheticism, though never in musical treatises, even if they profess to be theoretical. With all the science of our time, is there any branch so superficially taught as music? As if it could be treated merely as an abstraction—as if humanity and art were not dependent on one another! Even here, our educational books are loosely worded; one thing is never the consequence of another,—still less is everything the consequence of one thing,—as it must be in legitimate theory. . . .

Yours most sincerely,
M. HAUPTMANN.

41.

LEIPZIG, October 13th, 1867.

DEAR AND HONOURED SIR,—

I must send you a little word of gratitude for your kindly recollection of my jubilee on the 12th September. It is impossible to thank everyone, as I should like to, and cards are too mechanical for my taste. All I can do is to decimate my army of friends, after the fashion of a successful general who decorates every tenth soldier, or of an unsuccessful one, who reckons every tenth man dead. Even this is too impersonal for me, but there is something more human about it; one looks out the best letters—no very difficult task, when they stand in the front rank, as yours does—and down they go! I received far more compliments than I deserved, and my friends

have been only too good to me. May Heaven requite them
all! I am keeping some of the congratulations over for to-day,
my 75th anniversary. Many a man does not live to be so old,
many a man is younger at seventy-five than at seventeen—so
it's all one in the end! It takes thirty years to make a
generation. If a man has written *Don Juan*, or painted the
Sixtine Madonna, by the time he is thirty, he may die
content; what matters the larger figure? We should not
satisfy ourselves, if we lived to the age of Methuselah. Life
is never more than a beginning. . . .

42.*

Leipzig, *September 9th*, 1864.

. . . Melody, that is progression, is the Alpha and
Omega of music, and everything else is only in between. It
sounds too much like Bellini perhaps, but I see the good side
of it very distinctly, and sometimes you really feel more
comfortable with Bellini than with one of those grand people,
whose aims are so very high, and whose music is so very ugly.
Beauty is, for the moment, very much out of fashion; music
avoids her like poison. The passing moment is not enough
for beauty and melody; it is not music, it is a transitory
thing, caught and held fast that we may look at it; music
lays claim to the whole, the passing moment as well as what
comes after. Music in the guise of architecture, the permanent in the transitory—this is a very fine condition of
existence, and the only one that is charged with life. People
find fault with harpsichords and pianos, because the tone is
not sustained, but when you strike a note, and it becomes the
universe, dying away into that universe which we call nothing,
then you realise something which no other instrument, not
even the voice, conveys. It is something elemental, indefinite,
natural, and therefore inartistic. Ole Bull understood the
effect of it better than any one; he would make a long
Diminuendo, and then go on holding his bow over the strings,

---

* These Letters are addressed to Carl Kossmaly, a well-known *Kapellmeister.*

so that the audience thought that they were still listening, long after he had ceased to play, and the restrained applause burst forth all the more vehemently afterwards. Maria Weber used to do the same, with a very long *Arpeggio-crescendo* and *decrescendo*—from the softest *pianissimo* up to *fortissimo*, and down again. It was a favourite device of his, in the days when he was a pianist—simple enough—but he did it well, and it never failed to bring down the house. The stiff, stony tone of the organ makes such effects as these impossible,—and that is why I greatly dislike it, as an accompaniment to the voice. If tone, when it is not well sustained, is, taken by itself, inartistic —sustained tone, taken by itself, is equally so. And yet I would rather have the organ played naturally; I dislike those artificial swells, those affected *nuances*, by means of which every other organist forces his sentimentality upon one. If the tone of the organ be stony, let the player content himself with producing a sculpturesque effect; let him stick to form, and not attempt colour! The true sculptor will not complain that his art is defective, because it does not enable him to represent the colour of eyes, cheeks, lips, and draperies. To my mind, it is a defect in modern organ music, that one should be allowed to feel the want of *crescendo* and *diminuendo*, as one never does in the writings of Bach, nor in those of others who lived before him. It would as soon occur to one, to want colour in an antique. Style, or rather the want of style, is this; proportion or disproportion between the means available and the objective requirement, in every sense of the word. It is this which gives the style of the orchestra, of the theatre, of chamber and quartet music, and of the symphony—but not the style of Bach, Handel, Mozart, &c. Everything which enables one to recognise the author is mannerism, however great it may be. . . .

M. HAUPTMANN.

43.

LEIPZIG, *July 15th*, 1865.

DEAR FRIEND,—

. . . *Tristan und Isolde* has really seen the light at last, and everyone is in a state of morbid over-excitement accordingly. I don't suppose any opera ever had such a hard time of it. With so many difficulties in the way, people can scarcely expect that it should be done often, and it will be some time yet, before the world in general is clear as to that present Future which, so they say, has never found its true sphere until now. Do you remember the Berlin *flâneur*, who was so very grand about that country estate of his by the sea-shore? "You can't see a single mountain, a single hill, a single tree, a single bush," &c., and when it was objected, that you must be able to see something: "Oh no! you never see a thing. *It's all country.*" Well, *Tristan* is just like that! It is hard to believe that it has done anything much for the cause it represents. According to Wagner's own purpose, the whole domain of music, taken in its widest sense, seems to me desolate—the more desolate, the nearer he gets to it—the more desolate because, everything granted, he stands no longer on artistic ground, but on the natural earth, covered with manure—demanding as he does, reality alone. The whole tendency of his poem is false to art, and that is what seems to me so hopeless. They think it is degrading art to speak of *play;* and yet to conquer materialism, to lift the burden of labour, to lighten the weight of passion, to turn work into *play*, this is the highest function— the *irony* of art, as people say. The very fact that music keeps time is in itself ironical ; passion does not observe this rule ; if it did, it would lose its weight, like stone when it is thrown into the form of an arch. The architect plays with the forms of nature, and the hard granite blossoms into a flower. I daresay we shall soon hear of the great and permanent success of W.'s opera. Well, that won't alter, not our opinion, but our conviction (for it is more than an opinion) that it does not stand on the right foundation ! *Prendre le mors aux dents* means that the horse is running away; of course, if once he gets the bit between his teeth, there is nothing to be done, but it is not a comfortable gallop, for you never know whether you won't get your neck broken. The real Pegasus wears a bridle. There is such a thing though as an unbroken advance, not *ventre à terre*, but at a foot's pace. Jean Paul has a capital illustration of it. Pastor Schmelzle's horse goes at a foot's pace through the streets of Vienna, and even the postman, who has to deliver his letters in those great six and eight-storied houses, keeps up with him; but slowly as it goes, he cannot stop the beast, and when he shouts out "Wo!" all the passers-by roar with laughter; nobody understands the poor fellow's distress. Music that moves slowly, slowly, in everlasting 4/4 measure,— perpetual Recitative and declamation,—may become horribly wearisome. A great deal of *Lohengrin* gets along very much in the same style as Schmelzle's horse; all the modulations from A to Z and back again only make it more tiresome. Recitative has no metre, only rhythm and accent—a valuable and naturally artistic quality, which ought not to be sacrificed to the *a tempo* used to mark the beginning of the actual piece, when it starts upon the course measured out for it. Here the old state of things is certainly more poetical, and the new is very prosaic, as compared with it. Recitative has many forms which ought to be retained: they were founded on vocal expression by word of mouth, and grew up naturally of their own accord, with Recitative.

I hope you and your family have been keeping well, all this time. When I was younger, I used to suffer very much from my head; now that's all right, my legs won't do their work. It was said to be rheumatism at first, but now it has taken up its position and means to stay, like the French garrison, which remained at Ancona, to keep it safe, long after the inhabitants had begun to wish their friends were in Jericho. There is a great *Männergesangfest* at Dresden next month; 2,200 singers have sent in their names. It is scarcely possible to imagine the effect of such a number. Perhaps it may be very fine,—only the music which they do must be clear and simple. . . .

Yours,

M. HAUPTMANN.

44.

LEIPZIG, *May 14th*, 1866.

DEAR KOSSMALY,—

  . . . They are fond of giving historical Concerts at the *Gewandhaus*, and many an interesting piece of music, which has fallen into undeserved neglect, is now being brought to light. Some of the finest works of our foremost men—Bach, for instance—have only become known of late years. They were allowed to moulder in dusty cupboards, while he was still alive, and during the period that followed, people cared so little about them, that it is a mercy they were not thrown into the waste-paper basket. A famous old opera is the only thing that cannot be revived. Operatic writers must be content with a momentary success. Excellent as they may be musically, *Idomeneo* and *Medea* are dead, and cannot rise again. No art depends so much upon the present as music, although her laws are eternal, and must remain the same for all time.

M. HAUPTMANN.

45.*

LEIPZIG, *June 6th*, 1853.

DEAR HERR MAIER,—

  . . . When I pay my morning visit to the *Conservatoire* and am deafened by millions of pianos and that hateful, though necessary grinding process called practising, which is the death of all music, I can't help feeling mystified. It is hard to realize brilliant players, such as Mozart and Beethoven, working mechanically their nine hours *per diem*, as our unhappy boys must do, if they mean to excel. But with those great ones, we can't help feeling, that playing and music went together and

---

* These Letters are addressed to J. J. Maier, formerly Secretary to the Minister of the Interior at Carlsruhe, afterwards Teacher of Counterpoint at the Munich Conservatoire, and Curator of the Musical Department of the National Library at Vienna. He is known as the editor of many important works by the ancient masters (English Madrigals, &c.).

were indivisible. Would that technique were possible, entirely apart from the art itself! It seems so strange, that mere mechanism should ever ripen into music! Composition is quite another matter with them. One class is devoted to pure counterpoint, another to pure composition. The composition class takes no notice of counterpoint, the pupils are not taught to let the one affect the other—everything that pleases is permissible, they are told—and they consider themselves let out of jail, so to speak, into beautiful Nature. To be sure, this beautiful Nature is often ugly enough, for such vulgar, harsh, unmusical stuff as our youngsters treat us to now and then, was never before heard of. It is nothing but vexation at their own inability, set to music.

46.

LEIPZIG, *April 14th*, 1854.

DEAR HERR MAIER,—

. . . On Good Friday we are to have a performance of Handel's *Israel in Egypt;* I have just heard a part of it rehearsed in the *Thomaskirche.* There's health and strength for you! What poverty-stricken stuff is our best modern music, by the side of it! How we strain for effect, and miss all the simplicity and repose, which are associated with every bar of this Oratorio, even in its most vigorous movements! And how splendid is the organ accompaniment, if not made unduly prominent! It is such a mercy to be quit of the flutes and clarinets, and two or four horns—not to mention the *cornet à piston,* &c. We never know how fine drums and trumpets can be, until we have them combined with a powerful chorus and organ. The organ is out of place in weak, nerveless music, depending entirely on *crescendos* and *decrescendos,* reviving only to fall back again into *pianissimo;* it wants to draw a deep breath. For such choruses as those in the *Israel,* there is nothing like it; all our instrumentation is child's play by the side of it. We have the further privilege of using Mendelssohn's own organ part; he put it in when he was editing the Oratorio for the English edition of Handel's works.

47.

LEIPZIG, *May* 30*th*, 1861.

Sad news, dear Maier! Everything may work together for good on the whole. Faith may be unshaken, but it is no safeguard against trouble, and the loss is our own. The clergyman at Cassel thanked God for taking his dear wife to Himself—in the papers. From such affectations of piety, He who created us susceptible of joy and sorrow, would Himself turn away. To believe that everything happens according to the good pleasure of God, helps us to submit and to conquer, but it is not against the good pleasure of God to grieve over a heartfelt loss, even while we believe.

48.

LEIPZIG, *August* 29*th*, 1861.

DEAR HERR MAIER !—

I have received your volume of English Madrigals, and am quite delighted with them. They are extremely graceful, and they are so modern, that one may go on for pages, and never find out that they were not written by a living composer. Our amateurs will prefer these to most others, and I confidently reckon on their popularity. I don't know whether you, or someone else, arranged the German words, but it is very well done. I daresay a good deal of it is literal translation, but both skill and taste must have been brought to bear upon it. Considering its date, I have scarcely ever met with music which had so little of the date about it. You feel the quiet charm of real musicianship. . .

Have you got Mendelssohn's Letters yet? My copy arrived yesterday, and but for other business, I should probably have finished the volume at one sitting. These letters only represent the two years that he spent in Italy and France, 1830-1832 ; they are so clever and so original, that it is a delight to read them. I do hope that Paul Mendelssohn will give us another volume, but there is no hint of that in the first; it would be a real pity to stop here. Most of the letters published now-a-days, depend entirely for their interest on the personality of the writer; Mendelssohn's, characteristic as they are, have something besides. They are full of that genial cultivation, which left its mark on everything that he *il. It was of great service to him also as a composer, fc *he did not produce so instinctively as many other writers. In after days at Leipzig, when he was recasting the *Walpurgisnacht*, which he had written in Rome twenty-five years before, he used to say: "What rubbish to call me a master! Think of taking all this time to finish a work to my liking! Had I been really a master, I should have run it off the reel." The image, the thought was there, but years passed before he could find the expression.

49.*

LEIPZIG, *September 15th*, 1857.

HONOURED SIR,—

. . . Your collection of old German hymns is an interesting one, and you have put them together in a very practical way. The old fogies cannot complain, that they are not appreciated now-a-days. They are appreciated as highly as if they were curiosities. Anything and everything has its value, the saucepan as well as the god, and an archæological interest attaches not merely to works of art, but even to the uninspired handiwork of any ancient craftsman. There is a certain feeling of safety about it, of absolutely reliable *savoir faire*, as there is in the architecture of old Gothic churches, even when they are not of the first order. Every detail is in its right place, and whether or no the spirit of genius be felt, it leaves upon the mind the impression of a whole, not as in later days, of a combination. The birth and growth of Polyphony, as shown even in the most inferior music of the old time, is not enough remembered now-a-days; we ought to take it as allopathic

---

* This Letter is addressed to G. Rebling, Organist of the *St. Johanniskirche* at Magdeburg.

medicine, when we are going in for too much compact harmony. I do not say we should imitate it, for no good ever comes of imitation,—but it ought to be recognised.

With all our just recognition of what was good in former days, with all our meritorious striving to preserve it for our own benefit, it must not be forgotten, that this very need of the time shows that the Present is defective. Transcendental though it be, it is not sufficient unto itself, like the Roccoco Period, when that too was the Present, and owned and could invent its own appropriate music, and wanted nothing more. We live between the Future and the Past; there is enthusiasm for both, but only criticism for the Present.

50.*

September 9th, 1854.

DEAR RIETZ,—

Herr S. sends me to-day some copies of the lithographed portrait of your humble servant. As your collection is not confined to birds of Paradise, but includes every variety of crow, please accept this gray-black or black - gray enclosure, and stick it into your album or your waste paper basket, whichever you like. Many of my friends say it's a good likeness, *tant mieux* for the artist, *tant pis pour moi!*

Yours affectionately,

HAUPTMANN.

51.

LEIPZIG, *November 17th,* 1860.

CHER FRÈRE EN APOLLON !

Such was the style of address used by the French Academicians, and I adopt it to-day, in my congratulatory letter to the new member of the Royal Prussian Academy of Arts. I heartily wish you joy of your new honours. *Excelsior,* say I ! I maintain it's a fine thing, to have a long list of

---

* These Letters are addressed to Julius Rietz, the distinguished *Hof-Kapell-meister* at Dresden.

alphabetical distinctions tacked on to your signature. They may say if they please:

> Deck your wig with flowing locks,
> Case your feet in tragic socks,
> Still you are the man you were!

Quite so! You were a fine fellow without them, they are merely signs of recognition; "the man's the man for a' that." . . .

A word or two about our musical doings here! At the first Concert of the *Euterpe*, we had nothing but Bach and Handel; the *Gewandhaus* followed it up with Wagner's Overture to *Faust*. This was rather amusing. One Society wished to show that it thought of something besides the Future, the other, that it was not entirely wedded to the Past. . . . The second Part of yesterday's Concert was made up of the music to *The Midsummer Night's Dream*, the music alone without recitation. This is a mistake. Even if we know what it all means on the stage, we want to be reminded of it; the speeches give point to the details, and mark the division of scenes. When Spohr's *Faust* was brought out at Frankfurt, Börne said that the story of the opera would hang together more coherently, if the dialogue were omitted. It is not so with Shakespeare's play. . . .

52.

LEIPZIG, *September* 18*th*, 1865.

. . . I am glad that you have been able to give several performances of Cherubini's *Requiem*. In former times one would never have ventured on such music; not that people were unwilling to listen to it, but the Conductors could not and dared not put it before them. This state of things prevailed to a greater extent in the days of old Frederick Augustus, than it has since. Peters has just published the great eight-part Credo, a noble and effective work. None of the musicians that we remember could have produced such music. Cherubini began it in Italy, between 1770 and 1780, and, after a lapse of twenty years, took up the work again in

Paris, and finished it. So even are the style and the workman-ship, that you cannot detect the join. He is as full of feeling as he is free from sentimentality; it is this which makes his music last. Fifty years, more or less, do not affect him; he is his own counterbalance. Formal he may be, but never dry; nay, much of the charm of modern Harmony originated with him. As an Italian, he had two privileges to start with; his classical form (*i.e.*, his large and regular construction), and his independent melody. The consequence is, that his full harmonies never obscure the transparency of his art. Though too intent on over - refinement in Harmony, the main division of his form is not affected; its movement is always healthy and natural. . . .

53.*

CASSEL, *December* 27*th*, 1838.

DEAR FRIEND,—

After racking my brains to devise an historical programme, consisting of music of the earlier and middle periods, I have come to the conclusion that this is not the way to set about it. We must cling to the works—not to the names—which have come down to us. There is plenty of music by the Netherlanders and the early Italians, from Palestrina down to Leo, Durante, and Scarlatti, and it is easily accessible everywhere, but it is only for the voice; the last named men wrote operas, as well as sacred and chamber music with instrumental accompaniment, but it has all disappeared, with the exception of a few fragments, which perhaps are still to be found in ancient libraries. As regards Opera, it is hardly safe to go back farther than Gluck. There are things by Lulli and Rameau, which used to interest me very much; for a time, I was rather in love with Lulli's *Roland*, and had whole scenes of it copied in our notation, so as to read it with greater ease; but everything that he and Rameau aimed at is centralised, and comes to maturity in

---

* These Letters are addressed to Wilhelm Speyer, a Frankfurt merchant, the pupil and friend of Spohr. He was a well-known writer of Songs.

Gluck.　He forsook the common Italian *bravura* style for that
of the French, which suited his principle of musical declamation better; and when once he had adopted it, he
cleansed and brought it to perfection.　I don't think Lulli
and Rameau are suitable for a large audience, for though it
may affect a transient interest in history, yet your large
audience demands music in the first place, and that interminable Psalmody—small doses of which are impossible—would
pall upon them.　Of all tho operas written between 1760 and
1780, and discussed by Hildegard von Hohenthal, as if they
were *chefs d'œuvre* that would last for ever, not a note has
reached our ears.　To begin with, they consist almost entirely
of Recitatives and Arias which no modern singers, in Germany
at least, could sing.　As for their style, Mozart's *Idomeneo*
represents it at its best—as the Greek imitations represent
Egyptian antiquities.　The antiquities have not lost their
peculiarity, but they are more pleasing than they were in the
original; it is the normal in a more perfect form.　As regards
Opera, it is certainly best to make a beginning with Gluck and
Mozart, both Germans, yet representing, one the French, the
other the Italian School.　Besides, the older things—French
works at least—cannot be given without the addition of strings
and wind instruments, whereas the works of Gluck and
Mozart may be done just as they are.　As examples of sacred
music and Oratorio in Germany, Bach and Handel, as a
matter of course!　Telemann, Keiser, Fux, and many others
shared their celebrity whilst they were still alive, and that is
no mean fame; but all the best and deepest thought of the
age is summed up in these two, and though it would doubt-.
less prove interesting to musicians, to be made acquainted with
famous works that have long since perished, the public at large
cares as little about them as about their authors.　.　.　.
To come back to earlier days, I think I should omit the Netherlanders.　Palestrina, though an Italian, combines all their
virtues, softens down their roughness, and steeps it in
a certain grace, which makes it more acceptable to modern
taste, but even Palestrina might easily prove too strange for a
large audience, and I would rather propose Leo's eight-part
Miserere, with cuts.　It is just old enough for nineteenth

century listeners, and musically it was a great success, when we did it here. According to this standard of fitness, it is not judicious to go much more than a hundred years back, and even then, only such specimens must be selected as are in their own way quite perfect, and we must not attempt instrumental music, nor vocal music with instrumental accompaniment. Between S. Bach and Haydn, there is another gap in the history of Music, which is filled only with names. The dead must be allowed to rest in peace. Most of Emanuel Bach's vocal music belongs to the wearisome Cantata style, and though he did something for orchestration, in the way of developing form, he was only preparing the way for Haydn. . . . I have studied the music of the most different ages with very great interest, and when I had once lived myself into a particular period, or into the mind of a great master, it never failed to give me the keenest pleasure, and I could not understand, how such beautiful things should leave others cold and unsympathetic. But when I came back to them again, after less earnest preparation, I did not find it so easy to revive this feeling, although it never affected my belief in their beauty, when once I had felt it. If Mozart had been born at Rome in the sixteenth century, he would have written like Palestrina—if at Venice in the seventeenth, he would have resembled Gabrieli. If he were to be born to-day, he would write as people did not write sixty years since, and yet everywhere he would be the same great composer. The personality of the artist is the really effective thing in a work of art, but it takes some time to get accustomed to a strange costume, and in music, which is supposed to express only the mind and heart of man, anything *passé*, anything which reminds us in the very least of fashion, immediately becomes intolerable ; that is why music ages so fast.—I am very sorry that I cannot be of greater assistance to you, and that my advice should be almost entirely negative. . . .

Yours most sincerely,

M. HAUPTMANN.

54.

HONOURED SIR,—

Your representative, Herr Schädel, has done me
the high honour of offering me the post of Conductor to the
Frankfurt *Cäcilienverein*. The confidence reposed in me,
and the kind way in which it has been expressed, call for my
deep gratitude. I have only a general knowledge of your
circumstances, but I cannot imagine an able musician better
employed than in devoting his best powers to the interests of
so excellent an institution. The impressions I derived from
some performances of the Society, when Schelble was its
conductor, are among the most pleasurable that I remember.
I should speak with less certainty, if I were drawing upon
youthful memories, which are so often falsified, when one
comes to examine them in after years; but I heard those
performances at a time of life when I had learned to care
only for good music—*i.e.*, to care for very little. Schelble was
the soul of this well-organized body. I know no living
musician to compare with him as a conductor. He was not
only a most cultivated man, but he had this further important qualification, that he was himself a trained and highly
accomplished vocalist. His perfect intonation helped the
Choir more than any amount of talk, gesticulation, or playing.
Add to this, his mastery of the piano! To be sure, others
may equal him in that respect, but I never found the two
gifts combined in such perfection; he could take a whole score
in with his eyes, and give it out again with his fingers. Then
there was his quiet, dignified demeanour, and his remarkable
talent for conducting; one felt that here, for once, was an
ideal leader. Turning from him to myself, I am alas! forced
to admit, that I fail almost entirely in the most necessary of
these qualifications. I cannot sing, I am a poor pianist, and
I have so little natural talent for conducting, that I could never
pretend to be the worthy successor of a man like Schelble.
I reckon good pianoforte playing as an indispensable

requisite. . . . I cannot account it a disadvantage, that it prevents the conductor from beating time. All the good Societies that I have ever known, did without the conductor's stick, and they had better do so, as soon as they are up to it. By the way, there is something very unmusical in forcing your audience to see every division of time written in the air, as well as marked in the music, the essence of which is, to combine what is divided. Goethe complains of the audible beating of time in the Italian Churches, and asks what we should think of a sculptor, who insisted on adorning every joint of his statue with a patch of red cloth. But the visible beating of time is not much better, only we happen to be more accustomed to it. . . .

Yours most sincerely,
M. HAUPTMANN.

55.*

LEIPZIG, October 31st, 1865.

DEAR WEHNER,—

. . . I am glad to hear that you got on well with Rossini; I can quite believe it. He is a complete circle, he always did whatever he meant to do. We must go back to the very early days of his career for unfinished work of any kind; music became natural to him at an unusually early age. He formed himself on no special model; he never had the slightest difficulty in expressing any of his thoughts, for his head and his hand went together. We have composers who are good enough in their way, but oh! what labour it costs them to master their subject! A fellow brings you his composition, and you feel inclined to say: "Go back, and spend as many months working the work out of it, as you spent weeks working it in! Do you want the whole world to see how dreadfully difficult you found it?" Where does Rossini show difficulties of workmanship? Yet the workmanship is often

---

* This Letter is addressed to Arnold Wehner, a pupil of Hauptmann's, both in Cassel and at Leipzig, afterwards Choirmaster of the Cathedral at Hanover.

very remarkable—but then it is not Counterpoint to a *Cantus firmus*, there is nothing that has been added or placed in opposition; the contrasting elements appear to emanate, the one from the other, and a sense of unity is obtained.

Weber's Biography is full of passages which show his utter contempt for Rossini, but that depreciation is a weakness of Weber's. Perhaps after all, Rossini doesn't like Weber.

> " Reader, how dost thou like me ?
> Reader, how do I like thee ? "

as the poet Logau says. Where Rossini is strong, Weber is weak; he is incomplete and incoherent, so much so, that Hofmann used to say, he often failed to find the conclusion of his melodic premise. I fancy that Rossini was much keener in recognising what was positively good in Weber, than Weber was to appreciate the same qualities in him. No one will ignore Weber's geniality; he has introduced many fresh elements into modern music, but the motive and the character of music are not the question here—we are talking about the construction. There he is beaten by many whom he looked upon as his inferiors. And yet it is a quality which, considered with reference to the whole, is of equal importance with harmony. His want of thorough scholarship gives a *dilettante* air to his music. Meyerbeer, who was also a pupil of Vogler's, was far more successful in getting rid of the unsound harmonies of his master. Weber is not quite free from certain 6/4 harmonies; Meyerbeer went through the Italian School.

M. H.

56.*

Leipzig, August 20th, 1851.

Dearest Wolff,—

  . . . Bogumil Goltz has been here again. He is a first-rate fellow. It would not do for everybody to be like him, but once in a way, it is delightful to meet such a

---

* This Letter is addressed to Johannes Wolff, a distinguished architect.

character, and it would be pleasant to know that he was in the neighbourhood, as a sort of concentrated spirit in the midst of the all-surrounding phlegm ; he is the essence of rum, in water, sugar, and lemon—the ordinary bitter-sweet of ordinary life. He is rather overwhelming, when you are only a short time with him ; but he is a real conversation-alist, and it is possible to enjoy capital talk with him, when he has once found out, that there really is a man behind the words of the other speaker, and has begun to listen to what you say. He spent the whole of his one day here with us, and from morning to evening inclusive, he talked a good big book — if one could only have stenographed it. He never wearied me ; it was too attractive and too exciting. That is just the difference between talk and chatter. Chatter so soon becomes intolerable, that you long to be quiet, to hear your own thoughts again ; but when you are talking to a man who really thinks and feels what he says, you think and feel with him, and it never tires you, because it is not all on one side. Goltz is not only an intelligent, he is a rational man, who knows that whatever he may assert, the contrary of that assertion is, in a certain sense, always true notwithstanding ; he is therefore willing to include it, and to allow for anything in it which is positive. He is, *pro* and *contra*, poetry and philosophy, at one and the same time; he is *pro* and *contra* Goethe and Hegel, but he only opposes everything that he is *not*. Of course there is plenty for so clever and eloquent a man to talk about, for either he must not begin at all, or he must go on and on for ever, because he is fain to contradict himself perpetually, that he may steer clear of the contradiction of onesidedness. I should greatly like to meet him again, but there is little chance of it, unless publishing affairs should call him hither.

57.

DEAREST WOLFF,—

Thank you very much indeed for your kind
present. It is a two-fold joy, first because of its contents,
and secondly, as a token of remembrance from the author.
It naturally contains the principle of your earlier writings,
but here you have expressed it in the form of an answer
to your opponents—as the negation of a negation—so that it
really makes for something positive. One part of Goethe's
Farbenlehre is entirely polemical, and it is always better to
meet than to ignore your adversaries, because some people,
who are not capable of reasoning out a subject, so as to
see that two contrary opinions cannot be held concerning
it, always incline to think that each has something to
justify it, and such people as these take the side of whatever
book they may chance to have read last. Confusions like this
are even more harmful in architecture than in music. A score
which is based on unsound principles, is certain to be shelved
sooner or later, and what is false never lasts ; an audience
may be taken in, but not mankind at large. An ugly building
however remains ; nobody knocks it down, because, æsthetically, it is all wrong. By-and-bye, people will say : " What a
pity it was built so ! " but the eye gets accustomed to it,
and this in itself is bad. Most of the things we see are
bad ; how then are we to preserve and cultivate our taste for
what is good ? Besides, the public taste for architecture is
corrupt ; it is easier to find a naturally good judge of any
other art. Every house that has columns in front of it is
known as " a handsome house." In the *Alexander Newsky
Perspective*, one of the principal streets of St. Petersburg, no-
one is allowed to build a house that has not got porphyry
columns to it, so that there may be nothing but "handsome houses." And yet, it is doubly hard to make even a
grand house handsome in this style, if the facade is to form
an exterior which shall properly correspond with the

interior of it. It never occurs to the *dilettante* architect, that the materials of which a building is made, ought to have some connection with the idea of the building; he would not allow it, even if one tried to convince him; he considers his own taste an infallible guide, and never cares to enquire into the conditions which would bring his work into accordance with Nature. The proportion of the expression to the means, in the sphere of technical æsthetics, the proportion of the expression to the object to be expressed, in the wider sphere of literature and art—this is what I call style. Style belongs to the different crafts, not to the different craftsmen. The craftsmen are distinguished by their individual mannerisms. Even Goethe has his mannerisms, but then he has his style too—not the Gothic style, but the style of the things he represents, working as he does, from the real to the ideal. He was quite young, when Merck wrote thus to him: "Your one effort, your incontrovertible tendency is *to give poetic form to reality.* Other people try to realize poetry and imagination, so-called, and the result is mere rubbish." Goethe's advice to every man, to be in his own way a Greek, points the same moral. But such advice as that is often misunderstood. People catch the word "Greek," and they think you mean columns and hexameters, when all you meant was truthfulness of representation. . . . False art may often possess a charm, which is wanting in true art, inasmuch as the latter has to content herself with beauty unadorned, and beauty, which is harmonious concord, only appeals to a cultivated sense of harmony. The charm which consists in pure feeling awakes an easier echo, addressing itself directly to the senses. It has inspired the so-called "fine passages" in music. *Don Juan* has no "fine passages," and "fine passages" will not sustain a work for any length of time; they are details for detail's sake, they have no meaning in the whole. I don't understand what Semper means by his architectural embodiments of ideas. I remember a work on architecture by Le Doux—of course you are acquainted with it: "*La Ville de Chaux,*" in which the same thought occurs. A cooper lives in a house made like a cask, with hoops round it! Heaven be thanked, that such embodiments as these remain upon paper! Le Doux's actual work—suburban houses, if I mistake not—was as prosy and commonplace as could be.

I wish they would hold a conference of Architects in Leipzig, it would be such a pleasure to see you here for a few days. Of course you would have to bring your wife, let the other architects do as they would! . . .

EXTRACTS FROM THE UNPUBLISHED LETTERS
OF HAUPTMANN.

Schröder-Devrient has been re-engaged for three years, beginning from the autumn. They may run her down if they please, but we know that without her the Dresden Opera would collapse. She is still the one Armida in Germany. If she be "an old house," she is still a grand specimen of architecture, the beauty of which has been but slightly impaired by the ravages of time. Her singing and acting too are architectural; it is this which makes her so different to all other *prime donne*. I don't care much about her delivery of particular passages, nor the way in which she sings Schubert's Songs, but I do care about the definite form, with which she invests any *rôle* in any given Opera, and the way in which she sustains it at an equal height throughout. These powers she still retains, and as the effect of them is never lost upon an audience, it is always safe for a manager to re-engage her. Compared with others, she is like an old Greek statue by the side of lay figures in a Journal of Fashion, which only survive until the next number is out. Devrient was quite splendid as Donna Anna,—I don't wish for a better. She sang *very well*, much better than she used to; she is greatly improved, and her acting is surpassingly fine and effective. It is not *her* fault, if her great gifts divide her from the others in a manner that is not favourable to the *ensemble :* and besides, she does raise those around her to the highest level they are capable of attaining. Next year she goes to London; they have promised her £10,000! "That's a good one," as I have heard you* say, when making a fluke at billiards.

At Liszt's house, I saw one Part of Raimondi's triple Oratorio, *Potiphar, Jacob, and Joseph ;* each part is to be performed singly, and then the whole three all together ! An illustration this, of the absurdities a *virtuoso* may commit,

---

* Spohr.

when he can do nothing better. The score, sent me by Liszt, is 5 feet high and 5 feet broad. The three orchestras have their full complement of wind instruments, trombones and ophicleides; therefore there are nine trombones, three ophicleides, twelve horns, and so on, all going at once,—and each of us has only one pair of ears, and they cannot even take in two things at a time! There is some technical skill in it, nothing else.

The worst of over-seasoning is, that it vitiates the taste: purity seems vapid by comparison. We get accustomed to anything, and it may become second nature to walk on stilts.

Frau X. has a fine voice, and she sang Constanze's air well enough, but her roulades were rather thick and clumsy. If a vocalist fails to make her roulades delicate, she misses the real meaning of ornamentation. They are like the twisted pillars of the later Middle Ages. "The wreath around the pillar winds," but the pillar itself was never meant to wind.

Absolutely perfect singers do not exist now-a-days. Good singers like Ney and Viardot have their position, or are indifferent about it. Viardot gives another Concert here next Saturday. Her execution is marvellous, no difficulties are too great for her, and she keeps her tone throughout, though her voice is less agreeable than Ney's. Sometimes she illustrates character at the expense of beauty.

If Goethe is anxious to praise a thing, he uses two terms—"goodness" and "dignity" (*Werth und Würde*). They are not convertible terms, and, taken together, they mean a great deal. If we want to sum up everything that is estimable and praiseworthy, we may add a third term—grace. Thus we have goodness, dignity, and grace, and these three qualities make any number of binary combinations possible—goodness and dignity without grace, goodness and grace without dignity,

dignity and grace without goodness. . . . The three qualities are never present in equal force; dignity prevails over grace, grace over dignity, and so on. You may classify compositions in this way, and composers too, if you take them in the lump. Handel, for instance, is pre-eminently dignified, whereas Bach is worth everything in the sphere of morals; they are so great, that in neither of them do we feel the want of the other two qualities, which make up the sum total. Bellini is graceful rather than anything else; his dignity, &c., is questionable, and there are many like him. Many of our German composers have nothing but a sham dignity, which goes a very little way, in the long run. If we are only to be allowed one of the three virtues, grace will get the best of it—for gracefulness alone makes the fortune of hundreds of thousands of songs and drawing-room pieces. It keeps afloat on its own uncertain element, as the water-lily blooms on the surface of the lake, but once faded, it sinks to the bottom.

———

" Pretty good ! " is the worst that can be said of a work of art. It had much better be abominable at once, for then no one would bring it out, no one would care to hear it. But " Pretty good ! " is good enough for so many people, and, as it is, we are deluged with things that are " Pretty good ! "

———

Robert Schumann, who is a most industrious composer, has lately written a Cantata in three parts, *Paradise and the Peri;* most of the libretto is by T. Moore. The performance will be in November. I heard one of the rehearsals with a small chorus and quartet. It seems to be very fresh and spirited. How it will sound as a whole, I do not yet know; it hangs together without a break ; even the three parts are scarcely divided, and there are no Recitatives nor metrical numbers. The phenomena of this modern Romantic Music, or whatever they call it, suggest the vegetable kingdom. Schumann's construction is that of a tree—a branch more or less, and what does it matter ? Mozart's is that of the human body : you cannot add an arm or a leg.

We have got a young Viennese called Joachim here, a born *virtuoso* on the violin. He is thirteen years old, and all but perfect. I wish you* could hear him, but still more do I wish that he could hear you.

To-morrow, there is to be a performance of Hiller's Oratorio, *The Destruction of Jerusalem*—a respectable work, with very beautiful solos, and about twenty fine choruses, which ought to recommend it favourably to Choral Societies. . . . I suppose it is difficult for a composer, whose name is not already well known, to win the public ear with a work of this kind. Otherwise, the fact that it has not been given on so many occasions, when the most leathery fare was dished up instead of it, would be truly astonishing. It leaves a good deal to be desired, but, on the whole, it is tasteful and full of spirit, and after Mendelssohn's, I think it bears the palm among modern oratorios.

We had the *Antigone*, with Mendelssohn's music, the other night. I daresay the whole performance, theatre, dialogue, dresses, and music, would have seemed very odd to an ancient Greek, but to us it was most enjoyable. It lifts one into a right noble sphere of Art. Oh, the pity of it ! And yet it is never pitiful, as it would be in modern tragedy. They say that Mendelssohn's music is not altogether the music of the Greeks, but I should like to know, how he could have kept up the fire if it had been; the long and the short of it is, that every man must make his own music, if it is to speak to the heart. Perhaps it is the rich figures for stringed instruments, not the stringed instruments themselves, which give the impression of polychrome on the more plastic surface of poetry.

It is curious that in Bach's sacred music, in every one of his Cantatas, the first chorus is always the most important and effective, and is only followed by passages for single voices, concluding with a chorale. The old gentleman was not

---

* Spohr.

nearly so anxious about an effective *Finale* as we are now-a-days—nor indeed as Handel was, for Handel cared a great deal about effect. Both men of genius, humility is the strong point of the one ; proud self-consciousness that of the other. The *Jubilate* appealed to Handel, the Penitential Psalms to Bach.

———

However interesting a composition may be, if it is not satisfactory as a whole, the layman will feel this as well as the *connoisseur*, and it will die a natural death. It is not the esteem of *connoisseurs* which preserves good music and damns bad music, but rather the general feeling for what is good, as it exists in the masses, that is, in the ideal Man ; the very best works of the most gifted men are just good enough for him. Ugly buildings are allowed to stand, pictures are left hanging, books are preserved in libraries, but music has to be performed first of all—and to bring about this result, great works must be approved of by a large majority. From very early days, only the best of its time has survived, never the second best.

———

"Talent is industry," Mendelssohn used to say, and he never would allow, that talent could exist under any other conditions. There is an element of truth in this, if it be rightly understood; but long continued, permanent industry is also a sign of utter want of talent. Who, that had the smallest insight in matters of Art, but would do anything rather than torment himself and others, by making mechanical exercises, which lead to nothing, the principal business of his life ?

———

There are very clever amateurs whom one would, nevertheless, dissuade from entering the profession. How much rather then, amateurs who want to begin at the beginning ! Yet such people often think they cannot possibly do anything else, and they actually become useless members of society, because they delude themselves into the idea, that they would be happier in the most modest circumstances, as musicians, than they could be in any other condition of life.

The devil take all intrigues ! It is intolerable, to have to do with people, who affect to be so honourable, that one thinks one is doing them an injustice, to suppose that they could be capable of a falsehood, though afterwards they turn round and laugh at one for a greenhorn. But there are such people, and deception is the whole charm and enjoyment of life to them. They care for nothing but the wisdom of the serpent ; they leave the harmlessness of the dove to their adversary, and devour him with great self-complacency, digesting him easily enough, as the sustenance appointed by Nature for serpents.

The monetary prospects of a composer are not, as a rule, promising. He must be a popular man, and much sought after, if he is to earn as much as a second-rate teacher of the piano, whose lessons are miserably paid. I do not wish to discourage young people from learning composition, if they have any gift that way, but I should always advise them to make themselves practical musicians, in one line or another, at the same time. To choose poetry alone for one's vocation is no easy matter ; one ought to qualify oneself for something else besides verse-making. And it is just the same with composition. The great majority of composers are not known as composers only ; in their own homes, they are something over and above—teachers, *virtuosi*, members of the orchestra, conductors, *Kapellmeister*. Composition is generally the employment of their leisure hours, and it is none the worse for that. The unity of a work need not suffer, because a man cannot write it off all at once. Nay, it may gain in concentrated tension on that very account,— becoming lax and nerveless, if the writer have unlimited time at his disposal. Neither too much nor too little is the best, or rather the only good rule, with time as with everything else, I expect.

He who has tried to do anything will have gained this much, at any rate, even if he does nothing ; he will know how difficult it is, he will know that respect is due even to partial success. It is not difficult for a man to praise what is best and highest, without understanding it. Voltaire used to say : "He who does not know how to appreciate Regnard" (a comic writer, who was formerly very popular), "does not deserve to admire Molière." If only our youngsters, who wear themselves out in the struggle to appear men of genius, and think they can never be mysterious nor deep enough, could see that the highest level they ever reach is far far below that of an ordinary composer, whose music sounds well, and has contrived to hold its own ! When I see them turning up their noses at the easy, popular music of the Italians, I tell them straight out, that they will never do anything half so good. I cannot say there is any decided tendency towards the Music of the Future in the *Conservatoire*, but a sort of enjoyment of obscurity seems to lie in the spirit of the age itself. It is such a pity, that the lads will not work steadily, and think that study corrupts the pristine freshness of their genius. Art never comes to anything, unless it be founded on the golden base of handicraft, upon which the ancients reared their temples so securely, that they are still standing. Just such an inspired craftsman was Sebastian Bach ! He always meant to do the ordinary thing, and yet, all that he did was extraordinary. Nevertheless, had it been *altogether* so, it would have perished, and we, after the lapse of many years, should have known nothing about it ; even what was extraordinary would have been lost in what was *unordinary*.

Joachim stands by himself. It is not his technique, it is not his tone, it is not anything that anybody could describe ; it is the reserve of all these qualities, so that you hear, not Joachim, but the music. With all his depth of character, there is a rare modesty about him ; he never makes a fuss about himself, but he does make an effect, which is recognised everywhere.

Our Winter Season began again last night, but I was not well, and could not make up my mind to go. The *Eroica*, *Meeresstille und glückliche Fahrt*, Beethoven's E flat Concerto, Airs from *Fidelio* and *Der Freischütz*—all excellent—all excellently done—only one knows it all beforehand. I often wish for something different to start with, something unfamiliar, no matter whether of the past, the present, or the future—not because I am tired of my old friends and acquaintances, but simply because I should like to see them in new surroundings. Then, too, it is bad for the public to hear nothing but No. 1. It spoils their critical sense. They are petrified into speechless admiration, and any change in the programme puts them out, because they don't know what they are expected to say to it. We have twenty Concerts; we do not want to hear all the nine Symphonies every winter. It really is too much of a good thing. Where there is nothing but the best, the best no longer exists. If every day were Sunday, what would become of the Sabbath ? Nature does not arrange all her highest peaks in a row; she divides them with hills and valleys. An Italian likes a bouquet that is all flowers, without a single green leaf, and yet it is the green leaves that set off the glowing beauty of the blossoms.

Our forefathers were not antiquated of set purpose ; their temples look antiquated to us, because they were built to last for a long time. I suppose it is the same with other arts; what is good to begin with, stands growing old, and remains good for all time. Bach and Handel are not classics because they are old ; they have grown old because they are classical. Study the moderns ! said Schumann, the ancients are contained in them. Study the ancients ! said Goethe, their age is a proof of their value, a sign that there is something in them ; and Goethe is probably right. Much that is modern may *appear good*, but the old *must be good*, or it would not have lasted so long.

I am of one mind with Hauser, that Palestrina is even more difficult to sing than Bach. Indeed, I know only too well, that it is much easier to secure a tolerably good performance of one of Bach's pieces, especially when all goes smoothly and people have their hearts in the work, than it is to master the least little fragment of Palestrina. The voices must be neither too loud nor too soft, and the music must be thoroughly felt and understood. If the performers do not love it, they cannot sing it, and such warmth of feeling is seldom found even in the conductor, and cannot be relied upon to last. The music, taken on its own merits, is, strictly speaking, not so much music as Sacred Music. Great artist though he was, Palestrina never intended to captivate his hearers by his art. The Sacred Music of after ages, whether instrumental or vocal, is more egotistic, less independent of everything save the service, and of everyone, save the officiating priest. Comparatively speaking, it is written more for the Concert Room than the Church. Of course, we must not aim too high, or we should banish Art from the Church altogether, painting as well as music, and nothing would be left but the bare walls of the Moravian Brethren, which are unrefreshing enough, and never could represent abstract truth to any but the members of a limited sect, accustomed to set so little store by their place of worship, that its architectural ugliness does not disturb them. Architecture is not an independent art, like painting and music, as is proved by the fact that a beautiful church does not hinder abstract devotion, as a picture or a piece of music does; it is only an ugly church, built on false principles, that disturbs us. If it be beautiful, we are at home in it at once; if it be ugly, we have to get accustomed to it, before we can ward off the troublesome distraction, caused by a thousand evidences of false taste.

In former days, people were too fond of abusing the wearisome "Psalmody" of the old French School of Opera, that flourished in the time of Lulli and Rameau. Those men employed a kind of lumbering Recitative, which hooked itself on to the metrical feet of the verse with a lot of harmonic ballast. It was like wading through a marsh. The accompaniment was very inconvenient, still, it was always an accompaniment. In modern declamatory music, the orchestral parts are very often written first; the voice, the words, are huddled in anyhow, whether they fit or whether they don't, with the result that nine times out of ten they don't, at least, if one has any regard for truthfulness of expression. But if truthfulness of expression has gone, how can it be musical declamation any longer? What is there left?

I cannot quite make out, how certain persons, when irrefragable truth has shown their dicta to be absurdly narrow, or ridiculously visionary, persist in their false faith. Do they really believe in it? I can hardly believe so. They talk such rubbish about the special branches of the one universal Art, they seem to have no idea whatever of that essential and necessary development, which is the condition of real Art. They would have us plant trees head downwards, with boughs and branches in the earth, that the roots might grow up in the air. They want the boughs to grow together again, to preserve unity, as if they had not preserved unity in the very fact of their development. If poet and composer are to be one person, what is to become of the singer, the scene-painter, the dancer, the chorus, the orchestra? Will all these people be able to enter so thoroughly into the mind of the composer, that they can represent the unity of his work? I do not like a musician to be his own librettist; a man does not marry himself; alliance must come from the union of opposites, if a new and independent being is to be born. Don't confuse the sexes! Don't expect any healthy art, where the necessities of contrast are lost sight of—subject and form, poetry and art, substance and formation. They have no idea how to express the general in the particular, and so they go on spinning cobwebs!

It does not in the least surprise me, to find Bach often setting the veriest trash to fine music. As a rule, his Cantatas consist of an old Hymn, the first and last Strophe of which is sung as a Chorale, varied at first, and then simple. All the intermediate part is twined and twisted anyhow into Recitatives and Solos, and these are often as ugly as you could wish. It would be easy to find beautiful passages about "putrifying sores and ulcers." The painters of the seventeenth century were often forced to depict the most hideous martyrdoms, and they tried to make up for it to themselves and to Art in general, by the beauty of the heads and figures of the spectators, that they might have something healthy to represent. Not so Bach, who sets the whole gamut of disease to healthy music. I fancy a composer of our time would be driven to despair, if he were asked to set any one of the dozens of librettos which Bach had to deal with. No doubt they were not all equally bad, and we may make exceptions. Such texts, however, are generally earlier in date, for in his day Poetry was at a very low ebb. Nor did he always, as I think, keep clear of the flourishes then in vogue, although they did no harm to the depth and grandeur of his work, as a whole.

Bülow certainly *plays* everything, the most tremendous things included, which are not play at all to most people. It is a sign of disease, and of general morbidity, that there should be so little playfulness, in the good artistic sense of the word, about our compositions. Our feelings torture us; we are so material, that we cannot rise above them. We have no unfettered sympathy with the real creations of Art. Our highest point is naked passion, devoid of self-control. A bull-fight, at which the spectators are not ranged in a circle, but thrust into the arena itself, so that they dare not leave go each other's hands, for terror of the savage beasts—this is our modern Art. And not music alone; poetry, painting, sculpture, are too often affected in the same way. French artists, whose power of technique is abnormal, introduce terror wherever they can. A well-known picture by Biard represents a boat in the Arctic Ocean, attacked by hungry Polar bears, against which a few sailors can hardly hold their own; but it is a wonderful composition. Kiss's *Amazon*, a painful subject for sculpture, is just as bad; the *contours* are ugly, and one cannot get a firm grasp of the whole from any standpoint. What is the good of such things? What thought do they suggest beyond themselves? And what does the music of the day express, except the diseased mind of the composer? His diseased mind is nothing to me, and nothing to Art in general. He ought to work his own cure, before he tries to appear as an artist.

———————

"Sweet peace comes over me, I know not how," whenever I think of Mozart. It is possible that he may appear again every 500 years, but as I shall not appear again every 500 years, for me he is there to all eternity. I am not ashamed to own, that to this day the thought of *Figaro, Don Juan, Die Zauberflöte,* and *Così fan tutte,* makes me cry like a child.

———————

. . . It is plain that everyone who passes judgment on anything, passes judgment on himself at the same time.

A LIST OF MORITZ HAUPTMANN'S PUPILS.

CASSEL.

1.	1822.	GERKE, O.	...	...	... of	Lüneburg.
2.		LINDENAU ...	...	...	... ″	Hamburg.
3.		OCHERNAL ...	...	...	... ″	Bremen.
4.		GEORG	...	...	... ″	Frankfurt-a.-M.
5.		POTT	...	...	... ″	Oldenburg.
6.		BLASCHEK ...	...	...	... ″	Cassel.
7.		DAVID, FERD.	...	...	... ″	Hamburg.
8.		RIES, H. ...	...	...	... ″	Bonn.
9.		MOSENTHAL	...	...	... ″	Cassel.
10.		NOHR, F. ...	...	...	... ″	Gotha.
11.		PACIUS	...	...	... ″	Hamburg.
12.	1823.	HERMANN ...	...	...	... ″	Nordhausen.
13.	1824.	HOM	...	...	... ″	Aschaffenburg.
14.		CURSCHMANN, C. F.	...	...	... ″	Berlin.
15.		BIERMANN ...	...	...	... ″	?
16.		RADELFAHR	...	...	... ″	Hamburg.
17.		BURGMÜLLER, NORB.	...	...	... ″	Düsseldorf.
18.		VON DITTFURTH, F	...	...	... ″	Rinteln (Hesse).
19.		WIEGAND, J.	...	...	... ″	Cassel.
20.		CARL	...	...	... ″	Rudoldstadt.
21.	1825.	SEIFARTH ...	...	...	... ″	Hamburg.
22.		KUFFERATH	...	...	... ″	Düsseldorf.
23.		FRANZ.	...	...	... ″	Celle.
24.		HARTMANN	...	...	... ″	Coblenz.
25.	1827.	SCHMIDT	...	...	... ″	Rinteln.
26.		BENDER	...	...	... ″	Cassel.
27.		LANGE	...	...	... ″	″
28.		BUHLMANN, P.	...	...	... ″	Hamm.
29.		BRAND	...	...	... ″	Rudoldstadt.
30.		MOHR, C. ...	...	...	... ″	Copenhagen.
31.		WEITZMANN, C. F.	...	...	... ″	Berlin.
32.		SCHEUERMANN	...	...	... ″	Arolsen.
33.		KRAUSHAAR, O.	...	...	... ″	Cassel.
34.		GRAHN	...	...	... ″	Cassel.
35.	1828.	CART, R. ...	...	...	... ″	London.
36.		EICHLER	...	...	... ″	Leipzig.
37.		GRENZEBACH, E. ...	...	...	... ″	Cassel.
38.	1829.	PFFIFFER, K.	..	...	... ″	″
39.		EICHBERGER	...	...	... ″	″
40.	1830.	NEBELTHAU, F.	...	...	... ″	″
41.		REITER, E.	...	...	... ″	Wertheim.

42.	1831.	KIEL	...	...	...	... of	Detmold.
43.		MOAWKS	...	...	...	... ″	London.
44.		VOIGT, C. ...	...	..	... ″	Hamburg.
45.		MAIER, A. ...	...	...	... ″	Ansbach.
46.		GÖRINK	...	...	... ″	Coburg.
47.		BERNINGER	...	...	... ″	Mainz.
48.		ABEL	...	...	...	... ″	Greifswald.
49.	1832.	HIRSCH	...	...	...	... ″	Cassel.
50.		CROSCHEL ...	...	...	... ″	Düsseldorf.
51.		ALT	...	...	...	... ″	Cassel.
52.		LINDEN, G.	...	...	... ″	Hagen, near Nürnberg.
53.	1833.	BRAND	...	...	...	... ″	London.
54.		HAUSSMANN	...	...	... ″	Hanover.
55.		HARRASS ...	...	...	... ″	Arnstadt.
56.		WOLFF	...	...	...	... ″	Krefeld.
57.	1834.	CRAMER	...	...	...	... ″	Brunswick.
58.	1835.	MANSBACH ...	...	...	... ″	Cassel.
59.		HILL	...	...	...	... ″	New York.
60.		BÄRWOLF ...	...	...	... ″	Gotha.
61.		BÖHME, F.	...	...	... ″	Gandersheim.
62.	1836.	HERION, A.	...	...	... ″	Carlsruhe.
63.		HAUCK	...	...	...	... ″	St. Petersburg.
64.		HORNZIL ...	...	...	... ″	Lemberg.
65.		DÖHLER	...	...	...	... ″	Buttstedt.
66.	1837.	WEIDEMÜLLER	...	...	... ″	Gotha.
67.		TIETZ, PH.	...	...	... ″	Hildesheim.
68.		GACKSTATTER, F. ...	...	... ″	Rothenburg.
69.		DERSKA	...	...	...	... ″	Bohemia.
70.		BÜDING	...	...	...	... ″	Cassel.
71.		VON LADOWSKY	...	...	... ″	Warsaw.
72.		SCHNEIDER	...	...	... ″	Schweinfurt.
73.	1838.	BOTT, J. J.	...	...	... ″	Cassel.
74.		NEUMANN ...	...	...	... ″	Cologne.
75.		WALLBRÜL	...	...	... ″	Bonne.
76.		JACOBI	...	...	...	... ″	Göttingen.
77.		BÄHR, O. ...	...	...	... ″	Cassel.
78.		LUMINAIS ...	...	...	... ″	Paris.
79.		HÜLLS	...	...	...	... ″	Münster.
80.	1839.	HORSLEY, CH.	...	...	... ″	London.
81.		WIEGAND, FRL.	...	...	... ″	Cassel.
82.		STÄHLE, H.	...	...	... ″	″
83.		JOBST	...	...	...	... ″	″
84.		EISENBAUM	...	...	... ″	Warsaw.
85.		MÜLLER ...	...	...	... ″	Münster.
86.		EPSTEIN ...	...	...	... ″	Cassel.
87.	1840.	BESOZZI, S.	...	...	... ″	Paris.
88.		LEHMANN ...	...	...	... ″	Nürnberg.
89.		WEHNER, A.	...	...	... ″	Göttingen.
90.		EGELING ...	...	...	... ″	Cassel.
91.		WENIGMANN	...	...	... ″	Cologne.

92.	1841.	BARTHEL ...	...	...	... of	Sondershausen.
93.		SCHUCHT, J.	...	...	... ″	″
94.		MAHR ...	...	...	... ″	Hildburghausen.
95.		OESTERLEY, F.	...	...	... ″	Göttingen.
96.		MORRIS, FRANK	...	...	... ″	London.
97.		BECKER ...	...	...	... ″	Detmold.
98.		FIRNHABER	...	...	... ″	Wiesbaden.
99.		SCHÜRMANN	...	...	... ″	Bielefeld.
100.		SOUCHAY ...	...	...	... ″	Lübeck.
101.	1842.	UNGER ...	...	...	... ″	Göttingen.

LEIPZIG.

102.	1842.	NAUMANN, EMIL ...	...	...	″	Bonn.
103.		BABCOOK ...	...	...	″	New York.
104.	1843.	JOACHIM, J.	...	...	″	Pesth.
105.		HAUSER, M.	...	...	″	Vienna.
106.		GOLDSCHMIDT, O. ...	...	...	″	Hamburg.
107.	1844.	SPEYER, Frl. A. ...	...	...	″	Frankfurt-a.-M.
108.		JOSEPHSON, J. A. ...	...	...	″	Stockholm.
109.		RUBINSON ...	...	...	″	″
109A.		BREUNUNG, F.	...	...	″	Broderode.
110.	1845.	DRESSEL, O.	...	...	″	Frankfurt-a.-M.
111.		WILLIS ...	...	...	″	Boston.
112.		VON KÖNIGSLÖW, O.	...	...	″	Hamburg.
113.		VON WASIELEWSKI	...	...	″	Dantzig.
114.		CAESARIO ...	...	...	″	Detmold.
115.		HASSLINGER	...	...	″	Vienna.
116.		GROSKURT ...	...	...	″	Göttingen.
117.		VON BÜLOW, H. ...	...	...	″	Dresden.
118.		KITTAN, G.	...	...	″	Flössberg (Saxony).
119.	1846.	WIENROTH...	...	...	″	Carlskrona (Sweden).
120.		WARPURG ...	...	...	″	Hamburg.
121.		KUHLAU ...	...	...	″	Leipzig.
122.		TAUSCH, J.	...	...	″	Dessau.
123.	1847.	BRADBURY, B.	...	...	″	New York.
124.		TUFFTS ...	...	...	″	Boston.
125.		ASHER, J. ...	...	...	″	London.
126.		REISS, C. ...	...	...	″	Frankfurt-a.-M.
127.		LIST ...	...	...	″	Konigsberg. (?)
128.		MÜLLER ...	...	...	″	(?)
120.		VON POGOJEFF, FRL.		...	″	St. Petersburg.
130.		DROUET ...	...	...	″	Coburg.
131.		KADE, O. ...	...	...	″	Dresden.
132.		VOLLMER ...	...	...	″	Munster.
133.		BROWN, MISS	...	...	″	London.
134.		HAYMANN ...	...	...	″	Breslau.
135.	(1848?)	KALLIWODA, W. ...	...	...	″	Donaueschingen.
136.		KREISSMANN, A. ...	...	...	″	Bückeburg.
137.		COSSMANN, B.	...	...	″	Dessau.
138.		STECHE ...	...	...	″	Leipzig.

139. (1848?)	Von Perfall, K., Baron	...	of	Munich.
140.	Martens	...	"	?
141.	Giehne, H.	...	"	Carlsruhe.
142.	Samson, Frl.	...	"	Holland.
143.	Metzler	...	"	Leipzig.
144. 1849.	Maier, J.	...	"	Carlsruhe.
145. } 146. }	Labitzty	...	"	Vienna.
147.	Mason, W.	...	"	New York.
148. 1850.	Von Kolb	...	"	Augsburg.
149. 1851.	Naumann, Ernst	...	"	Leipzig.
150.	Gunther, Dr. H.	...	"	"
151.	Röntgen, E.	...	"	Deventer (Holland).
152.	Ehmant, A.	...	"	Frankfurt-a.-M.
153.	Capel	...	"	London.
154.	Nowotny, A. J.	...	"	Budweis (Bohemia).
155.	Bahre	...	"	Altona.
156.	Udbye, M. A.	...	"	Drontheim.
157.	Parker, J. E.	...	"	Boston.
158.	Koch, Frl.	...	"	Minden.
159.	Weber, Frl.	...	"	?
160. 1852.	Van Eycken, J. A. ...	...	"	Amersfort (Holland).
161.	Richter, H.	...	"	Dresden.
162.	Schubert	...	"	Hamburg.
163.	Perkins	...	"	Boston.
164.	Löw, R.	...	"	Bâsle.
165.	Friedenthal	...	"	Breslau.
166.	Leupharth	...	"	Lisbon.
167.	Hilf, Arno	...	"	Elster.
168.	Heisse, P.	...	"	Copenhagen.
169.	Nater, J.	...	"	Zürich.
170.	Dessoff, F. O.	...	"	Leipzig.
171.	Von Hornstein, R. ...	...	"	Constance.
172.	Thooft, W. F.	...	"	Rotterdam.
173.	Japha, G. J.	...	"	Königsberg.
174. 1853.	Fendrich, K.	...	"	Zürich.
175.	Berger, F.	...	"	London.
176.	Bache, J. E.	...	"	"
177.	Von Adelung	...	"	Livonia.
178.	Von Ehrenstein, J. W. ...	...	"	Dresden.
179.	Billeter, A.	...	"	Männedorf, near Zürich.
180.	Jadassohn, S.	...	"	Breslau.
181.	Mertke, E.	...	"	St. Petersburg.
182.	Faltin, F. W.	...	"	Dessau.
183.	Von Holstein, F. ...	...	"	Brunswick.
184. 1854.	Homer	...	"	New York.
185.	Von Senger, H.	...	"	Weissenhorn, near Ulm.
186 1855.	Zillinger, G. J.	...	"	Doeshorgk (Holland).
187.	Von Wilm, P. N.	...	"	Riga.
188.	Oesterley, H.	...	"	Göttingen.

189.	1855.	Dräseke, F. ... ... of	Coburg.
190.		Muth-Rassmussen ... ... ″	Copenhagen.
191.		Von Maczewski ... ... ″	Mitau.
192.		Zocher ... ... ″	Leipzig.
193.		Widmer ... ... ″	Zürich.
194.		Billig, F. D. ... ... ″	Nordhausen.
195.		David, J. ... ... ″	Odessa.
196.		Schneider, C. ... ... ″	Breslau.
197.		Pratt, G. W. ... ... ″	Boston.
198.		Dietel, J.... ... ... ″	Zeulenroda (Reuss).
199.		Rossbach, Sen. ... ... ″	Klingethal (Saxony).
200.	1856.	Rossbach, Jun. ... ... ″	″ ″
201.		Hachmann... ... ... ″	?
202.	1857.	Graben-Hoffmann, G. ... ... ″	Posen.
203.		Grün ... ... ″	Pesth.
204.		Barnett, J. F. ... ... ″	London.
205.		Grebe, Th. W. ... ... ″	Cassel.
206.		Stange ... ... ″	?
207.		Fint, Chr. ... ... ″	Silzbach (Würtemberg).
208.		Rubener, C. ... ... ″	Sonnerstadt, near Bamberg.
209.		Rogers ... ... ″	Scotland.
210.		Reichel ... ... ″	?
211.		Hompenius, J. A.... ... ... ″	Zwolle (Holland).
212.		Böhme, M. ... ... ″	Weimar.
213.		Rollfuss ... ... ″	Dresden.
214.		Thielemann ... ... ″	Copenhagen.
215.	1858.	Bache, W.... ... ... ″	Birmingham.
216.		Von Davidoff, C.... ... ... ″	Moscow.
217.		Zitzhold ... ... ″	Brunswick.
218.		Naumburg, C. W. ... ... ″	Leipzig.
219.		Rischbieter, W. ... ... ″	Brunswick.
220.		Schmidt ... ... ″	Oldenburg.
221.		Prince Trouskay... ... ... ″	Russia.
222.		Wallerstein ... ... ″	Frankfurt-a.-M.
223.		Schulz ... ... ″	Arolsen.
224.		Seiss ... ... ″	Dresden.
225.		Hornemann ... ... ″	Copenhagen.
226.		Lammers, J. ... ... ″	Osnabrück.
227.		Graf Du Moulin, E. ... ... ″	Bavaria.
228.	1859.	Weiss, E.... ... ... ″	Göttingen.
229.		Krause, E. ... ... ″	Stettin.
230.		Howard, R. ... ... ″	Leipzig.
231.		Hauptmann, Helene ... ... ″	″
232.	1860.	Fabricius, E. F. ... ... ″	Wiborg (Jutland).
233.		Borchers ... ... ″	Kiel.
234.		Wilfer, A. ... ... ″	Bohemia.
235.		Weissenborn, Chr. F. ... ... ″	Leipzig.
236.	1861.	Krumbholz, Th. ... ... ″	Neudietendorf.
237.		Fischer, L. Chr.... ... ... ″	Bückeburg.
238.		Kleffel, A. A. ... ... ″	Pösneck (Saxe-Meiningen).

239.	1861.	RUDORFF, E.	...	...	...	of	Berlin.
240.		JERVIS-RUBINI, E.	...	...	//	London.
241.		VAN EDISDEN, G. ...	...	...	//	Utrecht.
242.		PAUL, Dr. OSC. ...	...	...	//	Freiwalden in Silesia.
243.	1862.	VON. STARZEWSKI, M.	...	...	//	Lemberg.
244.		HORNIKEL, C. R. ...	...	...	//	Lichtenstein.
245.		THUREAU, H.	...	...	...	//	Göttingen.
246.		RÖHRICH, J. R.	...	...	...	//	Alt-Ruppin.
247.		BING	...	...	...	...	//	Ofen (Munich).
248.		MARTIUS	...	...	...	...	//	Meiningen.
249.		DAVID, P. ...	...	...	...	//	Leipzig.
250.		HAUBOLD, G. F.	...	...	...	//	//
251.		HECKER	...	...	...	...	//	Brunswick.
252.		V. ASANTSCHEWSKY, M.	...	...	//	Moscow.
253.		GLEISTEIN, W.	...	...	...	//	Begesack (Bremen).
254.		HILL, J. W.	...	...	...	//	Boston.
255.		VON BERTHA, A. D.	...	...	//	Pesth.
256.		KÖNIG, G. F.	...	...	...	//	Bern.
257.		NIEDERMAIER, L. ...	...	...	//	Hildesheim.
258.		SCHLEEMÜLLER, H. G.	...	...	//	Königsberg.
259.		VON DEMIDOFF	...	...	...	//	St. Petersburg.
260.		KOCH, W. ...	...	...	...	//	Dantzig.
261.		FELCHNER, A.	...	...	...	//	Königsberg.
262.	1863.	BREUER, L.	...	...	...	//	Pesth.
263.		GEIBEL, ST.	...	...	...	//	Leipzig.
264.		SCHEUERMANN, PH. A.	...	...	//	Dayton in Ohio.
265.		LANGER, B.	...	...	...	//	Pesth.
266.		D'ESTER, C. F.	...	...	...	//	Ballendar, near Coblentz.
267.		WEISS	...	...	...	...	//	Königsberg.
268.		GRECKY, M. W. ...	...	...	//	Posen.
269.		BORETZSCH, J. F. ...	...	...	//	Altenburg.
270.		IHLE, C. L.	...	...	...	//	Köthen.
271.		WILLERBACH	...	...	...	//	Königsberg.
272.		CLAUS	...	...	...	...	//	Riga.
273.		BOAS, CH. L.	...	...	...	//	Arnheim (Holland).
274.		PETERSEN ...	...	...	...	//	Sweden.
275.		KUNDE	...	...	...	...	//	Dresden.
276.		VON STOCKHAUSEN	...	...	//	Hanover.
277.		HATELY	...	...	...	...	//	Scotland.
278.		CLAY, F. ...	...	...	...	//	London.
279.		EGERTON, S. S. ...	...	...	//	//
280.		EMERY	...	...	...	...	//	America.
281.		BROWN	...	...	...	...	//	New York.
282.		WILHELMJ, A.	...	...	...	//	Wiesbaden.
283.	1864.	VON CONSTANTIN, O.	...	...	//	St. Petersburg.
284.		VON CHRISTIANOWITSCH, A.	...	//	//
285.		BAUCH, E. B.	...	...	...	//	Lichtenstein (Saxony).
286.		WEBER, K. G.	...	...	...	//	Bern.
287.		VON FAMINZIN, A.	...	...	//	St. Petersburg.
288.		BERGMEIER	...	...	...	//	Munich.

289.	1864.	HAUSMANN, G.	...	...	... of	Dresden.
290.		WALKERLING, R. ...	...	...	... "	Göttingen.
291.		NODSKOU ...	...	...	... "	Denmark.
292.		CALDICOT...	...	...	... "	England.
293.		LEAF, J. A.	...	...	... "	London.
294.		KRAFFT, E.	...	...	... "	Leipzig.
295.		CANTOR	...	...	... "	St. Petersburg.
296.		HAASE	...	...	... "	Köthen.
297.		RAST	...	...	... "	Königsberg.
298.		VON MIHALOVICH...	...	...	... "	Pesth.
299.		SCHÖNE, Dr. A. ...	...	...	... "	Dresden.
300.	1865.	RAMANN	...	...	... "	Hamburg.
301.		NESSLER, B. E. ...	...	...	... "	Strasburg.
302.		VON DAVIDOW, M.		...	... "	Moscow.
303.		LAHSE	...	...	... "	Weissenfels.
304.		VON GUMPERT, O.		...	... "	Glogau.
305.		RÖNTGEN, J.	...	...	... "	Leipzig.
306.		TOTTMANN, A.	...	...	... "	Löbau.
307.		FÖRSTER ...	...	...	... "	Prague.
308.		SCHMELZ, R.	...	...	... "	Cassel.
309.		COURTNY ...	...	...	... "	London.
310.		MATTHEWS, W. E.		...	... "	"
311.		COWEN, F. H.	...	...	... "	"
312.	1866.	ELZIG	...	...	... "	Freiberg.
313.		LANKAU	...	...	... "	Dresden.
314.		COCROFFT, J.	...	...	... "	Manchester.
315.	1867.	TOPFER	...	...	... "	Altwasser, near Salzbrunn.
316.		WILMSEN ...	...	...	... "	Düsseldorf.
317.		THIERFELDER, A....	...	...	... "	Mühlhausen.

A CATALOGUE

OF THE PUBLISHED COMPOSITIONS OF

MORITZ HAUPTMANN.

Compositions marked with the number of the work.

Op. 1. Six German Songs with Pianoforte Accompaniment. New edition. Leipzig, Peters.

      1. From *Der Zauberring*, by La Motte Fouqué: *Vöglein dort im klaren Blauen* —2. From the same: *Zur Sommerzeit da schlagen weit.*—3. From the same: *O ! Flügel mir.*—4. *Minnelied*, by H. Voss : *Der Holdseligen sonder Wank.*—5. *Die Freude*, by Matthisson : *Sanft säuseln die Lüfte.*—6. *Der Geist der Harmonie*, by Matthisson : *Von fernen Fluren weht ein Geist.*

Op. 2. Deux Duos concertants pour deux Violons. Dédiés à Monsieur Louis Spohr. Leipzig, Peters.

      1. G minor.—2. A major.

Op. 3. Gretchen before the Mater Dolorosa, from Goethe's *Faust*. Song with Pianoforte Accompaniment. New edition. Leipzig, Peters.

      Ach neige, du Schmerzenreiche.

The same arranged for Orchestra by Franz von Holstein. Score and Orchestral Parts. Leipzig, Fritzsch.

Op. 4. Anacreontiche del Vitorelli col accompagnamento di Pianoforte. Dedicate a Son Eccelenza la Signora Principessa Repnin, nata Contessa Rasoumowsky. Leipzig, Peters.

      1.—*Guarda, che bianca luna.*—2. *Lascia che questo labbro.*—3. *La terza notte è questa.*—4. *Zitto ! quei due labbrucci.*—5. *Non l'accostar all' urna.*—6. *Ecco di Gnido il tempio.*—7. *La vidi, oh che portento.*—8. *Veglai la notte intera.*

Op. 5. Trois Sonates pour Pianoforte et Violon. Dédiées à Madame la Baronne Caroline de Malsbourg. Leipzig, Peters.

      1. G minor.—2. E flat major.—3. D major.

Op. 6. Sonatine pour Piano et Violon (F major). Dédiées à Mademoiselle la Comtesse Hélène de Kwilecka. Vienna, Schreiber (formerly Spina).

Op. 7. Deux Quatuors pour deux Violons, Alto et Violoncelle. Vienna, Schreiber.

1. E flat major.—2. C major.

Op. 8. Divertissement pour Violon et Guitarre (C major). Vienna, Schreiber.

Op. 9. *Salvum fac regem, Domine,* for Four-part chorus. New edition. Score and Parts. Leipzig, Siegel.

Op. 10. Three Easy Sonatinas for Pianoforte and Violin. Leipzig, Siegel.

1. C major.—2. G major.—3. F major.

Op. 11. Amor timido (Shy Love). Parole di Metastasio, per Canto con accompagnamento del Pianoforte. Nuova Edizione. Vienna, Schreiber.

Che vuoi, mio cuore.

Op. 12. Twelve Compositions for the Pianoforte. Second Edition. Vienna, Schreiber. (Called in the First Edition : Douze pièces détachées pour le Pianoforte.)

First Series : 1. Ecloge.—2. Gigue.—3. Ländler.—4. Canon.— 5. Ländler.—6. Ecloge.

N.B.—Six Numbers appeared first in *Mühling's Museum für Pianoforte-Musik und Gesang.* Halberstadt, Brüggemann.

Op. 13. *Salve Regina* a quattro voci pieno con Organo o Pianoforte ad libitum. Partitura e 4 parti. Berlin, Simrock.

Op. 14. Eight Poems for Single Voice with Pianoforte Accompaniment. New Edition. Vienna, Schreiber.

1.—*Lied,* by E. Schulze : *Wehe nur, du Geist des Lebens.*— 2. *Frühlingslied,* by Hölty : *Die Luft ist blau.*—3. *Lied,* by E. Schulze : *Kleine Blumen, kleine Lieder.*—4. *Abendlandschaft,* by Matthisson : *Goldener Schein deckt den Hayn.*—5. *Frühlingsreigen,* by Matthisson : *Freude jubelt, Liebe waltet.*—6. *Zweifel* von Seidel : *Mir fluthet im Herzen ein Meer.*—7. *Lied der Liebe,* by Matthisson : *Durch Fichten am Hügel.*—8. *Nachruf,* by G. Schwab : *Nur eine lass von deinen Gaben.*

Op. 15. Offertorio a quattro voci pieno con Organo o Pianoforte ad lib. Score and Parts. Leipzig, Siegel.

Lauda, anima mea.

Op. 16. Trois Duos pour deux Violons. Vienna, Schreiber.

1. G major.—2. D minor.—3. A minor.

Op. 17. Trois grands Duos pour deux Violons. Dédiés à Monsieur Antoine Rolla, maître de concert de S. M. le Roi de Saxe. Seconde Edition. Offenbach, André.

1. B major.—2. D major.—3. B minor.

Op. 18. Mass for Chorus and Solo Voices. Score and Parts. Leipzig, Siegel.

     Kyrie.—Gloria.—Credo.—Sanctus.—Agnus Dei.

Op. 19. Twelve Songs with Pianoforte Accompaniment. Dedicated to Herr Franz Hauser. New edition. Offenbach, André.

     First Series : 1. Goethe's *Ganymed : Wie im Morgenglanze du rings mich anglühst.*—2. *Du bist wie eine Blume,* by H. Heine.—3. *Wo ich bin, mich rings umdunkelt,* by H. Heine. — 4. *Mit Veilchen,* by F. A. Lecerf : *Süsse Blumen, dürft' ich euch begleiten.*—5. *Es fällt ein Stern herunter,* by H. Heine.—6. *Neue Liebe, neues Leben,* by Goethe : *Herz mein Herz, was soll das geben?* Second Series : 1. *Frühlingsglaube,* by Uhland : *Die linden Lüfte sind erwacht.*—2. Ghasel : *Von der Schöpfung an hört man die Vögel singen die Liebe.*—3. Sonnet of the 13th Century, after Herder, St. d. V.: *Ach könnt' ich, könnte vergessen Sie!*—4. *O Tannenbaum! Du edles Reis,* by Uhland.—5. Ghasel : *Wer hätte sie gesehn und nicht auch sie geliebt.*—6. Ghasel : *Mein Herz ist zersplittert.*

Op. 20. Concerto facile pour le Pianoforte accompagné de deux Violons, Alto et Violoncelle (E flat major). Leipzig, Peters.

Op. 21. Goethe's *Auf dem See,* for Four Solo Voices and Four-Part Chorus. Dedicated to Herr J. N. Schelble. Pianoforte Edition and Vocal Parts. New edition. Leipzig, Breitkopf and Härtel.

     Und frische Nahrung, neues Blut.

Op. 22. Six German Songs with Pianoforte Accompaniment. Dedicated to Herr Friedr. Nebelthau. Leipzig, Breitkopf and Härtel.

     1. *Komm heraus, tritt aus dem Haus!* by F. Rückert.—2. *Wenn ich in deine Augen seh',* by H. Heine.—3. *Du siehst nicht, wer hier steht,* by F. Rückert.—4. *Morgenlied,* by Uhland : *Noch ahnt man kaum der Sonne Licht.*—5. *An den Mond,* by Goethe : *Füllest wieder Busch und Thal.*—*Verfliesset, vielgeliebte Lieder.*

Op. 23. Trois Sonates pour Pianoforte et Violon. Dédiées à S. A. Madame la Princesse Sophie Volkonsky. Leipzig, Peters.

     1. B major.—2. B major.—3. D minor.

Op. 24. Dodici Ariette per voce di Mezzo-Soprano con accompagnamento di Pianoforte. Dedicate alla Signora Susetta Hummel. Leipzig, Breitkopf and Härtel.

     Parte prima. Sei Anacreontiche del Vitorelli : 1. *Lucido vaso io mando.*—2. *Seppi, che al dubbio lume.*—3. *O Platano felice.*—4. *In solitaria stanza.*—5. *Aveva due canestri.*—6. *Ascolta, o infida.*

     Parte seconda. Sei Canzonette del Metastasio : *Già la notte s'avicina.*—2. *Nò, la speranza più non m' alleta.*—3. *Io lo so, che il bel sembiante.*—4. *L'onda che mormora.*—5. *Se tutti i mali miei.*—6. *Non so dir se pena sia.*

Op. 25. Six Songs by Goethe, for Soprano, Alto, Tenor, and Bass. Dedicated to Herr Dr. Felix Mendelssohn-Bartholdy. Score and Parts. Leipzig, Peters.

 1. Im Sommer: *Wie Feld und Au.*—2. Wandrers Nachtlied: *Ueber allen Gipfeln ist Ruh'.*—3. Mailied: *Zwischen Waizen und Korn.*— 4. Haidenröslein: *Sah ein Knab' ein Röslein stehn.*— 5. Frühzeitiger Frühling: *Tage der Wonne; kommt ihr so bald?*—6. Geistergruss: *Hoch auf dem alten Thurme.*

 1, 3, 4, and 5 arranged for Single Voice with Pianoforte, by E. Brissler.

Op. 26. Six Songs by Fr. Rückert, with Pianoforte Accompaniment. Leipzig, Peters.

 1. Mein Alles: *Du meine Seele, du mein Herz.*—2. Gute Nacht: *Die gute Nacht, die ich dir sage.*—3. Beruhigung: *Du bist die Ruh', der Friede mild.*—4. Sommerlied: *Seinen Traum lind wob Frühling kaum.*—5. Leitstern: *O mein Stern! nah und fern.*—6. Trennung: *O weh des Scheidens, das er that.*

Op. 27. Tre Sonetti del Petrarca per voce di Mezzo-Soprano con accompagnamento di Pianoforte. Leipzig, Peters.

 1. Sonnet cxxxi.: *Or che'l ciel e la terra.*—2. Sonnet cxxxii.: *Come'l candido piè.*—3. Sonnet xv.: *Piovon mi amare lagrime.*

Op. 28. Twelve Songs with Pianoforte Accompaniment. Leipzig, Peters.

 First Series: 1.—*Liebchen über Alles*, by Gerhard, after R. Burns: *Wär' ich mit dir auf jener Höh'!*—2. *Meine Jean*, by the same: *Von allen Winden in den Welt.*—3. From *Genoveva*, by L. Tieck: *Dicht von Felsen eingeschlossen* (D minor).—4. *Hatem*, from *Der Westöstliche Divan*, by Goethe: *Was wird mir jede Stunde so bang.* 5. *Suleika*, ditto: *Ach! um deine feuchten Schwingen.*—6. *Sehnsucht*, by Goethe: *Was zieht mir des Herz so?*

 Second Series: 7. *Liebesboten*, by Fr. Rückert: *Die tausend Grüsse, die ich dir sende.*—8. *Diora*, from *Der Schatz des Rampsinit*, by Platen: *Durch die Lüfte, schmerzbeklommen.*—9. *Am Ufer des Doon*, by Gerhard, after R. Burns: *Ihr Hügel dort am schönen Doon.*—10. *Liebliche Maid*, by the same: *Früh mit der Lerche Sang.*— 11. *An Cassili's Rande*, by the same: *Der holde Lenz ist wieder wach.*— 12. *Mary schlummert*, by the same: *Fliess, murmelnder Afton.*

 N.B.—No. 10 appeared first as the supplement to No. 28 of the *Salon*, Cassel, Hotop.

Op. 29. Three of Petrach's Sonnets for Mezzo-Soprano, with Pianoforte Accompaniment. (Second set of Sonnets.) New edition, with Italian and German text. Leipzig, Siegel. (First edition with Italian title, Casella, Appel.)

 1. Sonnet xxviii.: *Solo e pensoso.*—2. Sonnet xcviii.: *Quel vago impallidir.*—3. Sonnet clxxxvii.: *Quando'l sol bagna in mar.*

Op. 30. Mass for Solo Voices, Chorus, and Orchestra. Dedicated to His Majesty Frederick Augustus, King of Saxony. Score and Parts. Complete edition for the Pianoforte, arranged by the Composer. Leipzig, Peters.

 Kyrie. — Gloria. — Graduale. — Credo. — Offertorio. — Sanctus.— Agnus Dei.

Op. 31. Three Songs with Pianoforte and Violin Accompaniment. Dedicated to Herr Professor Dr. Carus. Leipzig, Peters.

    1. *Meerfahrt*, by H. Heine : *Mein Liebchen, wir sassen beisammen.* —2. *Nachtgesang*, by Goethe : *O gieb, vom weichen Pfühle.*—3. *Der Fischer*, by Goethe : *Das Wasser rauscht, das Wasser schwoll.*

Op. 32. Six Four-Part Songs for Soprano, Alto, Tenor, and Bass. Dedicated to Herr Stadtsyndicus Dr. Ferd. Oesterley, of Göttingen. Score and Parts. Leipzig, Breitkopf and Härtel.

    1. *Sängerfahrt*, by Eichendorff : *Laue Luft kommt blau geflossen.*— 2. *Zigeunerlied*, by Goethe : *Im Nebelgeriesel, im tiefen Schnee.*— 3. *Frühlingsliebe*, by C. Keil : *Wenn der Frühling kommt.*—4. *Abendlied*, by Fr. Rückert : *Ich stand auf Berges Halde.*—5. *Frühlingsreigen*, by Matthisson : *Freude jubelt, Liebe waltet.*—6. *Waldeinsamkeit*, by L. Tieck : *Waldeinsamkeit, die mich erfreut.*

Op. 33. Six Hymns for Soprano, Alto, Tenor, and Bass (Chorus and Solo Voices). Score and Parts. Leipzig, Kistner.

    1. Morgengesang : *Kommt ! kommt ! lasst uns anbeten.*—2. Bittgesang : *Herr ! Herr ! du wollest deine Barmherzigkeit.* — 3. Trauungslied : *Ich und mein Haus, wir sind bereit.*—4. *Gott mein Heil.*—5. Leben in Gott : *O der alles hätt' verloren.*—6. Abendlied : *Die Nacht ist gekommen.*

Op. 34. Motet : *Nimm von uns, Herr Gott*, &c., for Chorus and Solo Voices. Score and Parts. Leipzig, Siegel.

Op. 35. Six Sacred Songs for Two Sopranos and Altos. Score and Parts. Leipzig, Peters.

    1. Morgenlied : *Der schöne Tag bricht an.*—2. Trost : *Wenn in Leidens Tagen.*—3. Gebet : *Gott deine Güte reicht so weit.*—4. Abendlied : *Der Mond ist aufgegangen.*—5. Gottvertraun : *Lass mich dein sein und bleiben.*—6. Bleib bei uns : *Ach bleib bei uns, Herr Jesu Christ.*

Op. 36. No. 1. Motet : *Komm heiliger Geist*, for Solo and Chorus. No. 2. Motet : *Herr unser Herrscher*, for Solo and Chorus. No. 3. *Ehre sei Gott in der Höhe !* Motet for Male Voices, with Accompaniment of Two Horns and Three Trombones ad lib. New edition. Score and Parts. Leipzig, Seigel.

Op. 37. Six Songs with Pianoforte Accompaniment. Dedicated to Herr Emil Trefftz. Leipzig, Siegel.

    1. *Mignon*, by Goethe : *Kennst du das Land ?*—2. *Minnelied*, by Hölty : *Holder klingt mir Vogelsang.*—3. *Erster Verlust*, by Goethe : *Ach wer bringt die schönen Tage.*—4. *Die Kindheit*, by Matthisson : *Wenn die Abendröthe.*—5. *Die Schiffende*, by Hölty : *Sie wankt dahin.*—6. *Seufzer*, by Hölty : *Die Nachtigall singt überall.*

N.B.—1, 4, and 6 appeared first in *Mühling's Museum.* Halberstadt, Brüggemann.

Op. 38. Cantata : *Herr ! Herr ! Wende dich zum Gebet !* for Chorus and Solo Voices, with Accompaniment for Organ and Four Trombones. Score and Parts. Leipzig, Siegel.

Op. 39. " St. Cecilia's Day," Hymn for Double-Chorus and Solo Voice, with Pianoforte Accompaniment. Dedicated to the *Cäcilienverein* of Cassel. Score and Parts. Leipzig, Siegel.
Ueber die entlaubten Haine.

Op. 40. Three Motets : No. 1. *Herr, höre mein Gebet.*—No. 2. *Macht hoch die Thür, die Thor macht weit.*—No. 3. *Walte, walte nah und fern.* For Chorus and Solo Voices. Score and Parts. Leipzig, Siegel.

Op. 41. Three Motets : No. 1. *Christe, du Lamm Gottes.*—No. 2. *Gott sei uns gnädig und barmherzig.*—No. 3. *Lobe den Herrn, meine Seele.* For Chorus and Solo Voices. Leipzig, Siegel.

Op. 42. Six Sacred Songs for Four-Part Chorus, from Friedrich Oser's *Kreuz-und Trostlieder.* Score and Parts. Leipzig, Siegel.
1. *Nimm mir Alles, Gott mein Gott.*—2. *O theures Gotteswort.*— 3. *Herr, Herr, wess soll ich mich getrösten.*—4. *Du bist ja doch der Herr.*—5. *Wie ein wasserreicher Garten.*—6. *Sei still dem Herrn und wart' auf ihn.*

Op. 43. Three Sacred Pieces for Chorus and Orchestra : No. 1. *Nicht so ganz wirst meiner du vergessen.*—No. 2. *Und Gottes Will' ist dennoch gut.*—No. 3. *Du Herr zeigst mir den rechten Weg.* Score, Pianoforte Edition, Orchestral and Vocal Parts. Leipzig, Breitkopf and Härtel.

Op. 44. Three Choral Hymns for Soprano, Alto, Tenor, and Bass. Score and Parts. Leipzig, Siegel.
1. Zuversicht : *Hart scheinest du gesinnt.*—2. Gebet : *Gott sei uns gnädig.*—3. Bei der Trauung : *Auf euch wird Gottes Segen ruhn.*

Op. 45. The Eighty-Fourth Psalm : *Wie lieblich sind deine Wohnungen.* Motet for Chorus and Solo Voices. Score and Parts. Leipzig, Siegel.

Op. 46. Two-Part Songs. Words by K. F. H. Strass. Dedicated to his sister Julia. Score and Parts. Leipzig, Breitkopf and Härtel.
1. Freie Natur : *In's düft'ge Heu will ich mich legen.*—2. Sehnen : *In die Lüfte möcht ich steigen.*—3. Nachtgesang : *Es feiert die Flur.*— 4. Unter Lindenbäumen lass uns ruhn.—5. Waldlust : *Auf dem Rasen im Walde.*—6. *Wie ist mir so wohl und so heiter.*—7. Mailied : *Willkommen uns, o schöner Mai.*—8. Ständchen : *Schläfst, Liebchen, schon ?*—9. Andenken : *Wo ich wandle, wo ich bin.*—10. Abschied : *Liebchen, mein Liebchen, Ade.*—11. *Wogende Wellen wallen empor.*— 12. Liebesboten : *Holder Mond, noch scheide nimmer.*

Op. 47. Six Four-Part Songs for Soprano, Alto, Tenor, and Bass. Dedicated to Julius Rietz. Score and Parts. Leipzig, Breitkopf and Härtel.

1. *An der Kirche wohnt der Priester*, after Klaus Groth.—2. *Hell in's Fenster*, after Klaus Groth.—3. *Der Lerchenbaum*, from *Volkslieder der Polen*, by W. P. : *Lerchenbaum, mein Lerchenbaum.*— 4. *Wenn Zweie sich gut sind*, after Klaus Groth : *Kein Graben so breit.*—5 *Im Holz*, after Klaus Groth : *Wo das Echo schallt.*—6. From *Mirza-Schaffy*, by Friedrich Bodenstedt : *Neig', schöne Knospe, dich zu mir.*

Op. 48. Motet : *Wer unter dem Schirm des Höchsten sitzet* (Psalm xci., vv. 1, 2, 4, and 16), for Chorus and Solo Voices. Score and Parts. Leipzig, Siegel.

Op. 49. Twelve Songs for Four-Part Male Chorus. Words by Friedrich Rückert. Score and Parts. Leipzig, Breitkopf and Härtel.

First Series : 1. *Schön ist das Fest des Lenzes.*—2. *Ihr Engel, die ihr tretet.*—3. *Götter ! keine frostige Ewigkeit !*—4. *Du Herr, der Alles wohl gemacht.*—5. *Nun wünsch' ich, dass die ganze Welt.*— 6. *Aus der Jugendzeit.*

Second Series : 7. *Frühling ! vollen, vollen Liebesüberfluss.*— 8. *So freudelos, so wonneblos.*—9. *Komm, verhüllte Schöne.*— 10. *Ich will die Fluren meiden.*—11. *Wohl wünsch' ich, dass der Frühling komme.*—12. *Wunderbar ist mir geschehn.*

Op. 50. Twelve Canons in German and Italian, for Three Voices, with or without Pianoforte Accompaniment. Dedicated to Her Majesty Queen Maria of Hanover. Score and Parts. Leipzig, Breitkopf and Härtel.

First Series : 1. *Tu sei gelosa, è vero.*—2. *Sempre, sempre.*— 3. *Perchè, perchè, se mia tu sei.*—4. *Perchè mai, tu mio bene.*— 5. *Clori ! Clori !*—6. *O cari boschi.*

Second Series : 7. *Chiedi tu.*—8. *Quanto son dolci i palpiti.*— 9. *Pur nel sonno.*—10. *I primi fior del maggio.*—11. *Su, cantiamo.*— 12. *Ah tu sai, ch' io son felice.*

Op. 51. Motet : *Herr ! wer wird wohnen in Deinem Haus ?* for Chorus and Solo Voices. Score and Parts. Leipzig, Siegel.

Op. 52. Motet (From Psalm cxi.) *Ich danke dem Herrn von ganzem Herzen*, for Chorus and Solo Voices. Score and Parts. Leipzig, Siegel.

Op. 53. Three Choral Hymns (From the Psalms), for Soprano, Alto, Tenor, and Bass. Score and Parts. Leipzig, Siegel.

1. *Meine Seele ist stille zu Gott.*—2. *Gott sei mir gnädig.*—3. *Herr, ich schrei' zu dir.*

Op. 54. First Series : Six Easy Sacred Songs for Two Sopranos and Altos. 1. *Vom Himmel hoch.*—2. *Nun lasst uns* (Helene H.)—3. *Nun ist es Zeit.*—4. *Herr, der du mir das Leben.*—5. *Der Tag ist hin.*—6. *Allein Gott in der Höh'.*

Second Series : Six Choral Hymns for Two Sopranos and Altos. Score and Parts. Leipzig, Siegel. 1. Morgengesang : *Auf geht des Ostens Thor.*—2. Osterlied : *Preis sei dem Vater.*—3. Busslied : *Hier bin ich Herr.*—4. Himmelfahrtslied : *Christ fuhr gen Himmel.*—5. Pfingstlied : *Komm, komm du Geist.*—6. Dreifaltigkeitslied : *Der Du bist drei in Einigkeit.*

Op. 55. Six Songs for Four-Part Male Chorus, from Friedrich Oser's *Naturlieder.* Score and Parts. Leipzig, Breitkopf and Härtel. 1. Sommermorgen : *Frischer, tauiger Sommermorgen.*—Im Wald : *O Wald, O Wald ! wie ewig schön.*—3. Himmelslicht : *Silberumsäuseltes Wolkengebilde.*—4. Abendruhe : *Ueber den Hügeln hin.*—5. Sommerandacht : *Schaut der Mond so leuchtend nieder.*—6. Nordsturm : *Nordsturm komm'.*

Op. 56. Three Choral Hymns for Soprano, Alto, Tenor, and Bass.—No. 1. *Ich komme vor Dein Angesicht.*—No. 2. *Gott, heilige Du selbst mein Herz.*—No. 3. *Ich weiss es, Herr !* Score and Parts. Leipzig, Siegel.

Op. 57. *Sei mir gnädig, Gott !* For Two Four-Part Choruses and Four Solo Voices. Score and Parts. Leipzig, Siegel.

Op. 58. Two Ave Marias for Mezzo-Soprano, with Pianoforte Accompaniment. Leipzig, Kistner. (No. 1 of the Posthumous Works.) 1. Canzonetta alla Madonna di Frascati : *Maria, alta regina.*—2. Ave Maria : *Ave Maria, gratia plena.* N.B.—No. 2 appeared first with Organ and Pianoforte Accompaniment in *The Töpfer-Album.* Leipzig and Winterthur, Rieter-Biedermann.

Op. 59. Twenty-Five Album Canons, edited by S. Jadassohn. Leipzig, Kistner. (No. 2 of the Posthumous Works.)

Op. 60. Overture to the Opera of *Mathilde.* Arranged as a Pianoforte Duet by S. Jadassohn. Leipzig, Kistner. (No. 3 of the Posthumous Works.)

COMPOSITIONS NOT MARKED WITH THE NUMBER OF THE WORK.

I. Polonaise and Rondo for the Pianoforte. *Mühling's Museum für Pianoforte. Musik und Gesang.* Halberstadt, Brüggemann.

II. Dorpdans for the Pianoforte. *Album von de Maatschapij tot Bevordering der Toonkunst,* No. 17. Amsterdam.

III. *Bleib' erster Lieb', o Herz, getreu.* Song with Pianoforte Accompaniment. *The Mozart Album.* Leipzig, Kahnt.

IV. Song with Pianoforte Accompaniment. From L. Tieck's *Genoveva.* Cassel, Luckhardt.

> *Dicht von Felsen eingeschlossen.* (C minor.)

V. Romance from the Opera *Mathilde,* with Pianoforte Accompaniment. Franz Hauser's *Gesanglehre.* Leipzig, Breitkopf and Härtel, 1866.

> Mathilde : *Dort, wo in reine Lüfte.*

VI. Recitative and Cavatina from the Opera of *Mathilde,* with Pianoforte Accompaniment. Hauser's *Gesanglehre.* Leipzig, Breitkopf and Härtel.

> Malekadhel : *Dies also ist der Ort.*
> Cavatina : *O holder Stern.*

VII. For Van Dyk's *Landleben.* Song with Violin (or Flute) and Pianoforte Accompaniment. Hauser's *Gesanglehre.* Leipzig, Breitkopf and Härtel.

> *Aure amiche.*

VIII. *Weihnachtslied,* for Soprano, Alto, and Bass, with Pianoforte Accompaniment. *Deutsche Jugend.* Vol. iii., No. 3. 1873, Leipzig, Dürr (Posthumous Work).

> *Nun schwebt auf Engelsflügeln.*

MISCELLANEOUS WORKS.

1. Erläuterungen zu Joh. Sebastian Bach's Kunst der Fuge. Leipzig, Peters, 1841. Second Edition, 1861.

2. Die Natur der Harmonik und der Metrik. Zur Theorie der Musik. Leipzig, Breitkopf and Härtel, 1853. Second Edition, 1873.

3. Die Lehre von der Harmonik. Mit beigefügten Notenbeispielen. Posthumous Work. Edited by Dr. Oscar Paul. Leipzig, Breitkopf and Härtel, 1868.

4. Briefe an Franz Hauser. Edited by Professor Dr. Alfred Schöne. Two Vols. With Portrait. Leipzig, Breitkopf and Härtel, 1871.

5. Opuscula. Miscellaneous Essays. Leipzig, Leuckart, 1874.

6. Briefe an Ludwig Spohr und Andere. Edited by Dr. Ferdinand Hiller. New Series. Leipzig, Breitkopf and Härtel, 1876.

Aufgaben für einfachen und doppelten Contrapunct. Compiled from the notebooks of Hauptmann's pupils, for the use of teachers, by Ernst Rudorff. Leipzig, B. Senff.

INDEX.

Parish Alvars. II., 196.

Pergolese (Pergolesi), Giovanni Battista, born at Naples 1710, pupil of Leo and Durante, died 1737; wrote Operas and Sacred Music. I., 153.

Peri, Jacopo, an Operatic Composer living in Florence about 1600. I., 97.

Pfeiffer, Dr. II., 217.

"Philister" (Der), by Clemens Brentano. See Brentano.

Pistor. I., 116.

Pixis, Franzilla, née Göringer, sang in Opera and at Concerts 1833-4, born at Lichtenthal near Baden-Baden, adopted daughter of Pixis, the Violinist. I., 116, 161.

Platen, Poet. I., 141-2.

Pleyel, Marie Camilla, a famous Pianist; appointed to the Brussels Conservatoire 1847. I., 211.

Pohlenz, Christian Aug., born 1790, died 1843; Organist, Teacher of singing, and Director of Music at Leipzig. II., 1, 6, 190.

"Prinz Eugen," Opera by Capellmeister G. Schmidt. II., 65.

Proch, Heinrich, born at Vienna 1809, and appointed Capellmeister 1837; Violinist and Writer of Songs. II., 132.

Proske, Canonikus; a very learned musician. II., 102.

Quanz, Joh. Joachim, born 1697, went to Berlin 1741, died 1773; Flute player and friend of Frederick the Great. II., 79.

Queisser, Carl Traugott, Trombone player, born near Grimma, 1800, became a member of the Leipzig band 1824; died 1846. I., 37.

Rabelais, Regis' translation of. I., 207-8.

Racine. II., 207.

Raff, Joachim, Composer, born in Switzerland 1822; went to Wiesbaden 1857. II., 168.

Rahel Varnhagen. I., 123.

Raimondi. II., 269.

Rameau, Jean Philippe, born at Dijon

1683, died in Paris 1764; a well-known Theorist and writer of Opera. II., 130, 246, 259, 260, 277.

Raphael. I., 29, 57; II., 194, 210, 223.

Rauch's Monument to Frederick the Great. II., 78.

Regnard. II., 275.

Reicha, Anton, born at Prague 1770, died in Paris 1836; a Theorist. I., 204.

Reichardt, Joh. Friedr., born at Königsberg 1752, died near Halle 1814. Composer and writer on Music. I., 147; II., 200.

Reinecke, Carl, born at Altona 1824, became Capellmeister at Leipzig 1860; Pianist and Composer. II., 146, 183.

Reissiger, Carl Gottlieb, born at Belzig 1798, died Capellmeister at Dresden 1859; wrote Operas, Songs, and Sacred Music. I., 37, 39, 202; II., 16, 49, 99, 109, 204.

Richter. See Jean Paul.

Richter. II., 236.

Riedel, Carl, Professor, born near Elberfeld 1827; Theorist and Founder of a Gesangverein at Leipzig. II., 106, 117.

Riepel, Theorist and Conductor at Ratisbon; died 1782. I., 12.

Ries, Ferd., born at Bonn 1784, died at Frankfurt 1838. Beethoven's only pupil; wrote Operas, Symphonies, and Chamber Music. I., 10, 24, 161, 187.

Rietz, Julius, born at Berlin 1812, Capellmeister at Leipzig 1847-60, when he went to Dresden; eminent as a Cellist, Conductor, Composer and Teacher. II., 73, 131, 137, 144-5, 206-7, 257.

Rochlitz, Friedr., born at Leipzig 1770, died 1842; a well-known amateur and savant. I., 3, 121-2, 124 5, 137; II., 103-4, 199.

Rode, Pierre, born at Bordeaux 1774, died in Paris 1830; Violinist and Composer. I., 58; II., 37-8.